CERTIFIED FITNESS INSTRUCTOR/ PERSONAL TRAINER
career starter

Lauren Starkey

LEARNINGEXPRESS

New York

Library of Congress Cataloging-in-Publication Data:
Starkey, Lauren B., 1962–
   Certified fitness instructor/personal trainer career starter / Lauren Starkey.—1st ed.
   p. cm.—(Career starters)
   ISBN 1-57685-420-5 (pbk. : alk. paper)
1. Personal trainers—Vocational guidance—United States. 2. Personal
trainers—Employment—United States. 3. Personal trainers—
Certification—United States. I. Title. II. Series.
   GV481.4 .S83 2002
   613.7'1—dc20   2002011288

Printed in the United States of America
9 8 7 6 5 4 3 2 1
First Edition

ISBN 1-57685-420-5

For more information or to place an order, contact LearningExpress at:
   900 Broadway
   Suite 604
   New York, NY 10003

Or visit us at:
   www.learnatest.com

About the Author

Lauren Starkey is a writer and editor, specializing in educational and reference works, with over ten years of experience. For eight years, she worked on the Oxford English Dictionary, and she is the author of *Hotel/Restaurant Management Career Starter*. For over a decade she has been involved in the fitness industry as an owner of a fitness consulting business and a certified aerobics instructor. Ms. Starkey lives in Essex, Vermont, with her husband, Gorden, and children, Emma, Graham, and Cameron.

Contents

Introduction

Why Become a Fitness Instructor or Personal Trainer?

FITNESS INSTRUCTORS and personal trainers work in a booming industry. More people than ever before are exercising, and their ranks are expected to increase for at least another decade. Employment prospects in fitness will grow with them, but not only in sheer numbers—the types of positions held by certified instructors and trainers are becoming more varied as the number of available jobs gets larger.

It's not uncommon today to find fitness facilities in hospitals and large corporations. Exercise studios and gyms are opening to target specific segments of the population, such as women, kids, and seniors. Personal trainers make house calls, and sometimes even help their clients design their own home gyms. The division between instructors and trainers is becoming blurred, as more instructors get certified to train, and trainers learn to teach classes. The two jobs are highly complementary.

Those already employed in the fitness industry report an extremely high level of job satisfaction—higher, in fact, than just about any other profession. Instructors and trainers have varied schedules, rarely doing the same thing on Tuesday that they did on Monday. They don't sit behind a desk with a computer screen for company; rather, they spend most of their time working with people. An instructor might teach a yoga class in the morning, a stretch-and-relax class at lunchtime, and high intensity aerobics for the after-work crowd. He or she could also fit in some personal training clients between classes. This book introduces you to these exciting careers, in which you might find yourself working for a huge chain health club, hospital exercise center, fitness management company, yoga studio, or even a cruiseline.

Chapter 1 serves as a general exploration of the field. In it, you will learn what fitness instructors and personal trainers do, where they work, and what makes them successful. Also included are hiring trends and current salary information, sample job descriptions, and advice from current instructors and trainers.

Chapter 2 explains the importance of education, and how to decide what kind of program is right for you. It explains the importance of certification, and details a number of the most popular options. College and university study is also explored, with sample courses and tuition costs from schools across the country.

In Chapter 3, you will learn the possibilities for financing your education, including loans, scholarships, and grants. The differences between each option are explored, explaining eligibility, the application process, and how awards are given. You will also find out about the forms you need, where to get them, how to fill them out, and where to send them, and get some tips for simplifying and surviving the process.

Chapter 4 covers the job search process, beginning with a discussion about determining the type of job you really want. There is plenty of information on the best job prospects, and the easiest ways to find them, from classified ads to networking and Internet resources. Self-employment, an increasingly popular option for fitness workers, is also explored.

Then in Chapter 5, you will learn how to hone your job search skills. The crafting of winning resumes and cover letters that really get noticed, is explained, along with advice on how to handle interviews with more polish and less anxiety. Finally, you will discover how to evaluate the job offers you are sure to receive.

Chapter 6 takes you out of the job search and into the job market, showing proven ways to succeed in your new position. You will learn how to manage relationships with your superiors and your students and clients, as well as how to manage the liability risks that accompany work as a fitness instructor or personal trainer. Other topics covered include fitting into the particular culture of your new workplace, how to find a mentor, and how to promote yourself to get ahead.

In addition, throughout the book, you will find insights and advice from current instructors and trainers. The appendices at the end of the book offer helpful resources too: a list of professional associations, accrediting agencies, and state financial aid offices, as well as the names and contact information for two- and four-year schools that offer certificates and degrees in exercise science and related majors. Also included are books and periodicals you can refer to for additional information.

So turn the page and begin. This book will give you a great start toward a rewarding and challenging career as a fitness instructor or personal trainer.

CHAPTER one

CHOOSING A CAREER AS A FITNESS INSTRUCTOR OR PERSONAL TRAINER

In this chapter, you will learn about fitness instructors, including what they do, where they work, and what makes them successful. Jobs with large chain clubs, smaller clubs and studios, health care facilities, and corporate fitness/wellness programs are examined, along with sample job advertisements from many of these employers. You will also hear advice from a number of those already working in the field. Finally, the specific strengths and skills necessary to succeed as a fitness instructor or personal trainer will be explored in an interactive format.

THE FITNESS INDUSTRY is booming. Thanks to decades of research, the advantages of a healthy lifestyle that includes physical exercise are now widely understood and accepted. Not only are more individuals joining health clubs and other exercise facilities, but the medical community is espousing the benefits of exercise for the prevention and treatment of various diseases and conditions. Doctors and other medical professionals are prescribing workouts for their patients, both in and out of healthcare facilities.

An International Health, Racquet & Sportsclub Association's Annual Member Tracking Survey reveals that the number of health club members involved with personal training rose by 29% in 2000, while the number of members involved in yoga classes rose 16%. In addition, according to the

U.S. Department of Labor, a 36% rise in the employment of fitness instructors will occur during the decade ending 2010.

Add to this evidence of a rapidly expanding market the fact that, according to the National Endurance Sports Trainers Association (NESTA), there are very few people who more enjoy what they do for a living. NESTA cites a recent study that concluded that personal trainers/fitness instructors enjoy an 82% job satisfaction rating, compared to the population as a whole, which maintains a 71% job satisfaction rating. As Neil Reuben of the International Sports Sciences Association puts it:

> I have an incredible job. I work with personal trainers, who are such upbeat people; they're like cheerleaders who get their clients motivated. We are trying to make people's lives better, to help them, and do some good in the world. To know that you've made a lasting impact is a great feeling.

Whether you are interested in teaching a few classes a week, becoming a full-time personal trainer, or have any fitness career goal in between, this book will guide you on your path toward employment. You will find the most comprehensive look at the industry today, including exclusive listings of fitness publications, organizations, and websites. The information on self-employment options for instructors and trainers is invaluable if you are considering that option, and you won't find it anywhere else.

If you are still in school and have never held a job before, you will benefit from reading about how to conduct a job search, write your resume, tackle interviews, and evaluate job offers. If you are changing careers, you will find the specific health and fitness information you need to translate your prior experience into a new job in this industry. Discover how to get certified (or earn a degree) to maximize your employability, find great websites to visit, learn which organizations offer certifications and other benefits, and how to evaluate personal liability insurance policies.

WHO ARE FITNESS INSTRUCTORS AND PERSONAL TRAINERS?

Those who enter this exciting field have two important things in common: they understand on a personal level the importance and joy of exercise, and they love sharing that understanding with others. Fitness instructors are willing and able to claim the following characteristics:

- ▶ knowledge of the field
- ▶ necessary education and certifications
- ▶ ability to work well with others
- ▶ leadership qualities
- ▶ patience
- ▶ honesty and trustworthiness
- ▶ communication skills
- ▶ enthusiasm
- ▶ willingness to keep up with advances and trends in the industry

Personal trainers have many of the same qualities, and in addition to their qualities, are great coaches and motivators. They also have a thorough understanding of the body and how it works. Because the two jobs are similar in so many respects, it is often the case that individuals do both. In other words, those who work with individual clients at the gym in the morning may often be found in front of a class later in the day.

WHAT DO FITNESS INSTRUCTORS AND PERSONAL TRAINERS DO?

Fitness instructors lead groups of people in specific class formats. Because there are so many (see the next section), instructors often specialize in a few formats, such as kickboxing, step aerobics, or Pilates. Most classes involve aerobic conditioning, flexibility training (stretching), and/or muscle conditioning. During class, they set the pace for their students, providing an example of proper form or technique, while "cueing," or telling what will happen next.

Most instructors devise the framework of their own classes, including choice of music, choreography, and exercises to be done.

Personal trainers perform three distinct functions for their clients. First, they assess their level of physical fitness, helping them set realistic, desirable goals. Second, they develop a plan or set of plans that lead clients toward their goals. And third, they lead sessions in which the plan is followed. If they've "prescribed" an upper body workout consisting of three sets of nine different exercises, which target a variety of upper body muscles, the trainer leads the client through the exercises. He or she may demonstrate correct form, and otherwise help clients improve their technique. Trainers also keep records of their clients' exercise sessions, and provide analyses of their progress toward their goals.

Both fitness instructors and personal trainers play an integral role in the improvement of the health of their clients. According to a *Surgeon General's Report on the Danger of Physical Inactivity*, the benefits of exercise include:

▶ reducing the risk of dying from coronary heart disease and of developing high blood pressure, colon cancer, and diabetes
▶ helping reduce blood pressure in people with hypertension
▶ helping maintain healthy bones, muscles, and joints
▶ reducing symptoms of anxiety and depression and fostering improvements in mood and feelings of well-being
▶ helping control weight, develop lean muscle, and reduce body fat

As motivators, instructors and trainers keep their students and clients interested in staying fit and active. When regular exercise is performed, the body enjoys many of the benefits listed above. A healthier body can lead to a healthier mind, longer life, and better quality of life. Instructors and trainers love this aspect of their jobs—the knowledge that they are truly making a difference in others' lives.

TYPES OF FITNESS INSTRUCTION

As more of the general population engages in some sort of fitness activity, and those who have been exercising for years grow weary of repetition, the range and scope of fitness instruction expands to meet demand for variety. While just twenty years ago there were aerobics classes populated mostly by women, gyms for weight lifting populated mainly by men, and a much smaller number of ashrams (yoga facilities) and Pilates studios, today it seems the types of instruction available are limitless.

Trends include the introduction of sports such as cycling, rowing, and boxing to class formats that involve a number of participants led by a knowledgeable, enthusiastic instructor. Mind-body practices such as yoga, tai-chi, and Pilates are enjoying increasing popularity. Workouts are also being designed around techniques that used to be used only for patients in rehabilitation settings. And new types of classes and formats are being developed constantly. For instance, "sports yoga" is now gaining popularity. It aims to bring elements of traditional yoga to the general sports population by combining it with some of the features of standard group exercise classes.

The Originals

Current class formats owe much to their predecessors. The use of choreography and popular music with exercise that improves flexibility and aerobic capacity began over thirty years ago. Jazzercise was developed in 1969 by Judi Sheppard Missett, and is today the world's largest dance fitness program with more than 5,000 instructors teaching 19,000 classes weekly to 450,000 students in 38 countries around the globe. At about the same time, Dr. Kenneth Cooper published a number of books about aerobics and the benefits that may be derived from regular exercise that causes "windedness."

Thirteen years later, Jane Fonda made a video of her popular workout book and started the fitness craze of the 1980s. Fonda not only made 18 exercise videos for home use, but also opened studios bearing her name and built a multimillion dollar business around aerobics. Organizations such as the Aerobics and Fitness Association of America (AFAA) and The International Dance Exercise Program (IDEA) Health & Fitness Association were founded in the mid-1980s, and began certifying instructors to teach classes in styles similar to those of Missett and Fonda.

Since then, research in the field of exercise science has advanced rapidly. It is now known, for instance, that workouts with weights can be as important to overall health as those that focus on aerobics and flexibility. Strength training is becoming more popular as athletes and fitness enthusiasts embrace the trend and add weight workouts to their exercise regimens.

Sports Formats

Indoor stationary cycling classes have been offered in health clubs for over a decade, and remain popular. The first such program was created by cyclist Jonathan Goldberg ("Johnny G"), in the 1980s. Known as Spinning®, it uses specially designed bikes, music, and visualization to provide an intense workout. To be a Spinning® instructor, you must become certified by Johnny G's company, Madd Dog Athletics (MDA), and work for a facility that is licensed and authorized to offer the program (there are over 4,000 in 80 countries).

Because of Spinning®'s popularity, and the cost to clubs of licensing and authorization, a number of organizations offer their own versions of indoor cycling classes. These classes also use music and visualization techniques, and many employ heart rate monitors to further enhance the workout. You can become certified as an indoor cycling instructor by AFFA, the Cooper Institute, and other leading fitness associations.

Former professional kickboxer Thomas "The Promise" Trebotich began fitness kickboxing classes in the 1980s. He founded the International Sports Conditioning Association, which continues to train teachers in kickboxing class formats. Kickboxing is a cardio workout comprised of martial arts and dance moves; the punches and kicks are done to music, although the classes are usually less choreographed than regular aerobics (making them more popular with many men). Equipment such as weighted gloves and punching bags may be used, and self-defense moves are sometimes taught during the class.

Many fitness associations offer kickboxing certifications, including AFAA, AFPA, and IFA. There is also a form of the class taught in pools; certification in aquatic kickboxing is offered jointly through the Aquatic Exercise Association and the International Sports Conditioning Association.

Rowing is a newer addition to class formats that mimic outdoor sports. Think of a cycling class, and substitute rowing machines for the bikes. First introduced in 1997, rowing, or crew, classes are headed by an instructor, who uses music and visualization to lead students through an intense workout. Rowing exercises the legs, arms, back, abdomen, and glutes. It provides aerobic conditioning and strength training with a wide range of motion, and without impact to the body. A manufacturer of rowing machines, Concept 2, offers instructor certification in indoor rowing.

Mind–Body Options

As the population seeks to find release from the stresses of everyday life, many have looked to forms of exercise that involve a spiritual or centering component. Three of the most common practiced today are yoga, tai chi, and Pilates. Yoga is believed to be the most widely practiced of spiritual disciplines. As Georg Feuerstein explains, underlying this ancient practice "is the understanding that the human being is more than the physical body and that, through a course of discipline, it is possible to discover what this 'more' is." Today, according to Feuerstein, there are about 20 million Westerners practicing yoga. The number of ashrams, or centers in which yoga is taught and practiced, continues to grow.

Fran Scalessa, a yoga instructor in Summit, New Jersey, believes that its popularity hasn't yet crested. He notes, "people enjoy it, and see the benefits of what they're doing. As the population ages, I'm sure even more will come. Yoga delays the aging process, and the stretching and relaxation we do in class directly benefits my students." With the increase in interest, many fitness organizations are training instructors in yoga forms. While most purists would call classes like "fitness yoga" and "yoga ball" purely western derivations, they are becoming very popular in health clubs around the country, and those who participate cite relaxation and a sense of well-being as major benefits.

Tai Chi was derived from Taoism in China about one thousand years ago. It involves a form of martial arts known as "moving meditation," seeking to move from external, physical exercise to internal (spiritual, emotional) tranquility. Daily practice of tai chi is said to promote mental clarity and overall health, and improve balance and blood circulation. According to Jane Golden, a tai chi instructor in Sonoma, California, "it was brought [to the United States] in the 1960s, soon after the great doors of China opened to the world. Introduced by scholars through the universities, it spread across America slowly: first embraced by the counterculture; then by the martial artists;

and now by the mainstream." There are many tai chi centers around the country that train teachers to bring this ancient Chinese form to their classes.

The Pilates Method is an exercise program developed in the early twentieth century by German-born Joseph Pilates, who called it "Controlology." Using equipment that he designed himself (such as Universal Reformer, Cadillac/Trap Table, High and Low Chairs, all Barrels, Ped-O-Pul, Foot Corrector, Magic Circle) he became popular as a trainer and rehabilitative therapist for dancers in New York City. While dancers and other professional athletes have used Pilates for many years to achieve long, lean muscles, the program is now practiced around the world by those seeking to improve strength, flexibility, and overall health.

The Pilates method is designed to add strength without bulk. It is also said to correct postural imbalance, improve coordination and body awareness, combat stress and tension, and create a more streamlined body. Pilates is a slow and deliberate form of exercise, adhering to the Zen idea that less is more. It brings together the Eastern emphasis on mental concentration with the Western emphasis on physical activity, teaching students to pay attention to their bodies' movements, rhythms, and posture.

To become a Pilates instructor, one must attend a course or workshop to learn the techniques and use of equipment. However, there is no educational standard, so you will find instruction ranging from a weekend to a 750-hour commitment or more. As with other forms of exercise enjoying current popularity, many of the national fitness organizations offer "Pilates-like" certifications. AFAA's "Mat Science" workshops, for instance, teach instructors how to bring elements of yoga and Pilates to their students.

Rehabilitation Class Formats

There is a growing demand of the clinical population for safe, effective ways to maintain health, prevent disease, and rehabilitate from injury and illness. Doctors are more readily prescribing physical exercise to their patients, both for health maintenance and rehabilitation, creating a greater need for trainers and instructors who understand the physical limitations of their clients, and who can work with physicians to develop and oversee programs that meet clinical goals.

In addition to teaching and training the clinical population, exercise programs and equipment once designed specifically for rehabilitation and other medically based orientations are now moving into the mainstream. An example is the growing popularity of the stability ball, which was first introduced as a prop for physical therapy. The ball originated in Europe, and became favored in the United States in the 1960s with the medical rehabilitation community, who used it to treat patients requiring rehabilitation and back strengthening.

Known variously as an exercise ball, Swiss ball, Physioball, FitBall® or Resist-A-Ball®, the large (average 55 cm), inflated ball is now used in classes for flexibility training, yoga, interval work, kids, seniors, prenatal/postnatal women, strength training, cardio, yoga, and Pilates classes. The ISFTA (International Sports Fitness and Trainers Association) offers a certification in "Function-a-ball"™ that uses this piece of equipment in 150 different exercises.

Aquatic classes also have their beginnings in the clinical population. Underwater exercise involves resistance provided by the water without impact, making it ideal for those with orthopedic and neurological problems, traumatic injuries, arthritic pain, and fibromyalgia. Aquatic therapists use a variety of techniques including mild stretching exercises, flotation devices and watsu, a relaxation technique. While anyone may benefit from aquatic exercise classes, they are most often taught to groups who may have physiological limitations, such as some older adults and pregnant women.

As it became adapted for the general population, a water fitness industry grew up around it. Organizations such as the Aquatic Alliance International, Aquatic Exercise Association, and the National Academy for Health and Fitness promote water fitness and certify instructors to teach classes, as well as personal trainers to use the format with their clients.

HIRING TRENDS AND SALARIES

According to the Bureau of Labor Statistics (BLS), there were about 160,000 fitness instructors working in the United States in 2000. An industry survey placed the number of full-time employees at 141,000, and the number of part-time employees at 564,000. More than 60,000 of them were personal trainers. The BLS expects this number to increase by 36% during the deca ending 2010, placing fitness instructors and personal trainers in two of the fastest growing professions in the country. They attribute the anticipated increase to the growing interest in both personal training and many forms of exercise instruction.

The Department of Labor reports that the median hourly earnings of fitness trainers and aerobics instructors in 2000 were $10.96. The middle 50% earned between $7.65 and $17.84, while the top 10% earned $25.98 or more. However, the American College of Sports Medicine (ACSM) notes that salaries are difficult to predict, because they depend upon a number of factors. These include experience, geographic location, employment setting, certification, and market demand.

While they estimate a starting annual salary of between $18,000 and $30,000, the ACSM recommends that the "best way to gauge what salary you can expect is to speak with professionals who currently work in your field of interest. Since geography can heavily dictate salary, it is important that you speak with those who work where you are job-seeking. Again, it is important to emphasize that many factors, including those mentioned above, can impact this salary range."

THE IMPORTANCE OF TRAINING

As greater numbers of people seek employment in the fitness industry, the requirements set by employers get more stringent. Ten years ago you may have been able to walk into a health club in the morning, get a few hours of training from another instructor, and be teaching a class that afternoon. Today, it's more likely that you would need to walk in with a resume, request an interview, be quizzed about your education and experience, teach a sample class for a hiring manager, and then be considered for a position.

Tops on employers' lists is training. Whether in the form of certification or a college degree, it is a necessity for finding employment as a fitness instructor or personal trainer. "A commitment to education, certification and continuing education demonstrates that you are serious about what you do for a living and it sets you apart from less-qualified people," says Micheala Conley, president, HPRI, a job-searching service for fitness and health promotion professionals.

Certification

There are virtually no legitimate fitness employers who will hire an instructor or personal trainer who isn't certified. The good news is, there is a great variety of certifications available; check Appendix A's list of industry associations—each one with an asterisk after its name offers some type of certification. Certifications may be obtained through attendance at a workshop or course, home study, or a combination of the two.

You will first need to acquire basic certification in instruction and/or personal training (titles may vary with each organization). Then, you may move on to get specialty and advanced certifications. The latter include aquatic exercise, kickboxing, prenatal, step aerobics, indoor cycling, and weight training. Certifications are valid for three years, and may be kept current by securing continuing education credits.

Certification will prepare you for employment by teaching relevant material including: basic anatomy and physiology, injury prevention, modifications for special populations, choreography, correct form, cuing, spotting techniques, CPR, and nutrition.

College Degrees

As with many other professions, fitness workers, and the industry in which they are employed, are becoming more professionalized. While you can still find an entry-level position as an instructor or trainer with just certification, employers are increasingly looking for college graduates. This is especially true of companies that offer full-time positions with promotion potential. "Most companies want someone with a degree in the field, and they will certainly give preference to someone with a bachelor's or a master's in exercise and sport science," says Linda Pejchar, owner of a recruiting firm for health and fitness professionals.

One of the reasons fitness employers prefer job candidates with college degrees is that these candidates not only have knowledge and skills learned in the classroom, but often graduate with a variety of work experiences as well. Most exercise science programs require students to complete internships, working at actual health clubs or other employment settings for college credit. Many also run their own health club right on or nearby the campus, affording even greater hands-on, work-study learning opportunities.

There are a number of other advantages to be gained by the job candidate with postsecondary training in fitness-related areas. Many schools hire those working in the industry to teach their classes, putting their students in contact with potential employers right away. Colleges and universities are frequently the sites of job fairs, where employers gather to interview and then hire graduating seniors. They also maintain relationships with area businesses that hire their graduates, and thus become an invaluable resource for job hunters.

All of this doesn't mean you won't be able to find a job if you haven't or can't go to college, but you may have a more difficult time than someone with a degree in hand. Because of the importance of formal training (and necessity of certification), two chapters of this book are devoted to the subject of your education and how to pay for it.

As you read through Chapter 2, remain flexible regarding your ideas about education. You may think now that you would like to jump into the job market right out of high school (and that may still be your course of action after reading this book), but be willing to consider other options. There are programs that take just a year to complete, and they offer some of the same benefits as longer programs.

If you haven't considered education beyond high school because you have always felt you couldn't afford it, Chapter 3 will take you through the financial aid "marketplace," explaining the types of aid available, where they can be found, and how and when to apply. However, if you didn't graduate from high school, your first step is to get a General Educational Development Certificate, or GED. In most states, you must complete a battery of tests in math, reading, grammar (including writing skills), social studies, and science. In addition to knowledge in these subject areas, you may be asked to document instruction in health, civic literacy, and career education.

To prepare for the GED tests, you can sign up for classes or individualized study offered in many communities through adult schools and non-profit agencies. Public television series often offer study materials, and you can receive educational support through phone contact and occasional teacher/student face-to-face meetings on campus. Technical colleges also offer these services and are often official GED test sites.

Some states recognize the "life experience" of adults who did not graduate from high school but who have learned skills equivalent to those expected of high school graduates. They evaluate and give credit for skills learned on the job, through raising a family, or from one's own self-directed learning. Check with your state's higher education department, listed in Appendix A, for more information about obtaining a GED in your area.

WHERE DO FITNESS INSTRUCTORS WORK?

The majority of fitness instructors are employed in health clubs, and, indeed, this is where many believe the scope of employment opportunities begins and ends. However, there are a number of new possibilities in the job market, many of which are experiencing rapid growth. Corporate fitness/wellness centers, located in business settings, are one such area: a 1997 study of fitness and exercise markets found there to be over 4,000; five years later, that number has grown significantly, to include not only corporations, but educational institutions, hospitals, and government agencies. All of these employers have realized that promoting the health and well-being of their employees makes good business sense: they perform better on the job, use their health insurance benefits less frequently, and take fewer sick days.

The health care industry presents another growing opportunity for instructors and personal trainers. According to the International Sports Sciences Association (ISSA), the number of hospital based fitness centers has doubled in the past few years. These centers all employ instructors and/or personal trainers. In addition, there are thousands of other health-care sites, including physical therapy and sports medicine clinics, which utilize fitness workers.

Another job possibility is self-employment. According to the Department of Labor, there are about 26,000 self-employed fitness workers, many of whom are personal trainers. Rapidly expanding areas for entrepreneurial fitness professionals include programs for older adults, long-term rehabilitation for people returning from surgery or injury, and working with young and seasoned athletes on developing sports-conditioning programs. "Partnering" with the medical community and health care providers for exercise therapy is a recent phenomenon that qualified fitness professionals are tapping. Learn more about self-employment in Chapters 4 and 6.

Once you enter the workforce, your overall job satisfaction will depend largely on how well you like the environment provided by your employer. Therefore, it is critical that you give consideration not only to the type of job you would like to have, but where and for whom you would like to work. There are important differences between large chain health clubs, small, family-owned gyms, city hospitals, and alternative health care centers.

Who Goes Where

Commercial health clubs currently claim 48% of all U.S. memberships in 2000. The total not-for-profit sector (YMCA's, JCC's, hospital-based clubs, residential, municipal, university, and military facilities) accounts for 39%, or 13.1 million members. A sizeable balance of 16% is represented by miscellaneous for-profit facilities: corporate fitness centers, aerobics studios, resorts, spas, hotels, and country clubs, a collective share that is significantly above the 1999 level of 13%.

Source: *International Health, Racquet, and Sports Club Association (IHRSA)/ American Sports Data Health Club Trend Report.*

While it is impossible to summarize all of the various work environments of fitness instructors, a description of some of the largest employers follows, including advantages and disadvantages of each. You will also find recent job advertisements for positions with these types of employers. While reading the following descriptions, keep in mind your reactions to each; you may already believe you know the type of employer you prefer, but may not be aware of the scope of opportunities available. For more information about these and other workplaces, see Chapter 6.

Corporate Owned (Chain) Health Clubs

Corporations are, because of their size, hierarchical. You will find in these organizations that there are often senior-level managers, who supervise junior-level managers, who supervise a staff of other employees. There are significant advantages and disadvantages to working in such a setting.

To begin with, you will be presented with a clear path for your career, including possibilities for raises and promotions. Corporations have many resources that smaller companies don't, so they can offer more to their employees. If you are interested in continuing your education, you may find that your employer will pay some or all of the cost associated with attending seminars, preparing for certification exams, or obtaining a college degree. You may also find that working for a corporation will provide:

► a higher salary
► better benefits if working full-time—more days of sick leave and vacation, superior insurance and retirement programs
► greater opportunity for advancement
► better equipment, so your job will be easier and you can be more creative
► larger schedules with a wider variety of classes

On the downside, large chain health clubs tend to focus much of their energy on signing up new members. To that end, nearly every employee is responsible on some level for sales. If you don't feel comfortable trying to get people to buy memberships, this could be difficult for you. In addition, some people feel suffocated by the hierarchy of corporations. Your job description will be very clear, and there will most likely be little opportunity to stray from it. Free-spirited types may find it difficult to fit in.

Largest Owners of Fitness Clubs

Company	Website	Number of clubs/centers
24 Hour Fitness Worldwide, Inc.	www.24hourfitness.com	437
Bally Total Fitness Holding	www.ballyfitness.com	400+
Gold's Gym Enterprises Inc.	www.goldsgym.com	550
YMCA of the USA	ww.ymca.net	2,400+
World Gym International	www.worldgym.com	200+
Powerhouse Gym	www.powerhousegym.com	240

Sample Job Advertisements

PERSONAL TRAINERS

No Excuses, Your Fitness Partners, Palo Alto, CA

Club/Company Description:

No Excuses is a private fitness studio serving residents and executives of Downtown Palo Alto and the surrounding communities (SF Bay Area).

Job Duties:

At No Excuses, management handles all aspects of marketing and sales, leaving the focus of our trainers on TRAINING and complete client service.

Job Qualifications:

Candidates must hold current certification with 4-5 years practical experience. In depth knowledge in the following areas: anatomy, kinesiology, understanding of Dr. Siff philosophy, Chek Scientific Back Training, Stability Ball and Core Training, Comparative Range of Motion. Trainer should have a passion for strength training and be able to provide creative and timely programming with a personal focus on continuing education.

Salary:

Commensurate with experience. Qualified Candidate can expect a range of $35-$50 per session!

GROUP FITNESS INSTRUCTORS

WOW! Work Out World

Monmouth, Ocean, and Middlesex Counties in NJ, USA

Club/Company Description:

Aggressive Upscale Fitness Centers...25,000 square feet in size and very rich in architecture. Currently five locations in NJ with a strategic plan for growth. Lots of services (ie. Dr's, Nurses, Chiropractor, Endermology, Personal Training, etc.)...Check our website at www.workoutworld.com

We are very focused and passionate about what we do and we accept nothing less from our team.

Job Duties:

Have Fun! Teach Classes! Get members excited and happy to be a part of WOW! Oh and by the way, Have FUN!!!

Job Qualifications:

Nationally Certified, CPR Certified, professional, passionate, likeable, caring, upbeat, and flowing with positivity. If you can WOW! a class then we want to hear from YOU!

Salary:

To be discussed.

The Fred Foster Fitness Company, Inc. (FFFC), Gaithersburg, MD

Positions:

Looking for experienced personal and group fitness instructors capable of working with in-home clients mostly in the Potomac, Bethesda and Rockville areas. Qualified candidates will be certified by a nationally recognized certification organization and/or hold a four year degree in a fitness related course of study. Each fitness instructor must be comfortable working with individuals and groups in settings that are not always ideal (i.e., WE DO NOT DO MUCH TRAINING IN GYMS AND WE DO NOT ALWAYS HAVE EQUIPMENT AT OUR DISPOSAL!). Candidates must commit to at least ten (10) hours per week and be able to train early to late mornings (0500 – 1200 hours) and/or evenings (after 1600 hours).

Independently Owned Clubs, Studios, and Management Companies

There are thousands of fitness facilities and businesses that are not owned by large corporations. In this category are included large clubs that bring in millions of dollars a year, $40' \times 40'$ storefront yoga studios, weight-training centers with boxing rings, and spas that cater to women only. There are also companies that have no facilities other than office space; they have contracts with various clients, hire instructors and trainers, and then send them out to the clients. All of these businesses have something in common—they are not owned or run by huge corporations.

Working for a smaller organization can bring a number of advantages. They may include a more relaxed work atmosphere, and the chance to work in a variety of areas, not necessarily in your job description. Whereas in a corporately owned facility, every phase of operation is dictated by upper management, there is more room for flexibility and creativity for instructors and trainers in independently owned locations.

In addition, you may find a personal, less formal setting, in which individuals are respected for their unique qualities. Independently owned clubs, gyms, and studios tend toward a team-like atmosphere. If one person is successful, everyone shares the success. You will most likely find in such a place a pleasant working environment that promotes growth and cooperation.

However, you may also find lower pay, fewer benefits, and less than state-of-the-art technology. In some smaller facilities, there is little chance for advancement simply because there aren't any job openings to move up into. In addition, there could be less job stability, as smaller operations fight to stay afloat in economic downturns that might be weathered more easily by large companies. Many are willing to put up with the disadvantages, though, as a trade-off for the many rewards to be had from this type of employer.

Sample Job Advertisement

GROUP CLASS INSTRUCTORS

Plus One Fitness, Chicago, IL

Club/Company Description:

Plus One is a comprehensive fitness and wellness management company specializing in the design, equipping, programming, and managing of corporate, hotel, and residential fitness centers. This latest corporate addition to Plus One's list of clients is located in the Sears Towers and includes the latest in fitness equipment, wellness programming, and training techniques with world class customer service.

Job Duties:

We are seeking teachers for all class styles, including Spinning, Kickboxing, Yoga, and Step classes.

Job Qualifications:

Instructors need professional certification and to be trained in CPR. Candidates must be energetic & professional with great customer service skills.

Salary:

$25.00 per hour

Corporate Fitness/Wellness Programs

The Wellness Councils of America (WELCOA)'s "America's Healthiest Companies 2000" included Union Pacific Railroad, Anheuser-Busch, The City of Austin, Texas, and Thomas Memorial Hospital in West Virginia. They represent just a handful of the thousands of corporations, government agencies, hospitals, and educational institutions that provide fitness programs to their employees. As word gets out about the benefits of such programs, the number and types of businesses who provide them increases. Those benefits include advancing employee health, lowering health care costs, and improving productivity and morale.

Many larger companies build fitness centers into their office space, and offer exercise classes, personal training, and other related services. Smaller companies may provide space such as empty conference rooms for classes after work or during lunch. They may also hire instructors to set up programs such as walking, running, team sports, and weekend ski trips. The instructor may be in charge of marketing the activities, supporting the individuals who sign up, and maintaining interest within the company.

Some employers hire their fitness workers individually, while others rely on corporate wellness companies that provide an entire package and oversee programs. These companies hire the instructors and personal trainers, and send them out to their clients on temporary or more permanent bases. Positions at these facilities may be numerous—in addition to a staff of trainers and instructors, there is typically at least one manager, and it's not unusual to find a nurse or other health care professional, too.

Many corporate fitness programs exist as part of an overall Health Promotion Program. This means that those hired to teach and train employees may also be responsible for coordinating such programs as smoking cessation, stress reduction seminars, company team sports, weekend ski trips, etc. One corporation with an in-house Health Promotion Program listed the responsibilities of its employees:

▶ fitness center management and staffing
▶ personal fitness assessment and body composition testing
▶ fitness programming (weight management, general conditioning and toning, strength training, body building, stretching, stress management, balance, sport specific)
▶ personal and group training sessions
▶ exercise classes (low impact aerobics, step, kickboxing, yoga, stretch, relaxation)
▶ outdoor training (walking/running groups)
▶ massage
▶ informative seminars on topics of interest

Sample Job Advertisements

Title of Position:

Corporate Health and Fitness Center Manager

Indianapolis, IN

Description of Position:

This position will oversee daily operations of corporate health/fitness/recreation facility. Duties include supervision of full-time and part-time employees, recreational sports programming, supervision of fitness center floor, fitness assessments and exercise prescriptions, and health promotion programming.

Educational requirements:

Bachelor's degree in health-related field required/Master's preferred; ACSM and/or other health-related certification preferred.

Other job qualifications:

Two to three years of staff supervisory experience required, two to three years experience in a worksite health setting, strong interpersonal and organizational skills.

Gybek Manufacturing, Tulsa, Oklahoma

Seeking Group Exercise Instructor for our Wellness Center.

The Group Exercise Instructor provides safe, fun, creative, and challenging group exercise instruction. The Group Exercise Instructor works closely with the Group Exercise Site Coordinator and Program Manager to provide variety of classes tailored our employees' needs.

Job qualifications:

Nationally recognized Aerobic/Group Exercise Instruction certification required

CPR and first aid certification required

Strong communication skills required

Reliable; prompt

Personable; positive attitude

Salary:

$19.00/hour

Healthcare Facilities

This is one of the fastest growing employers for the fitness industry, due in large part to the medical community's acknowledgement of the importance of exercise to the health and well-being of the population. Many physicians now "prescribe" exercise to their patients for overall improvement of health, as well as for disease and injury prevention. In addition, those recovering from injuries and surgeries require rehabilitation, which can often be administered by fitness professionals.

For instance, the Huntsville (Alabama) Hospital's Wellness Center offers assessments such as strength, flexibility, cardiovascular fitness, muscular endurance, body compositions, body measurements, blood pressure, and heart rate. Cardiac and cancer rehabilitation programs include exercise. They offer classes in Yoga, Pilates, Step aerobics, circuit training, water aerobics, stretching, indoor cycling, yogaball, kickboxing, and body sculpting.

In addition, they offer personal training. The personal trainer conducts an initial assessment, which includes:

- ▶ completion of health history
- ▶ review of personal goals
- ▶ determination and explanation of target heart rate
- ▶ explanation of strength and cardiovascular endurance
- ▶ explanation of sets, repetition, and weights

If you are interested in this sector of employment, you might consider becoming certified by an organization such as the American Academy of Health, Fitness and Rehabilitation Professionals. The AAHFRP offers certifications in Medical Exercise Specialist, Medical Exercise Program Director, and Post Rehab Conditioning Specialist (www.medicalexercisespecialist. com). You must first hold a "general" certification from one of the large, national certifying bodies before studying to sit for these certifying exams.

Some hospital-based facilities are run by companies that provide turnkey services, such as Healthtrax. These companies may physically set up the center, schedule classes, and staff the center. If interested, check out their website at www.healthtrax.com, or contact them at 2345 Main Street, Glastonbury, CT 06033. Tel: (860) 633-5572 Fax: (860) 633-7472.

Sample Job Advertisements

WOMEN'S HOSPITAL'S FITNESS CENTER
FITNESS INSTRUCTOR

Responsibilities:

Responsible for supervising and instructing members as they exercise on the floor. Assists the Fitness Coordinator with fitness assessments and exercise prescriptions. Performs other duties assigned by Department management according to policies and procedures and the mission of Women's Hospital.

Qualifications:

Bachelors of Science in Kinesiology or health related field. Six months supervisory experience in the health/fitness industry and/or one to two years experience in exercise instruction. Must be knowledgeable of exercise standards and guidelines established by the American College of Sports Medicine. CPR certification required. Other exercise certifications preferred. Must have basic understanding of exercise testing, training, and prescription and excellent communication skills.

Salary:

$10.61 - $16.45 per/hr, excellent benefits package.

Chester County Hospital Center
for Health & Fitness

Exercise Specialist (P/T) (04/15/02)

Responsibilities:

Exercise Specialist position in Hospital Based Medical Fitness Facility, located in West Chester, PA. Great entry position with abundant opportunity in an established and growing facility. Provide Exercise Specialist duties in a Medical Fitness Facility, including fitness assessments, exercise prescription and education. Ability to work with various populations and conditions including cardio-pulmonary rehabilitation, osteoarthritis, diabetes and ambulatory challenged.

Qualifications:

B.S. Exercise Science and 1-2 years experience. CPR certified. ACSM certification preferred.

OPPORTUNITIES FOR ADVANCEMENT

Fitness instructors and personal trainers with experience and education may decide, after a time, to seek different positions within the industry. You might want an opportunity to earn a better salary, gain more responsibility, or grow in a new direction. Perhaps the most obvious choice, and requiring the least effort, is to rise into management at the facility for which you are already working. While many health clubs require a bachelor's degree (and, in some cases, a master's degree) in exercise science, physical education, or a related area, to advance to management positions, it's not unheard of for instructors and trainers to get promoted without a degree.

Those who get promoted have a few basic characteristics in common. They know their employer's business and constantly seek out new information about how it is run and its current state of operation. They follow dictated procedures closely, not only playing by the rules, but also knowing them inside out.

Getting a promotion depends heavily on attitude. You need to stress customer service, showing genuine care for members and fellow employees, consistently. A positive attitude toward the changes that are inherent in the fitness industry is also essential. An employer doesn't respond well to an employee who gripes about his or her job; you will need to embrace the changes that upper management mandates and show that you are a team player. Employees who rise up into the ranks of management also take the time to get to know their superiors. Make an effort early on to have contact with upper management and make a positive impression.

When you feel you are ready to advance, don't wait for a superior to suggest a promotion. Be proactive about your career by applying for an open job with more responsibility and a higher salary. Positions you may be qualified to fill with certification and experience include:

▶ Corporate fitness director
▶ Fitness program director
▶ Personal training director
▶ Group exercise coordinator
▶ YMCA/Boy's and Girl's Club director
▶ Sport camp director

If you would like to utilize the knowledge and skills you obtained while working as an instructor or trainer, but seek a greater challenge or higher pay, you might consider any of the following positions. Some are compatible with work as a fitness instructor or personal trainer, while others might mean getting more education and pursuing different goals.

▶ Fitness franchise ownership
▶ Health club or studio ownership
▶ Pharmaceutical sales
▶ Sport marketing/merchandising
▶ Sport management/promotion/advertising
▶ Strength coaching for college/university athletic dept or professional athletic team
▶ Retail sporting goods sales
▶ Exercise equipment manufacturing; sales
▶ Intramural sports coordinating

If you are willing to go back to school and receive specialized training, your options become even greater. You might decide to work toward a bachelor's or master's degree, or take the courses necessary to qualify you for a desired position. Options include, but are not limited to:

▶ Clinical exercise programmer
▶ Cardiac rehabilitation therapist
▶ Sports nutrition specialist
▶ Nutrition educator
▶ Health and fitness educator
▶ Sports medicine practitioner
▶ Coach
▶ Physical therapist
▶ Occupational therapist
▶ Physician's assistant
▶ Sports journalist
▶ Athletic trainer
▶ Exercise physiologist
▶ Sport officiator

► Massage therapist
► Exercise technician
► Certified orthotist (prosthetics)

SKILLS INVENTORY

You have read about who fitness instructors and personal trainers are and what they do. You have learned where they work and how they can get ahead in their careers. Now, you can determine whether you are ready to seek a position as an instructor or trainer. This questionnaire was designed to get you thinking about the skills necessary to succeed on the job, including those you already possess, and those you may want to work on developing. It's a good idea to understand your strengths and weaknesses before you enter the job market, when there's plenty of time to turn your weaknesses around.

Read the following statements, determine your honest answer, and then circle true or false for each.

1. I enjoy fast-paced environments, and work best under pressure. T F
2. I like doing one thing at a time, completing each task before moving on to the next. T F
3. When faced with criticism, I usually get defensive. T F
4. In an emergency or crisis situation, I keep a level head and take charge. T F
5. I do my best work when I'm alone and can concentrate on the task at hand. T F
6. I'm good at motivating people, and bringing out the best in them. T F
7. I'm interested in workout trends, and love to experiment with new equipment and exercises. T F
8. Making people feel good about themselves is important to me. T F
9. I like working for someone who gives plenty of direction. T F
10. I'm glad school is over; I've got my diploma, and don't need to read much or study any more. T F
11. Irregular hours don't bother me; I've never considered myself a nine-to-fiver. T F
12. I'm very patient. T F

13. I don't want to make mistakes, so I prefer to wait until I understand exactly what's expected of me before proceeding with any task. T F
14. I like all kinds of music; the right song at the right time can really put me in a good mood and motivate me to work harder. T F
15. I get bored when I have to do the same thing every day; change keeps me energized. T F

Take note of your answers. The questionnaire is not an absolute measure of your suitability, but if you answered "true" to statements 1, 4, 6, 7, 8, 11, 12, 14, and 15, you already possess many of the skills necessary for success as a fitness instructor or personal trainer. If you answered "false" to any of these statements, begin thinking about ways to improve your skills. Education will help with some of them, as will an affiliation with one or more of the various industry associations. Remember, you will want to become the best possible job candidate you can be before making contact with potential employers.

Read on to discover how to prepare for your career as a fitness instructor or personal trainer. In the next chapters, you will learn how to get the education you need, how to pay for it, and how to get the most out of it. Then, discover where the instructor and trainer jobs are, and how to find and succeed in one.

THE INSIDE TRACK

Who: Alex McKechnie
What: Spinning Instructor/Personal Trainer
Where: Various New York Health Clubs
                  New York City

Having been an athlete and a dancer for most of my life, I found fitness instruction to be a perfect secondary career fit for me. I currently work about 40 hours a week as a full-time orthopedic physician assistant and 1–10 hours a week as a part-time spinning and weight training instructor at various New York City health clubs. Interestingly enough, the two positions aren't as dissimilar as one might think. Both jobs are health-oriented, and I've always believed that exercise is the best medicine.

In order to receive certification from The American Council on Exercise (ACE), I attended a preparatory course hosted by New York Sports Club and reviewed the training manual before taking the written exam. After obtaining my certification, I called several health clubs in my area to enquire about employment opportunities and used other, more experienced instructors as a resource. The best way to meet instructors is by attending their classes, where you can't help but get to know them.

An effective instructor should be fit, punctual, knowledgeable, and both mentally and physically prepared for each class, which includes having a microphone and the appropriate music. Since being an instructor involves a lot of human interaction, you should also be patient, enthusiastic, and friendly. Leadership skills are also extremely important; it's not easy to engage a class of strangers and make the experience fun even as you encourage them to push their physical limits. One thing to keep in mind while teaching fitness classes is that every student is different. Before starting a class, I always ask my students if they have any injuries, sensitivities, limitations, and/or pregnancies that I should be aware of and offer tips to make the class better for everyone, including those with special needs. Before starting a spinning class, I make sure that everyone is correctly set up on the bike and adjust each student as necessary. I also ask if anyone is training for anything, a triathlon, for instance, and do my best to offer them specific advice. Despite my efforts to cater to each and every individual, it's important to realize that no matter what you do, you can never please everyone, all the time.

One thing people often don't realize is that fitness instruction can involve a lot of creativity because there are so many avenues and niches to explore and develop as an instructor. The more cutting-edge you are, the more marketable you become, which is why I try to keep my music choices fresh and interesting. Since fitness classes are often taught in a vacuum, I also like to tie in real-world events during my classes. For example, when teaching my spinning class, I often make announcements about local races or engage the class in a conversation about the Tour de France.

Over the years, I've received my fair share of perks as the result of being a fitness instructor, like travel and TV exposure. But the most obvious perk is that you get paid to workout! Being an instructor has also given me the opportunity to meet a lot of great people and make new friends. Another added bonus is that, as a fitness instructor, you will always be able to find a job. I'm getting married and relocating soon, so teaching will help me meet people and get acclimated to the new city as I look for a new orthopedic physician assistant position. As an athlete, I am as dedicated to my own fitness goals as I am to those of my students, and fitness instruction will certainly help me stay committed to those goals even as I face a major life change.

CHAPTER two

GETTING THE EDUCATION YOU NEED

In this chapter you will learn why formal training is important. The types of instructional opportunities available to those seeking to enter the fitness industry, and the reasons for obtaining various levels of education will be explored. Included are sample courses and tuition costs from certifying organizations and schools around the country. You will discover how to choose a certification or degree program, by evaluating not only the curriculum and school or certifying organization, but your personal needs as well. Finally, there are tips on succeeding if you enroll at a college or university, including how to land an internship and how to prepare for exams.

IN CHAPTER 1, the dynamic growth of the fitness industry was explored, along with great employment opportunities for those seeking jobs as fitness instructors and personal trainers. How can you take advantage of those opportunities and begin your new career? The first step is education. While it may have been true ten years ago that you could walk into a health club in good shape, perhaps get some on-site training, and be teaching your first class or working with your first client within days or weeks, the climate of the industry has changed dramatically.

Today, it is highly unlikely that an instructor would be hired without, at a minimum, certification from a national organization. In fact, according to the U.S. Department of Labor, many fitness employers now require a college degree (associate or bachelor's) as a condition of employment—a far cry from the days when exercise classes were led by those with little or no training. There are a number of compelling reasons for this change, all pointing toward the need for fitness instructors and trainers to get educated before beginning a career in fitness.

WHY YOU NEED TRAINING

The first reason for choosing education before employment is that there has been an incredible amount of research and scientific study done in the area of exercise science. More than ever before, professionals know about the right ways to attain physical fitness while preventing injury and improving overall health. Instructors are expected to be knowledgeable about anatomy and physiology, the needs of special populations (such as the elderly and pregnant women), and even nutrition. Knowing the right ways to perform exercises, and which exercises work most efficiently to achieve desired effects, will not only help your students to achieve results more quickly, but will also keep them safer from injury and avoid wasting their time.

A recent study, conducted by the UCLA Exercise Physiology Research Laboratory and published in the February 2002 issue of the *Journal of Strength and Conditioning Research*, found that personal trainers with a college degree and certification were more knowledgeable than their peers with years of experience and no degree. The participants were given a questionnaire constructed for the study and designed to measure knowledge of nutrition, health screening, testing protocols, exercise prescription, and special populations. The researchers concluded that:

> Those with bachelor's degrees in exercise science and certification by the American College of Sports Medicine or the National Strength and Conditioning Association had the highest level of knowledge, compared to personal trainers with years of experience or other certifications. . . . As predicted, a personal trainer's years of experience did not translate into more knowledge. In fact, personal trainers with five or more years of experience had no greater knowledge than trainers with four or fewer years of experience.

The UCLA study concludes with the assertion that consumers should ask for education and certification credentials before hiring a personal trainer.

During an education in exercise science or a related field, instructors and trainers learn how to teach or train clients who make up a very diverse population. Once you begin your career, you will not only be asked to demonstrate the correct ways to perform exercises, but also be able to modify those exercises according to students' needs. You may have a class that has a mix of hard-core athletes and those just starting out on a fitness path. Your class should cater to both, and everyone in between. If someone in your class tells you that he or she has never lifted a weight before, you will need to guide them toward correct form and equipment while leading the rest of the class at a pace that gives seasoned participants a good workout as well. To perform with this level of expertise on the job, education is necessary, and must continue throughout your career as new methods and research data become available.

Second, there is a growing population of those requiring physical and recreational therapy. Doctors are prescribing various forms of exercise to their patients in order to rehabilitate, lessen the effects of disease and other conditions, and improve overall health. In order to serve this population, fitness professionals must work with the medical community to devise and provide appropriate treatment(s). Both groups are expected to perform with the same level of professionalism, knowledge, and skill. If you are thinking about tapping into the growing clinical side of fitness, consider obtaining a college degree, not only for the knowledge gained while procuring it, but also for the respect of those you will be working with.

Third, those participating in exercise programs are more sophisticated than they were a decade ago. The proliferation of information regarding health and fitness has not only educated those who go to school to study these topics, but the general population as well. You can expect many students to come to class armed with knowledge about what they want in a program, and a better idea of how to judge what you are doing against what they think you should be doing. This well-informed group also expects variation: they are not going to put up with the same routines week after week, or even the same class formats and styles. Introducing new pieces of equipment, exercises, choreography, and music is essential.

As the fitness industry becomes more professionalized, the need for highly qualified, educated employees increases. A degree or certificate will get you hired more quickly when entering the job market and increase your chances for promotion throughout your career. Fortunately, educators have kept up with the demand, so you won't have to look far for your education. There are dozens of national associations that offer certification programs, through hands-on workshop participation, home study, and various combinations of the two. Certificate and degree programs may be found at hundreds of community, junior, and four-year colleges and universities.

If you choose to obtain certification through a national organization such as AFAA, you will automatically become a member of that organization. Your membership can put you in touch with those in your field, both fellow instructors and the employers of instructors. From access to websites, newsletters, and magazines, you will learn about the wide variety of job opportunities available to you, and get a broader vision of what's possible for your future career. You might find you don't want to work for a large corporate-owned club. You might decide that health care facilities or educational institutions provide a work atmosphere you would enjoy.

In a degree program, you will have to take a variety of courses, often taught by those working in various capacities throughout the fitness industry. The diversity of what is taught and who teaches it will expand your ideas about what a fitness instructor's job can be.

Formal education will also make available to you vital job search and placement services. The job placement office can be a great source for internships during your schooling, which provide on-the-job training and possibly job offers once completed. Many schools offer courses in how to search for a job, and when your schooling is completed, you may find that a number of local employers actively recruit graduates from your program.

CERTIFICATION

Almost any position in fitness, from a once-a-week class instructor to a full-time personal trainer, requires certification as a condition for employment. Even if you hold a college degree in exercise science or a related area, you may be required to obtain at least one certification before you begin teaching. Neil Reuben of the International Sports Sciences Association likens fitness degrees and certification to law school and the bar exam—even after graduation, you need to pass an exam to work in your field.

There are hundreds of national organizations that offer various types of exercise certification, so it's important to shop around before making a commitment. There are a wide variety of programs themselves, methods through which certification is attained, and even the cost of the programs.

Certifications are available through home study, attendance at workshops, and various combinations of the two. While the workshop format remains the most popular route to certification, study-at-home, or correspondence, courses are being offered by more associations than ever before. Perhaps the most important reason for this change is the Internet: courses may be taught online and made available to those unable to attend a workshop due to geographic, economic, or other factors. The ease with which students can communicate with instructors and other students via e-mail and discussion groups brings correspondence courses into the twenty-first century.

Home study advantages include the flexibility of being able to learn the material at one's own pace and at times convenient to one's work, school, family, and other obligations. The practical part of the exams for correspondence students must either be performed at a workshop, or videotaped by the student and sent to the certifying organization for evaluation. Associations offering the study-at-home option include National Strength Professionals Association (NSPA), National Endurance Sports Trainers Association (NESTA), International Sports Sciences Association (ISSA), National Federation of Professional Trainers (NFPT), and National Academy of Sports Medicine (NASM).

No matter how they are obtained, however, all certifications must be kept current through participation in continuing education (CE), and many certifying organizations recognize each other's programs as valid CE credits. For instance, once you are certified by the American Fitness and Aerobics Association (AFAA), you can obtain six CE credits by becoming certified as a Spinning® instructor.

Your first step toward deciding on a certification should be to determine which one(s) you may need. Ask at clubs in your area for which you are interested in working which certifications they prefer. They may only hire employees who have attained certifications from one or two select organizations, or may be willing to accept any certification. If all of the facilities near you are authorized to offer Spinning®, you will need to obtain certification through MDA (see Appendix A for contact information). It pays to find out what's really necessary before making a decision; the financial commitment of plane fare, meals, and lodging for an out-of-town certification seminar might not be worth it if your future employer would hire you with a certification earned online.

Next, visit the websites of certifying organizations, and request that they send you more information. You should be able to learn online how certifications are achieved (either attendance at workshops, online or some other form of independent study, or a combination of the two), what they cost, and where workshops are scheduled to be held. Fees, study materials, and other important topics are also usually explained on associations' websites.

While doing your research, pay careful attention to the requirements each organization demands of its applicants. They range from no educational requirements to a college degree, and from no previous experience to years of employment in the field. You should also compare the benefits of certification, which vary from one organization to another. Many offer support when certification is attained (usually in the form of online access to information), networking, free listings on their website (for you or your club), and/or discounts on liability insurance and other products.

The following information regarding some of the larger organizations is included to get your research started. Consult Appendix A to find contact information (including websites, addresses, phone and fax numbers) for most of the associations offering certification.

Cardiopulmonary Resuscitation (CPR)

Almost every employer in the fitness industry requires training and certification in cardio-pulmonary resuscitation (CPR). Because exercise can, in rare cases, bring on sudden cardiac arrest (the leading cause of death in adults), especially to those who have underlying heart disease, it is imperative that those teaching classes or supervising exercise know CPR. The technique, invented in 1960, provides oxygenated blood to the heart and brain after cardiac arrest, keeping them viable, until expert medical care is available. According to the American Heart Association, performing CPR on a victim of sudden cardiac arrest doubles that person's chance of survival.

There are a number of ways to obtain CPR training and certification. First, check with a local hospital or rescue squad, both of which employ those trained to teach CPR. They may be able to tell you when classes will be held in your area. The American Heart Association and American Red Cross both train instructors and offer classes. Many college degree and certificate programs also offer CPR training as part of their curriculum, so their students graduate with CPR certification.

Increasingly, other groups and businesses are also teaching CPR, often competing with the Heart Association and Red Cross by offering lower prices. While most of these courses are legitimate and sound, there are a few that may not prepare you as thoroughly as they should. Check the American Council on Exercise (ACE) website (www.acefitness.org) for a list of acceptable CPR course providers (it is not comprehensive, but will give you a good idea of those whose programs are considered the best). Search the Internet with the term "CPR" to find more information, or log onto the Heart Association and Red Cross' websites: www.americanheart.org and www.redcross.org.

The American College of Sports Medicine (ACSM)

The ACSM offers certification in the following areas: Group Exercise Leader, Health/Fitness Instructor, Health/Fitness Director, Exercise Specialist, Program Director, and Registered Clinical Exercise Physiologist. All are obtained after successfully completing a written and practical examination. To take the Group Exercise Leader exam, one must hold current CPR certification and be familiar with all forms of group exercise (low, high, and mixed aerobics; step aerobics; slide; stationary indoor cycling; and interval, circuit, water, muscle conditioning, and flexibility classes). In addition, one must hold fitness certification from a nationally recognized organization; or have completed or be currently enrolled in group exercise-related college courses at a regionally accredited college/university; or have 300 hours of group exercise instruction experience.

The exam is drawn from the following textbooks: ACSM's *Guidelines for Exercise Testing and Prescription*, 6th edition; ACSM's *Resource Manual for Guidelines for Exercise Testing and Prescription*, 4th edition; and ACSM's *Health/Fitness*

Certification Review. They may be purchased through the ACSM website for $104.00. Attendance at a day-long Group Exercise Workshop is also recommended, at a cost of $220.00. The exam for ACSM members is $175.00 ($200.00 for non-members). More information about ACSM's certifications may be found on their website: www.acsm.org.

American Council on Exercise (ACE)

ACE offers certification as a Personal Trainer or Group Fitness Instructor. Benefits of certification include free listing on the online "Find an ACE Pro," discounts on liability insurance and other products, and access to job listings. Candidates must be at least 18 years old and hold current CPR certification. Certification is awarded to those who pass a three-hour exam testing knowledge in the following areas:

Personal Trainer
exercise physiology
anatomy
applied kinesiology
basic nutrition
fitness assessment
exercise programming
instructional and spotting techniques
effective communication and motivation skills

Group Fitness Instructor
anatomy
kinesiology
exercise physiology
nutrition
injury prevention
emergency procedures
effective communication
instructional techniques
motivation skills

To prepare for either exam, one may study independently from a textbook (ACE recommends three to six months be allocated for study), or enhance this study through attendance at a preparatory program. The cost is $175.00, and, unlike most others, ACE certification may be counted as college credit by your educational institution.

The American Fitness and Aerobics Association (AFAA)

The American Fitness and Aerobics Association has certified over 145,000 members since its inception in 1983. It offers a variety of certification workshops for group exercise instructors and personal trainers, all of which involve traditional and hands-on instruction, followed by written and practical exams. Requirements generally include current CPR certification, successful completion of the exams, and some experience teaching group exercise.

AFAA offers standard benefits to those who achieve certification. They include membership in the association, a subscription to its magazine, and discounts on liability insurance, supplies, and clothing. Certifications include basic, kickboxing, step aerobics, personal training, emergency response, and weight training. Once primary certification is acquired, a member can attend continuing education one-day workshops in many of the current format trends in fitness, including "mat science" (incorporating elements of Pilates and yoga), kickboxing and step choreography, aqua fitness, prenatal fitness, resistance training (class format), and senior fitness.

Certifications cost between $229 (kickboxing) to $399 (personal trainer), and the price of one-day workshops ranges from $99 (prenatal fitness) to $119 (aerobics choreography). Workshops are held at clubs and other facilities around the country. The AFAA website includes search capabilities that can help you find when and where certification workshops are scheduled to be held.

The Cooper Institute

For over thirty years, the Cooper Institute in Dallas, Texas, has been conducting research in exercise physiology and related health issues. It also certifies fitness professionals in the following categories: physical fitness specialist, master fitness specialist, and health promotion director. Specialty certifications are offered in counseling healthy behaviors, group exercise leadership, biomechanics of resistance training, providing dietary guidance, fitness specialist for older adults, special populations, fitness kickboxing, martial arts, indoor cycling, aquatics, and team building.

All of these certification seminars and workshops are held at the Dallas site, and in some cities around the country. If there is enough interest (i.e., a large enough group), Cooper Institute seminars may be held at clubs, workplaces, and other locations. In addition, the Institute offers three certifications through a home-study program: Providing Dietary Guidance, Martial Arts, and Biomechanics of Resistance Training. The cost of the home-study materials is $395.00, which is the same price as the certifications in workshop form. Basic certifications are obtained through five-day seminars, which cost $675.00. Specialty certifications cost between $295.00 and $395.00

International Sports Sciences Association (ISSA)

The ISSA sets itself apart from many other certifying bodies in that it not only prepares its students to perform on the job, but teaches them how to run their own businesses as well. Since many instructors and personal trainers work as independent contractors, this is an option worth consideration. Curriculum for the fitness trainer certification (one of nine certification and continuing education programs offered) includes the study of building a profitable business, in addition to anatomy, physiology, nutrition, and weight training technology.

The ISSA provides many services to its certified members, such as unlimited technical support, free business forms, listing on their online Trainer Locator, and discounts on liability insurance, nutritional supplements, and fitness products. Cost for certification is $595, which includes all texts, a video, study guide, and admission to a weekend seminar.

> **ISSA Certification and Continuing Education Programs**
> Certified Fitness Trainer
> Fitness Therapist
> Specialist in Performance Nutrition
> Specialist in Fitness for Older Adults

Specialist in Sports Conditioning
Specialist in Martial Arts Conditioning
Specialist in Adaptive Fitness
Endurance Fitness Trainer
Youth Fitness Trainer
Water Fitness Trainer
Golf Fitness Trainer

Jazzercise

Founded in 1969 by Judi Sheppard Missett, Jazzercise was the first program to train and certify instructors, and also the first to create industry teaching standards. It differs from other certifications in a number of ways. First, every certified instructor holds a franchise. That means instructors are free to set up their own businesses with the support of Jazzercise, Inc., and can rent a site at which they can teach their own classes, or employ many more "associate substitute" instructors. Second, every class is choreographed and set to music at a national level, so instructors must learn new routines by purchasing instructional materials and pre-recorded music. Third, franchisees must turn over 20% of their gross revenue monthly to Jazzercise, Inc.

The certification program is conducted through two to three-day work-shops, and requires advance study of:

▶ basic anatomy
▶ exercise physiology
▶ nutrition
▶ body composition
▶ dance technique
▶ injury prevention
▶ exercise leadership
▶ Jazzercise teaching technique
▶ Jazzercise routines (performed during practical exam)

Workshops begin with a 100-question written exam and a practical exam. After successful completion of the exams, seminars on operating the franchise are held.

The cost of certification (or "investment for a Jazzercise franchise"), including attendance at the workshop, study materials, ongoing marketing support through national headquarters, bookkeeping materials, is $650. Once a franchisee, there are a number of other costs (in addition to the 20% of gross revenues mentioned previously). Liability insurance must be purchased through Jazzercise, Inc. ($130 to $145 annually). Music for each new routine set costs $100 to $150, with an additional $38 to $74 per year for musicians' royalties. More information about Jazzercise franchises, including contact information for regional managers, may be found at www.jazzercise.com.

National Athletic Trainers Association (NATA)

The NATA offers certification to those who complete a rigorous set of requirements and pass a certification examination. Basic requirements include a high school diploma, current CPR or EMT certification, successful completion of athletic training course requirements (college level), a bachelor's degree from an accredited college or university, at least 200 hours of athletic training experience in practice or game coverage of football, soccer, hockey, wrestling, basketball, gymnastics, lacrosse, volleyball, rugby, and/or rodeo, and endorsement by an NATA-certified athletic trainer.

There is also an internship route to certification. Once requirements have been met, candidates apply to take the exam, which is offered at various sites across the country. An online self-assessment exam is available to help determine necessary areas of study when preparing for the certification exam. Cost of the self-assessment exam is $27; the certification exam is $300 for NATA members, and $350 for nonmembers. For more information, contact the NATA Board of Certification at staff@nataboc.org.

Pilates

There are dozens of studios across the country that offer Pilates certification. However, there is no standard for certification, so you will find courses ranging from one-day workshops to year-long programs requiring up to 750 apprenticeship hours. A basic course offered at a number of centers is "mat certification," which trains instructors in the various Pilates moves that can be done without equipment. More advanced courses teach the proper use of the various props used in the program.

Prices range from $325 for a two-day Mat Certification course at the Pilates Certification Center in North Carolina, to $4,200 for full Pilates certification from the Pilates Center in Boulder, Colorado. To find out where training and certification are offered, consult the directory of programs in Appendix C, and search the Internet with the terms "Pilates and certification."

Professional Fitness, Inc.

There is a group of organizations offering certification in exercise programs using a large (usually 55 centimeters) inflated ball, known variously as an exercise ball, Swiss ball, Physioball, FitBall®, or Resist-A-Ball®. Professional Fitness, Inc., the manufacturers of Resist-A-Ball®, have developed a number of certifications or "modules" that they offer in workshops around the country. They are accepted as continuing education credits by The National Academy of Sports Medicine (NASM), The National Strength and Conditioning Association (NSCA), The American Council on Exercise (ACE), and The Aerobics and Fitness Association of America (AFAA). Cost ranges from $40 to $90. Modules include:

▶ Resist-A-Ball® Basic Training
▶ Resist-A-Ball® Dynamic Flexibility
▶ Resist-A-Ball® plus Resistance
▶ YogaBall Instructor Training

The latter combines moves from yoga, Pilates, and balance and stability training with the use of the Resist-A-Ball®. The seminar teaches 24 postures which may be combined in a class format or used in personal training sessions to increase strength, flexibility, and help to reduce stress. It begins with a modified version of "sun salutations" and moves on to postures that specialize in strengthening the core and supporting muscle groups.

Spinning®

While there are a number of organizations that offer certification in indoor cycling (such as AFAA and the Cooper Institute), there is only one way to become certified as a Spinning® instructor. The creator of this program has trademarked it (see Chapter 1, page 6), so to participate, you must be certified by his company and work for a facility that is licensed and authorized to offer the program (there are over 4,000 in 80 countries).

Spinning® certification involves instruction in proper technique, class design, music selection, safety, and athletic and motivational coaching. You must attend an eight-hour orientation workshop, at a cost of $275 plus $29.95 for an instructor's manual. The workshop involves both classroom instruction and participation in both a form and technique class and a sample Energy Zone class. Students are then required to teach Spinning® for six months while studying the instructor's manual. At the end of this period, a take-home, open book test must be completed and sent to Mad Dog Athletics for evaluation.

Yoga

If your goal is to become a yoga instructor, you should be aware that there is currently a debate within the yoga community about the adoption of national certification standards. While no conclusions have been reached, the Yoga Alliance (www.yogaalliance.org), formed in 1999 to address the issue, has adopted minimum teacher training standards, and offers a Registry Mark to those teachers and training institutions that meet them (see chart on pages 46–47). You will note that training standards are offered at the 200- and 500-hour levels, and may be achieved through resident and non-resident programs. Consult Appendix C for a listing of many schools offering yoga instructor education.

Due to yoga's increasing popularity, some of the larger exercise associations offer certification in class formats that blend elements of yoga with stretching, martial arts moves, strength training, and the use of props. AFAA's "Mat Science" and "yoga ball" workshops (see the section on Professional Fitness, Inc.) incorporate many traditional yoga positions while maintaining a more casual approach suited to the athlete who wishes to add something new to his or her workout regimen.

Certification in these types of programs should not be confused with traditional yoga teacher training, which, as noted above, requires at least a 200-hour commitment. In addition, some groups within the yoga community, including the American Yoga Association, recommend that the teaching of yoga should not be attempted without having practiced it oneself for a number of years.

COLLEGE AND UNIVERSITY STUDY

There are many valid reasons for making the commitment to study at a college or university, the first being that your education will help to set you apart from many of those seeking the same jobs you are interested in. A degree or certificate tells your future employer that you are serious about your career, and want to start in the industry armed with knowledge and some experience (most programs require an internship, explained in detail on page 64).

If you are planning for your fitness career path to lead toward preventive or rehabilitative health care work, you will be working with doctors and other health care professionals. Holding a degree will not only help you perform better on the job, but will earn respect from your coworkers, who themselves went through many years of schooling before embarking on their own careers.

Certificates and Associate Degrees

Many community and junior (two-year) colleges offer programs in exercise science and related areas. A major difference between the two types of schools is that junior colleges offer degree programs, conferring associate degrees after a two-year course of study, while community colleges offer the option of studying for one year to earn a certificate or for two years to earn an

Yoga Alliance (www.yogaalliance.org) Minimum Teacher Training Standards

200-Hour Standards

Category	Required Hours	Description
Techniques	100 Hours	Includes asanas, pranayamas, Kriyas, chanting, and meditation. These hours include both training in the techniques and the practice of them.
Teaching Methodology	20 Hours	Principles of demonstration, observation, assisting/correcting, instruction, teaching styles, qualities of a teacher, and the student's process of learning.
Anatomy and Physiology	20 Hours	Includes both physical Anatomy and Physiology (bodily systems, organs, etc.) and astral/energy/subtle Anatomy and Physiology (chakras, nadis, etc.)
Philosophy, Ethics, & Lifestyle	20 Hours	Study of Yoga Scriptures (Yoga Sutras, Bhagavad Gita, etc.), ethics for yoga teachers, "living the life of the yogi," etc.
Practicum	10 Hours	Includes student teaching as well as observing and assisting in classes taught by others. Hours may be a combination of supervised and unsupervised.
Electives	30 Hours	Electives are to be drawn from the other five categories. These hours do not necessarily represent student electives: hours may be used according to a school's own particular emphasis.
Contact Hours	At Least 160 Hours	*Contact hours* means that the Teacher Trainer is physically in the presence of the student. Noncontact or independent study hours may include: assigned reading or other homework, nonsupervised study groups, observing yoga classes, etc.

Courtesy of Yoga Alliance

500 Hour Standards
NOTE: These hours are NOT in addition to the 200 hours above, but are a complete description for this level.

Category	Required Hours	Description
Techniques	150 Hours	Includes asanas, pranayamas, Kriyas, chanting, and meditation. These hours include both training in the techniques and the practice of them.
Teaching Methodology	30 Hours	Principles of demonstration, observation, assisting/correcting, instruction, teaching styles, qualities of a teacher, and the student's process of learning.
Anatomy and Physiology	35 Hours	Includes both physical Anatomy and Physiology (bodily systems, organs, etc.) and astral/energy/subtle Anatomy and Physiology (chakras, nadis, etc.)
Philosophy, Ethics, & Lifestyle	50 Hours	Study of Yoga Scriptures (Yoga Sutras, Bhagavad Gita, etc.), ethics for yoga teachers, "living the life of the yogi," etc.
Practicum	40 Hours	Includes student teaching as well as observing and assisting in classes taught by others. Hours may be a combination of supervised and unsupervised.
Electives	195 Hours	Electives are to be drawn from the other five categories. These hours do not necessarily represent student electives: hours may be used according to a school's own particular emphasis.
Contact Hours	At Least 350 Hours	*Contact hours* means that the Teacher Trainer is physically in the presence of the student. Noncontact or independent study hours may include: assigned reading or other homework, nonsupervised study groups, observing yoga classes, etc.
Teaching Experience	100 Hours	An additional 100 hours of teaching experience, outside of the 500 hours of training, are required before a teacher can enroll in the registry.

Courtesy of Yoga Alliance

associate degree. A sample program follows, showing the difference between the certificate and degree options.

Western Wyoming Community College's certificate program is geared toward students who are preparing to become fitness instructors and/or personal trainers. The associate degree program is also excellent preparation for a career in fitness instruction, but is obviously more comprehensive in scope and may be applied to a four-year program if the student desires to continue the course of study.

Both programs ready students to take national certification exams such as those detailed earlier in this chapter. They include classroom instruction as well as hands-on experience in settings such as health clubs, physical therapy centers, and hospitals. Tuition for Wyoming residents is $1,400 per year, while out-of-state residents are charged $3,752. Room and board costs are approximately $3,000 per year.

Required Courses for Certificate in Fitness Leadership

Principles of Biology (BIOL 1000)

Fitness Leadership (PEPR 2130)

Exercise Physiology (PEPR 2120)

First Aid and Safety (HLED 1221)

Nutrition (HOEC 1140)

Personalized Fitness I (PEAC 2005)

Personalized Fitness II (PEAC 2006)

Anatomy & Physiology I (BIOL 2010)

Anatomy & Physiology II (BIOL 2015)

One of the following: Interpersonal Communication (COMM 1030), Public Speaking (COMM 1010), or Listening, Conflict Management/Mediation (COMM 1050)

One of the following: Business Administration (BADM), International Business (BUSN), Management (MGT), or Marketing (MKT)

Weight Training (PEAC 1273)

Beginning Internship (HLED 2470)

Advanced Internship (HLED 2471)

Suggested course of study for
Associate of Science, Exercise Science, Degree

English I (ENGL 1010)
Technical Writing (ENGL 2010)
Fitness Leadership Training
Exercise Physiology (PEPR 2120)
Biology I (BIOL 1010)
Computer Info Systems (COSC 1200)
Nutrition (HOEC 1140)
Personalized Fitness I (PEAC 2005)
Weight Training (PEAC 1273)
Standard First Aid/CPR (HLED 1221)
Electives (two or three courses)
Exercise Science Beginner Internship
American & Wyoming Government (POLS 1000)
Problem Solving (MATH 1000)
Personalized Fitness II
Introductory Chemistry (CHEM 1000)
Anatomy & Physiology (BIOL 2015)
Anatomy & Physiology (BIOL 2016)
Communication Elective
Exercise Science Advanced Internship
General Psychology (PSYC 1000) or Wellness (HLED 1003)
Elective from SS, HUM, or App Art

Courtesy of Western Wyoming Community College

Bachelor's Degrees

If you wish to obtain a four-year college degree in preparation for a career in fitness, you should know that a number of majors, or concentrations of study, are available. The most popular for those entering the industry as instructors and personal trainers are *exercise science* and *physical education* (they are also the most widely offered majors). Most physical education degrees prepare students to teach in public schools (curriculum includes education courses geared toward youth classes), and graduate them with teaching certificates. Exercise science majors tend to concentrate more on adult populations.

However, if you are thinking of someday advancing your career within the industry, you may want to explore other majors in related areas. According to the National Center of Educational Statistics, over 77,000 degrees were conferred in the following fitness-related areas in 1997–1998: physical therapy, recreational therapy, kinesiotherapy, rehabilitative and therapeutic professions, sports and fitness administration and management, and kinesiology, in addition to physical education and exercise science.

The Department of Exercise Science at the University of California at Davis offers two areas of emphasis in its BS in Exercise Science degree, exercise physiology and biomechanics. The average yearly cost for an undergraduate degree is $16,000, including room and board. Course requirements for the exercise physiology emphasis degree are as follows:

Course Title	Credits
Anthropology 1	4
Biological Sciences 1A	5
Biological Sciences 1B	5
Chemistry 2A	5
Chemistry 2B	5
Mathematics 16A	3
Mathematics 16B	3
Exercise Science 45	3
Physics 7A	4
Physics 7B	4
Psychology 1	4
Statistics 13	4
Exercise Science 101	3
Exercise Science 101L	1
Exercise Science 102	2
Exercise Science 103	4
Exercise Science 104	3
Exercise Science 105	3

Cell Bio.& Human Anat.101	4
Cell Bio. & Human Anat. 101L	3
Neurobio., Physiology & Beh. 101	5
Neurobio., Physiology & Beh. 101L	3
Chemistry 8A (CHE 2B)	2
Chemistry 8B	4
Exercise Science 110	3
Exercise Science 111	3
Exercise Science 112	4
Exercise Science 113	3
Exercise Science 116	3
Exercise Science 117	3
Exercise Science 118	3
UD EXS Elective (graded)	3
Biological Sciences 102	3
Neurobio., Physiology & Beh. 112	3
Neurobio., Physiology & Beh. 113	4
Neurobio., Physiology & Beh. 140	3
Elective	4

Courtesy of the University of California at Davis

The Department of Health, Physical Education and Recreation at Jacksonville State University in Florida offers a Bachelor of Science (BSE) Degree with a major in one of four areas: health education, physical education, recreation administration, and exercise science and wellness. According to JSU:

The latter is intended primarily for those seeking a career in preventative and/or rehabilitative medicine. In the area of preventative medicine, graduates are receiving employment such as Physical Director-YMCA/YWCA, Corporate Wellness Programs, Hospital and Medical Center Wellness Programs, University Based Wellness Programs, Wellness Counseling Groups, Health/Fitness Organizations, and others. Primary responsibilities may include: health/fitness screening, exercise prescription development, teaching all facets of aerobics and weight training, nutrition/weight loss programming, stress management, smoking cessation, and others.

In the area of rehabilitative medicine, graduates are receiving employment in the areas of Cardiac Rehabilitation, respiratory, and Sports Medicine (i.e. physical orthopedic rehab). The primary responsibility in rehabilitative medicine is to engage in lifestyle modifications and physical improvements to enhance the lives of those who have experienced an anatomical or physiological setback.

Courtesy of Jacksonville State University

Tuition and fees, including room and board, total approximately $22,360 for the four-year program. Breakdown of coursework is as follows:

- ▶ 47 hours core curriculum
- ▶ 33 hours required department courses
- ▶ 9 hours department electives
- ▶ 2–8 hours of electives outside the department
- ▶ 18–24 hours of selected minor
- ▶ 6 hours of internship

You may graduate from Plymouth State College in New Hampshire with a Physical Education degree in one of six categories, including Health Fitness Administration. The program is designed to prepare students to pass certification exams such as those offered by the ACSM, the NSCA, and ACE. It also readies them for careers in corporate fitness, preventative or rehabilitative health care, health and fitness centers and/or recreational health/fitness programs. Tuition for the four-year degree totals approximately $16,880, and the suggested course of study is as follows:

PE255—Foundations of Physical Education
BI211—Human Anatomy and Physiology I
BI212—Human Anatomy and Physiology II
BI213—Human Anatomy and Physiology Laboratory I
BI214—Human Anatomy and Physiology Laboratory II

HE256—Personal Wellness

PE357—Kinesiology

PE358—Physiology of Exercise

PE373—Motor Development

HE220—Cardiopulmonary Resuscitation (CPR)

HE265—First Aid

PE356—Evaluation in Physical Education

PE372—Motor Learning

PE219—Beginning Swimming

PE241—Fitness Activities

PE235—Backpacking

PE281—Adventure Skills

PE217—Alpine Skiing

PE210—Golf

PE227—Square/Folk/Social Dance

PE202—Field Hockey

PE339—Coaching Soccer

PE241—Fitness Activities

PE264—Burdenko Conditioning

PE375—Physiology of Exercise Lab

PE383—Resistive Training

PE387—Fitness Testing Skills

PE478—Exercise Prescription

PE488—Physical Education Internship

HE375—Wellness Skills for Health Professionals

BU225—Introduction to Business Administration

BU245—Principles of Marketing

HE322—Applied Nutrition for Exercise and Wellness

Distance Education

Distance education—formerly referred to as *correspondence school*—is an option when pursuing associate and bachelor's degrees. Discussed previously in reference to obtaining certification, home-based study has become more appealing and accessible for career training in recent years, even for such a hands-on career as fitness instruction, because of the Internet and other forms of technology. It's not an option at every college and university, but there is a growing trend in this direction, as each year more schools offer the choice of distance learning.

Distance education differs from programs offered on-site at schools in that instruction is given through a variety of delivery systems, rather than the traditional teacher-and-students-in-the-classroom setup. Some rely heavily on the computer, providing web-based interactive lessons over the Internet, while others allow you to read texts and take exams at your own pace. Increasingly, interactive video broadcasts to distant sites are being used. They are usually referred to as web casts or net conferences, and involve your attendance in one location to watch an instructor giving a lesson from another. You have the opportunity to interact with your teacher and other students through the use of video cameras and monitors.

The most attractive feature of distance learning is flexibility; in most of these programs, you can work from your home, at your pace. You need to be highly organized, disciplined, and motivated to succeed in distance education, and some people shy away from it for these reasons. To find more information about distance learning, including general guidelines for choosing a program, and listings of colleges and universities offering this type of study, log onto www.distancelearn.about.com. In addition, conduct your own search of the Internet with terms such as "distance learning and exercise science" or "distance learning and physical education."

If you decide on home study as the means by which you will receive your education, use the same criteria spelled out below when choosing a program. Then also consider the type of delivery system used, and determine not only your own familiarity with the technology (if any), but also whether the institution provides student training and technical assistance during the course. Find out how much interaction takes place among teachers and students during courses—are teachers available via phone, e-mail, or meeting in person?

Ask the school for the names of former students whom you can contact for information about their experiences with the school. Get complete information on the course of study, and compare it with the curricula of schools you know to be reputable. Make sure that the distance education school you choose is accredited by an organization such as the Distance Education and Training Council (www.detc.org). The U.S. Department of Education can tell you about other accrediting agencies; contact them at 400 Maryland Avenue, SW, Washington, DC 20202-0498 (800-872-5327), or online at www.ed.gov. Finally, check with the Chamber of Commerce, the Better Business Bureau, or the attorney general's office in the state where the school is headquartered to see if it has had complaints lodged against it.

CHOOSING A COLLEGE PROGRAM

If you decide that an associate's or bachelor's degree is necessary for attaining your career aspirations, your next step will be selecting a school that best suits your needs, likes, and goals. You must consider the types of schools, overall sizes of schools, locations, and quality of programs. Would you prefer large classes held in lecture halls, or smaller classes in which you get to know your teachers? Do you want to go to a local school and live at home, or are you willing to relocate and perhaps live in on-campus housing?

You can explore these options and many others by using the guidebooks listed below, and checking out the resources listed in Appendix B. Another great source of information is experienced fitness instructors and personal trainers. If you don't know any, seek them out at a health club or other facility. Most will be happy to share their experiences with you. Ask where they went to school, what advantages they gained from their education, and what they would do differently in terms of their education if they were starting again. Finally, if you are still in high school, enlist the help of an experienced high-school guidance counselor or career counselor.

Which Educational Setting Is Right for You?

If you are interested in a certificate or associate's degree program, will live at home, and work while getting your education, you might consider a community college. These are public institutions offering vocational and academic courses. They cost less than both two- and four-year public and private institutions, and usually require a high school diploma or GED for admission (although some schools have "open admission" policies, meaning that they will accept all who apply). Most credits earned at community colleges can be transferred to a four-year college or university, to be counted toward a bachelor's degree.

Community colleges typically do not offer housing to their students, and are geared toward those who have other commitments in addition to education (most often work and/or family). The "commuter" component means that there may be less social interaction between students, as they may be on campus only to attend classes. Many courses are available on nights and weekends and on the Internet, to accommodate working students' schedules.

You can find out the location of community colleges in your area by contacting your state's Department of Higher Education (listed in Appendix A). They maintain lists of these schools that can be mailed to you or accessed through a website. If you prefer, check the Internet for community colleges through a search engine such as Yahoo, which lists them by state.

If your goal is to obtain an associate's degree, consider junior colleges, which are two-year institutions that confer these degrees in either arts or sciences (depending on the school, fitness majors may fall into either category). Junior colleges are typically more expensive than community colleges, because they tend to be privately owned; however, in exchange for higher costs, you may find better faculty-to-student ratios, more stringent admissions policies, and more rigorous academic programs.

Many two-year colleges offer campus housing and full-time programs to their students. You may find an active social life at these schools, with the opportunity to live and work with fellow students. Team sports and other activities are also found at many two-year colleges. The two-year degree (AA or AS) that you earn can be applied to four-year programs at most colleges and universities. Use the Internet or the best-selling guide *Peterson's Two-Year Colleges* to help you with your search.

Colleges and universities offer undergraduate (usually four-year) programs in which you can earn a bachelor's or master's degree in a variety of fields. Entrance requirements are more stringent than for community and two-year colleges; admissions personnel will expect you to have taken certain classes in high school to meet their admission standards. Your high school GPA (grade point average) and standardized test scores (most often the Scholastic Aptitude Test or SAT) will be considered. The section "Admissions Requirements," on page 62, contains more detailed information on exactly what is needed to apply to a four-year college or university.

There is enormous variety among four-year institutions regarding cost, campus atmosphere, selectivity, and other criteria. State or public colleges and universities may charge thousands of dollars a year less than their private counterparts, because they generally receive funding to offset expenses. You can pay as little as a few thousand dollars per year at such a school, as opposed to tens of thousands of dollars at a private institution. Some schools cater to the commuter crowd, and have little or no campus housing, while others insist that students live in dorms and eat in dining halls.

Another thing to consider when choosing a college is whether they have placement programs for fitness instructors and personal trainers. Do they have a relationship with those in the area who hire, in which the employers actively recruit on campus? Attending a school with such a relationship could greatly improve your chances of employment upon graduation.

Evaluating Your Needs

Thus far, this chapter has focused on the types of programs available and the schools that offer them. Before making a final decision, consider two more things: what you want from a school, and what the schools you are interested in are able to deliver. First, make a determination about what you want and need in terms of:

▶ location
▶ finances
▶ scheduling

Read through the descriptions of these concerns below, and make notes regarding your position on each of them. You may want to devise a checklist of those items you determine to be "must haves" from the schools you are considering.

Where to Get Your Training

There are excellent programs offered at schools throughout the country. To select one, you will need to decide where you want to be while getting your education. The best decision from a financial point of view may be to attend

Online College Guides

Most of these sites offer similar information, including various search methods, the ability to apply to many schools online, financial aid and scholarship information, and online practice test taking (ACT, SAT, etc.). Some offer advice on selecting schools, give virtual campus tours, and help you decide what classes to take in high school. It is well worth it to visit several of them.

- www.embark.com—a good general site
- www.collegequest.com—run by Peterson's, a well-known publisher of college guide books (they can also be found at www.petersons.com)
- www.review.com—a service of The Princeton Review. Plenty of "insider information" on schools, custom searches for school, pointers on improving standardized test scores
- www.collegenet.com—on the web since 1995, best for applying to schools online
- www.collegereview.com—offers good general information, plus virtual campus tours
- www.theadmissionsoffice.com—answers your questions about the application process, how to improve your chances of getting accepted, when to take tests

a school near your home, so you don't incur the added cost of room and board. However, you may wish to attend one of the more prestigious, competitive programs in the country, and be willing to relocate in order to attend it.

Since there are employment opportunities for fitness instructors throughout the country and abroad, where you go to school geographically probably won't have much impact on your ability to find a job. However, there are advantages to attending a school located in the job market in which you will later work. First, it will allow you to make contacts for future job hunting. Second, your school may help with job placement locally, and it may employ as teachers people who are in a position to hire you. Your instructors can thus be later sources of employment. Third, your networking possibilities will greatly improve. Although this subject is discussed in greater detail in Chapter 4, keep in mind that having friends from school when you are out in the job market can be a big help. You will also have former teachers and administrators to network with throughout your career.

Finances

Costs of the various programs, and the differences in costs between each type of school, have been touched on above. Now, you will need to think more specifically about what you can afford. While there are many sources of funding for your education (check out Chapter 3), and schools do sometimes offer full or partial scholarships, you will still need to spend some money in order to get a quality education.

When evaluating the schools in which you are interested, be sure to find out all the costs, not just tuition. You will have to purchase books, which can cost hundreds of dollars over the course of the program (even as much as a thousand dollars if you are considering a bachelor's degree). If you won't live at home, you will need to pay for room and board, which can total as much as your tuition at some schools. Will you need childcare while attending classes, or have to drive long distances to get to school? Consider those additional costs when calculating how much you will have to spend.

Don't rule out any schools in which you have an interest at this point. Just be sure to gather as much information as you can about the real costs of attendance. Read through Chapter 3 to understand all of your options regarding financing your education. Then, you will be prepared to make an informed decision about which program to attend in terms of what you can afford.

Scheduling

When making a choice about education, you should also think about your schedule, and the commitments you already may have made. For instance, do you currently have a job you would like to continue working at while you are in school? You will need to find a program that offers classes at times when you are not working. Will an internship interfere with your employment? It might be a good idea to speak with your employer about your plans and goals. He or she may be willing to offer some flexibility (and even possibly some help with tuition).

If you have young children at home, or some other responsibility that requires your energy and time, consider how you will manage both that responsibility and your education. Some schools offer low-cost childcare to their students. Or perhaps another family member or friend could help while you are attending classes or studying. Be sure to think through all of the potential obstacles to your training, and seek out ways to overcome them. The schools themselves may be a source of assistance as well, so don't hesitate to ask how other students have managed, or how the school can accommodate you.

Another option is part-time attendance. If you are under financial constraints, you can spread the cost of the program over a greater period of time. If you have young children at home, need to continue working while getting your education, or have another time constraint, part-time attendance can allow you the flexibility your busy schedule demands. But be aware that while both the financial and time commitments to the program are significantly reduced, it is only for the short term. In total, you will have spent the same, or more, time and money getting your degree or certificate.

Evaluating the Schools

At this point, you should be able to make decisions about the type of program and school you would like to attend, significantly narrowing down the number of schools that you are considering. After consulting the resources in this chapter and Appendix A, make a list of the school or schools offering what you want. Then, for each entry on your list, ask the following outlined questions. If you don't have enough information, call the school's admission director and ask the questions directly, or request more information in the form of school brochures, course descriptions, and other documents. Since many schools have their own websites, you may also be able to find your answers on the Internet.

► *What are the qualifications of the faculty?*
  There should be some faculty members with advanced degrees (M.A., M.B.A., Ph.D., J.D., etc.), and some with experience in the working world. The faculty should be accessible to students for meetings outside of the classroom.

► *What is the student-teacher ratio?*
  It is important that the student-teacher ratio not be too high. Education suffers if classrooms are too crowded, or if a teacher has too many students to hope to see everyone who wishes to be seen for a private conference. According to one of the top national accrediting agencies, the Accrediting Council for Independent Colleges and Schools, a reasonable student-teacher ratio for skills training is 30 students to 1 teacher in a lecture setting and 15 students to 1 teacher in a laboratory

or clinical instruction setting. At very good schools the ratio is even better than the ACICS recommends.

▶ *Is the school accredited?*

It's important that the school you choose be accredited. Accreditation is a tough, complex process and ensures sound educational and ethical business practices at the schools involved. It is a process that schools undergo voluntarily. Some accrediting agencies are national, some regional. The name of the agency giving accreditation for the school you are interested in will probably be plainly printed on the school's general catalog, or you can obtain the name of the agency by calling the school. In addition, each accrediting agency will send you, free of charge, a directory of the schools it accredits.

If you would like a directory, or have a question about the school you have chosen, call the agency that accredits that school. See Accrediting Agencies in Appendix A for contact information. Keep in mind that if you choose a school that is not accredited, you will not be able to get financial aid through any government programs.

▶ *What is the job placement rate?*

A school's job placement rate for graduates is extremely important. Usually schools offer placement services free of charge, often for the working lifetime of their graduates. All accredited private schools must place a percentage (determined to be "reasonable" by the accrediting agency) of their students in order to maintain accreditation. Many good schools boast placement rates of 90% or more, such as Bethany College in Lindsborg, Kansas, which has a current placement rate of over 90% for students in its Health, Physical Education, and Athletic Training department.

A good job placement office will offer:
- resume writing and cover-letter writing assistance
- job leads—full time, part time, permanent, and temporary
- networking opportunities with employers in the area (often begun as a part of an internship while the student is still in school)
- seminars on job hunting
- career counseling and simulated interviews
- lifetime placement assistance for graduates

▶ *Does the school have a good internship program?*

The value of internships is tremendous both as an educational opportunity, and as a way of gaining work experience during school. By working at a fitness facility for college credit, you will also be able to make a positive impression on your superiors, and come away with recommendations that can be used when applying for work after graduation. There is more information on how and why to land an internship on page 64.

ADMISSION REQUIREMENTS

After deciding upon the program you are interested in, admission requirements may be as simple as having a high school diploma (or GED), and filling out an application. Or, you may need high scores on the SAT or ACT, and have graduated within the top 10% of your high school class. Community colleges offering certificate programs and associate degrees are typically the easiest to get into. Many have an "open admission" policy, meaning that they will accommodate anyone interested in their programs. Others may ask that you take the SAT or ACT if you are applying for a degree, but may accept modest scores.

Colleges and universities require more of their applicants. You will have to fill out a lengthy application form (many schools share a common one), and may be given the option of completing and submitting it online. While some schools are more competitive than others, all will look at your grade point average (GPA) from high school, and your test scores (SAT or ACT). Therefore, you must arrange to have your high school transcripts and test scores sent to the schools to which you are applying. This may be done through your school's guidance department, and through the testing service at the time you are taking the SAT or ACT.

Your high school transcript may be compared with those of other applicants, as the college looks to see who has taken more rigorous courses. You may be required to write a personal essay, which highlights not only your writing skills, but also your ability to sell your personality, your activities, and your ideas.

More competitive schools receive far more applications than they have slots in their freshman class, so they can be highly selective. Others admit a higher percentage of applicants, because they get fewer applicants and maintain lower admission standards. For instance, Dover Tech Community College in Delaware offers an Associate in Applied Science degree in Exercise Science Technology. It accepts 100% of its applicants. North Carolina Central University, which has a physical education major, accepts 74% of those who apply, with an average high school GPA of 2.63.

In contrast, Florida Atlantic University, which offers a Bachelor of Science degree in Exercise Science and Health Promotion, requires applicants to have taken the following in high school:

English	4 years
Math	3 years
Natural Science	3 years
Social Science	3 years
Foreign Language	2 years

Minimum standards for grade point averages and SAT or ACT scores are linked. For instance, if the GPA is low, higher test scores must balance it. With a GPA of 2.0, SAT scores of 1050 (combined) or higher are needed. If a GPA is 2.9 or above, a student may be accepted with an SAT score of 860 or ACT score of 20.

San Diego State University also confers Bachelor of Arts degrees in physical education, and accepts 65% of those who apply. Average SAT scores are 940–1143 combined. 91% of the freshman class at the University of Michigan at Ann Arbor (which has a Sports/Fitness Administration major) graduated from high school in the top 25% of their class, with an average GPA of 3.7. Combined average SAT scores are 1180–1380.

To get an idea of how competitive the school(s) you are interested in is (are), check out the college websites listed previously—many have databases of thousands of schools through which you can search and compare results. They contain information about acceptance rates, selectivity, and other criteria.

If your GPA is low or it has been some time since you were last in school, you might want to consider taking courses at a community college first. This course of action will give you the opportunity to add positive grades to your transcript, and then apply as a transfer student to a four-year school. You will improve your chances for acceptance by showing admissions officers that you are capable of doing well at their school, and have the determination to do what it takes to achieve your goals.

If your test scores are low, or it has been more than five years since you have taken the SAT (scores are good for five years), consider enrolling in a test prep class before trying them again. You can find classes in the phone directory, or listed online (search for "SAT prep"). There are also many prep books, and prep sites on the Internet (some of them free), that contain sample questions and tests, and provide good information about how to improve your scores.

MAKING THE MOST OF YOUR TRAINING PROGRAM

Once you have chosen a program of study, completed the application process, and then been accepted, there are a number of ways to guarantee that the time, effort, and money you spend on the program are maximized.

Internships

Internships are a great way to get job experience before you enter the "real" workforce in your capacity as a fitness instructor. It is easiest to participate in an internship program if you are enrolled in school (certification seminars and certifying bodies generally don't afford this type of experience). However, it is possible to create your own internship, especially if you are willing to work for a specified period of time to gain experience while foregoing a paycheck.

Internships may be paid or unpaid, and be taken for college credit or simply as an educational experience. Finding an internship while in school is fairly easy, because most schools will place you, or help place you, in one. They have relationships with the health clubs, corporations, and other organizations that use interns, and place students with them year after year. Those who offer internships often look to hire students when they complete their courses of study. For a college internship, you may also have to attend a class with other interns, or prepare a journal detailing your work experience, or write a paper about it.

George Mason University, in Manassas, Virginia, offers a number of fitness internships for college credit. Students are placed in health clubs, corporate fitness centers, and health care facilities. They are required to work at least 400 hours during a 10–14 week period, complete weekly progress reports, attend monthly seminars, and complete a special project. In addition, students are visited and evaluated on-site by a member of the faculty, and must pass evaluations given by the internship supervisor at the midpoint and end of the internship.

If your educational institution doesn't offer internships, or can't provide the type of internship experience you want, there are a number of ways in which you can uncover an opportunity. Your school may hire those working in the fitness industry to teach some courses; if so, consider enrolling in them. You may be able to make a contact or contacts that could lead to an internship. The Internet is also a good source of information. There, you can learn about all stages of the internship experience, including identifying learning objectives, managing "office politics," self-monitoring and documentation, and how to use the internship to land a permanent job.

By searching the Internet with terms such as "fitness and internship," you will be directed to the websites of hundreds of companies that offer paid and unpaid student internships. You may also want to contact businesses such as Wellness Connection (www.wellnessconnection.techevolution.com), which provide listings of exercise and fitness-related internships across the country. Three other sites that offer listings of internships available nationwide are www.internships.com, www.internjobs.com, and www.vault.com.

The following books are also excellent resources:

- ▶ *Internship Success* by Marianne Ehrlich Green (VGM Career Horizons, $12.95)
- ▶ *Peterson's 2000 Internships* (Peterson's Guides, $24.95)
- ▶ *America's Top Internships, 2000 Edition* by Mark Oldman (Princeton Review, $21.00)
- ▶ *The Yale Daily News Guide to Internships 2000* by John Anselmi (Kaplan, $25.00)

When you locate specific internship opportunities, consider them carefully before making a choice. Some are great stepping stones toward employment, while others may give you a little work experience, but nothing else. When making your decision, some of the questions you will want answered include:

▶ How many work hours are required to receive credit?

▶ If applicable, how much does the internship pay?

▶ Will you be graded for your work? If so, by a college professor or the person you work under at the company you intern for?

▶ Do you have to arrange your own internship with the company or work through your school?

▶ Does the internship program at your school also require you to attend classes, write a paper, or make a presentation to a faculty member in order to receive credit?

▶ What will your responsibilities be on a day-to-day basis?

▶ Who, within the company, will you be working for?

▶ Will the internship provide real world work experience that's directly related to your chosen field?

▶ Will your participation in the internship provide you with networking opportunities?

Once you land an internship, consider it an audition for ultimately obtaining a full-time job. Always act professionally, ask questions, follow directions, display plenty of enthusiasm, volunteer to take on additional responsibilities, and work closely with your boss/supervisor. Upon graduation, highlight your internship work on your resume, because it will make you stand out to a recruiter for a number of reasons. First, it shows that you are already familiar with a professional environment and know what is expected of you. Second, you have proven yourself through performance to a potential employer (you may want to get a letter or recommendation and include it with your resume). Third, you have shown that, after evaluating the realities of the job, you are still eager to pursue it.

For all of the reasons detailed above, it makes great sense for you to participate in an internship. Claire Andrews, a director of programs at Casco Bay College in Portland, Maine, notes, "it's really important to me that the students do get out there, whether it's through a part-time job or through the internship, to get the practical experience. Otherwise, waving that certificate means nothing."

Getting the Most Out of Your Classes

Successful completion of your education depends upon a number of things, including your performance during internships, scoring well on tests, writing great papers, and even getting along well with the faculty and fellow students. The classroom is the setting in which most of these factors come together. You will attend class almost every day, providing plenty of opportunity to learn and prove yourself. There are three things you must do in order to get the most out of your classes:

1. complete all assignments before class
2. take good notes while completing assignments and during class; an outline-style of note-taking works best to organize information and make studying easier
3. as topics are introduced, ask questions about anything you don't understand (do not wait until exam time)

By completing your assignments on schedule, you will be able to get the most out of your time spent in the classroom. Undoubtedly, your instructor will base his or her lesson on assigned reading. If you have come prepared, the lecture will not only make more sense, but will build upon what you learned in the reading(s). You will also be able to participate in discussions, which may count toward your final grade. If there was anything in the assignment that you didn't understand, you will have the chance to ask for clarification.

If you never learned how to take good notes, you will need to acquire this skill while in school. Check out the resources in Appendix B for help, but also be on the lookout for a classmate who appears to be a great note-taker. If he or she is willing to share, you can learn by example. Many successful students find that they can reinforce the material covered by copying over their notes. Don't wait too long to do this, though, especially if your notes are sloppy and diffi-cult to read. Read through what you have written, and decide if the notes could be better organized. Then, copy them back into your notebook. The "cleaned up" version of your notes will help when it comes time to study for exams.

You may also want to highlight material in the margins of your notes that didn't make sense to you. During your next class, you can ask questions and get the clarification you need. Make sure you understand everything that is presented to you as quickly as possible. If you wait until exam time, it may be difficult under such pressure to take in large amounts of new information.

Preparing for Exams

Don't forget, good preparation throughout the semester will make studying for exams much easier. Studying for an exam should be about going over material you already know—not reading assignments for the first time or trying to learn a semester worth of work in a day or two. Begin preparing for an exam by reading over your notes. Look for any areas that you indicated you didn't understand at the time, and make sure you understand them now. If you don't, talk to your instructor or do some extra reading until the concept is clear.

Then try making an outline of the class. Organize the material in a way that makes sense to you, using Roman numerals for the main topics, capitalized letter for subtopics, and Arabic numerals to break down subtopics further. For more information, check the study guides suggested in Appendix B.

Most important, on the evening before the exam, relax, eat a good dinner, and get a good night's sleep. In the morning, eat a good breakfast (and lunch, if it's an afternoon test). Try to take a walk or get some other light exercise, if you have time before the exam. During the exam, stay calm and have faith in yourself and your abilities.

Your Social Life

Forging friendships with teachers and fellow students will not only make your time in school more productive and enjoyable, but can also make the transition from student to fitness instructor or personal trainer easier. Your teachers have knowledge and experience that may benefit you in school and after graduation. Most are more than willing to spend time with their students answering questions about current coursework or future career goals.

You and your peers in the classroom can help each other by studying together and creating an information "loop" that keeps everyone informed not only about what is happening in class, but throughout the school as well. After graduation, you can network together as you all seek employment. For these reasons, and to take a well-deserved break from your studies, take advantage of the social events at your school.

Depending on the institution you attend, those in the counseling and placement offices may also be a part of your social life. But don't wait for a social gathering to get to know them. Make it a point early in your academic career to visit these offices, greet those who work there, and find out the kinds of resources they offer. They can be an invaluable resource for finding internships, selecting courses that can help you find the right job in the future, and locating employment prospects.

Your education is the first, essential step on the road to becoming a fitness instructor or personal trainer. Don't view it simply as something to get through, as an ordeal you must overcome before you can begin work and start your real life. Whether you decide to work toward a certification or bachelor's degree, or any option in between, you will enhance your employability and professionalism by becoming as knowledgeable about your chosen field as you can be. Your future clients and students will reap the benefits of that knowledge, and your reputation will depend upon it.

THE INSIDE TRACK

Who:	Heather Peavey-Leone
What:	Personal Trainer
Where:	Dedicated Fitness
	New York City

I was always an athletic person, but after college, life was so uncertain and unpredictable that I started eating just to comfort myself. I cried every morning before work as I surveyed my size 14 clothes that no longer fit my expanding waistline. Finally, I decided to make a drastic change in my life, to become the healthy person I wanted to be. As a result, my husband and I began to follow a strict diet and exercise plan. Just three months later, I had lost 45 pounds. Through careful and consistent dieting and training, I reached my goal of losing 70 pounds. I never thought I had the strength to change my eating and exercise habits, but now I'm walking proof that we all have the power to set and achieve such goals. As a personal trainer, I hope to provide inspiration to others trying to accomplish the same goals.

In order to become a personal trainer, I obtained a dual certification from The American Council on Exercise (ACE) as a Lifestyle & Weight Management Consultant and as a personal trainer by purchasing the study materials from the company and passing a written test. After obtaining my certification, I bought some basic equipment, like dumbbells, a step, a physio ball, and stretch bands, and offered to train friends in my building for a discounted rate. Through word of mouth, I met new people who wanted to exercise, and, soon after, I was referred to Homebodies, an agency that sends trainers into client's homes.

A successful personal trainer must have the desire to help people make changes in their lives. Patience, organizational skills, and listening skills are very important. Understanding the body and knowledge of many different exercises for each muscle group is also imperative in order to keep the exercises safe and interesting. In the beginning, I worked with a more experienced trainer as an apprentice and gained valuable experience.

Currently, I work about 25–35 hours a week as a personal trainer in New York City, specializing in weight loss and strength training. I work with clients in their homes, fostering more personal attention and a measure of privacy. My training company is called Dedicated Fitness (www.dedicatedfitness.com), and my website has been a great way to show potential clients my before and after pictures and answer general questions about my program. A good website is a great marketing tool: it allows people to see you and understand your specialties.

A typical session with me includes a warm up, stretching time, a workout specific to the individual goals of the client, and a cool down. I vary the exercises to prevent boredom and burnout; most clients switch between strength training, kickboxing, plyometrics and balance work, Pilates, and stretching. During the first session with a client, I take measurements, check weight and body composition, and fill out a comprehensive health questionnaire. This allows us to create goals and develop the plan to reach them—together. Many of my clients are trying to lose weight, so I also provide assistance with diet modification. I highly recommend that everyone keep a food journal in order to have a clear understanding of what they're eating and which habits need to change.

Being a personal trainer is incredibly satisfying, but it's not easy. It's very difficult to juggle clients' schedules and to accommodate as many clients as possible in the few hours before and after the traditional workday. There is also a great deal of variability in your sessions from week to week. You are often subject to the busy schedules of successful people who frequently travel for business and pleasure, making them unavailable for their regular appointments. As a result, it is extremely important to set up late cancellation policies, which can be difficult to enforce. Clients forget that your appointment schedule is like a doctor's office: If they cancel without warning, they will be charged a cancellation fee. In the end, these kinds of variables make it very difficult to budget and plan for income, so you have to be prepared to work as much as possible, then enjoy the time off.

Another challenge is finding the time to focus on your own exercise goals. Contrary to popular belief, personal trainers don't really have the opportunity to work out all the time. After I have encouraged a client through their session, I often don't have the energy to push myself through my own. In the end, you have to make your own health and wellness a priority in order to better help others.

CHAPTER three

FINANCIAL AID—DISCOVERING THE POSSIBILITIES

IN CHAPTER 2 you learned how to find and succeed in the right training program for you. This chapter explains some of the many different types of financial aid available, gives you information on what financial records you will need to gather to apply for financial aid, and helps you through the process of applying for financial aid. (A sample financial aid form is included in Appendix D.) At the end of the chapter are listed many more resources that can help you find the aid you need.

YOU HAVE DECIDED on a career as a fitness instructor or personal trainer and you have chosen a training program. Now, you need a plan to finance your training. Perhaps you or your family have been saving for your education, and you have the money to pay your way. Or maybe your employer offers some money to help its employees attend school. However, if you are like most students, you don't have enough to cover the cost of the training program you'd like to attend. Be assured that it is likely that you can qualify for some sort of financial aid, even if you plan to attend school only part-time.

Because there are many types of financial aid, and the millions of dollars given away or loaned are available through so many sources, the process of finding funding for your education can seem confusing. Read through this chapter carefully, and check out the many resources, including the websites and publications listed on page 101. You will have a better understanding of where to look for financial aid, what you can qualify for, and how and when to apply.

Also take advantage of the financial aid office at the school you've chosen, or your guidance counselor if you're still in high school. These professionals can offer plenty of information, and can help to guide you through the process. If you're not in school, and haven't chosen a program yet, check the Internet. It's probably the best source for up-to-the-minute information, and almost all of it is free. There are a number of great sites at which you can fill out questionnaires with information about yourself and receive lists of scholarships and other forms of financial aid for which you may qualify. You can also apply for some types of federal and state aid online—you can even complete the Free Application for Federal Student Aid (FAFSA), the basic form that determines federal and state financial aid eligibility, online if you choose.

SOME MYTHS ABOUT FINANCIAL AID

The subject of financial aid is often misunderstood. Here are some of the most common myths:

Myth #1: All the red tape involved in finding sources and applying for financial aid is too confusing for me.

Fact: The whole financial aid process is a set of steps that are ordered and logical. Besides, several sources of help are available. To start, read this chapter carefully to get a helpful overview of the entire process and tips on how to get the most financial aid. Then, use one or more of the resources listed within this chapter and in the appendices for additional help. If you believe you will be able to cope with your training program, you will be able to cope with looking for the money to finance it—especially if you take the process one step at a time in an organized manner.

Myth #2: For most students, financial aid just means getting a loan and going into heavy debt, which isn't worth it, or working while in school, which will lead to burnout and poor grades.

Fact: Both the federal government and individual schools award grants and scholarships which a student doesn't have to pay back. It is also possible to get a combination of scholarships and loans. It's worth taking out a loan if it means attending the program you really want to attend, rather than settling for your second choice or not pursuing a career in your chosen field at all. As for working while in school, it's true that it is a challenge to hold down a full-time or even part-time job while in school. However, a small amount of work-study employment (10–12 hours per week) has been shown to actually improve academic performance, because it teaches students important time-management skills.

Myth #3: I can't understand the financial aid process because of all the unfamiliar terms and strange acronyms that are used.

Fact: While you will encounter an amazing number of acronyms and some unfamiliar terms while applying for federal financial aid, you can refer to the acronym list and glossary at the end of this chapter for quick definitions and clear explanations of the commonly used terms and acronyms.

Myth #4: Financial aid is for students attending academic colleges or universities. I'm going to a vocational training program so I won't qualify.

Fact: This is a myth that far too many people believe. The truth is, there is considerable general financial aid for which vocational students qualify. There are also grants and scholarships specifically designed for students in vocational programs. The financial aid you get may be less than that for longer, full-time programs, but it can still help you pay for a portion of your training program.

Myth #5: My family makes too much money (or I make too much money), so I shouldn't bother to apply for financial aid.

Fact: The formula used to calculate financial aid eligibility is complex and takes more into account than just your or your family's income. Also, some forms of financial aid—such as a PLUS Loan or an unsubsidized Stafford Loan—are available regardless of calculated financial need. The only way to be certain NOT to get financial aid is to NOT apply; don't shortchange yourself by not applying, even if you think you won't be eligible.

TYPES OF FINANCIAL AID

There are three categories of financial aid:

1. Grants and scholarships—aid that you don't have to pay back
2. Work-Study—aid that you earn by working
3. Loans—aid that you have to pay back

Each of these types of financial aid will be examined in greater detail, so you will be able to determine which one(s) to apply for, and when and how to apply. Note that grants and scholarships are available on four levels: Federal, state, school, and private.

Grants

Grants are normally awarded based on financial need. Even if you believe you won't be eligible based on your own or your family's income, don't skip this section. There are some grants awarded for academic performance and other criteria. The two most common grants are the Federal Pell Grant and Federal Supplemental Educational Opportunity Grant (FSEOG).

Federal Pell Grants

Federal Pell Grants are based on financial need and are awarded only to undergraduate students who have not yet earned a bachelor's or professional degree. For many students, Pell Grants provide a foundation of financial aid to which other aid may be added. For the year 2001–2002, the maximum award was $3,750.00. You can receive only one Pell Grant in an award year, and you may not receive Pell Grant funds for more than one school at a time.

How much you get will depend not only on your Expected Family Contribution (EFC), but also on your cost of attendance, whether you're a full-time or part-time student, and whether you attend school for a full academic year or less. You can qualify for a Pell Grant even if you are only enrolled part-time in a training program. You should also be aware that some private- and school-based sources of financial aid will not consider your eligibility if you haven't first applied for a Pell Grant.

Federal Supplemental Educational Opportunity Grants (FSEOG)

Priority consideration for FSEOG funds is given to students receiving Pell Grants because the FSEOG program is based on exceptional financial need. An FSEOG is similar to a Pell Grant in that it doesn't need to be paid back.

If you are eligible, you can receive between $100 and $4,000 a year in FSEOG funds depending on when you apply, your level of need, and the funding level of the school you are attending. The FSEOG differs from the Pell Grant in that it is not guaranteed that every needy student will receive one because each school is only allocated a certain amount of FSEOG funds by the federal government to distribute among all eligible students. To have the best chances of getting this grant, apply for financial aid as early as you can after January 1 of the year in which you plan to attend school.

State Grants

State grants are generally specific to the state in which you or which your parents reside. If you and your parents live in the state in which you will attend school, you have only one place to check. However, if you will attend school in another state, or your parents live in another state, be sure to check your eligibility with your state grant agency. Not all states allow their state grants to be used at out-of-state schools. There is a list of state agencies included in

Appendix A with telephone numbers and websites, so you can easily find out if there is a grant for which you can apply.

Scholarships

Scholarships are often awarded for academic merit or for special characteristics (for example, ethnic heritage, personal interests, sports, parents' career, college major, geographic location) rather than financial need. As with grants, you do not pay your award money back. Scholarships may be offered from federal, state, school, and private sources.

The best way to find scholarship money is to use one of the free search tools available on the Internet. After entering the appropriate information about yourself, a search takes place which ends with a list of those prizes for which you are eligible. Try www.fastasp.org, which bills itself as the world's largest and oldest private sector scholarship database. A couple of other good sites for conducting searches are www.college-scholarships.com and www.gripvision.com. If you don't have easy access to the Internet, or want to expand your search, your high school guidance counselors or college financial aid officers also have plenty of information about available scholarship money. Also, check out your local library.

To find private sources of aid, spend a few hours in the library looking at scholarship and fellowship books or consider a reasonably priced (under $30) scholarship search service. See the Resources section at the end of this chapter to find contact information for search services and scholarship book titles.

Also, contact some or all of the professional associations for the program you are interested in attending; some offer scholarships, while others offer information about where to find scholarships. If you are currently employed, find out if your employer has scholarship funds available. If you are a dependent student, ask your parents and other relatives to check with groups or organizations they belong to as well as their employers to see if they have scholarship programs or contests. Investigate these popular sources of scholarship money:

- ▶ religious organizations
- ▶ fraternal organizations
- ▶ clubs (such as Rotary, Kiwanis, American Legion, Grange, or 4-H)
- ▶ athletic clubs

▶ veterans' groups (such as the Veterans of Foreign Wars)
▶ ethnic group associations
▶ unions
▶ local chambers of commerce

If you already know which school you will attend, check with a financial aid administrator (FAA) in the financial aid office to find out if you qualify for any school-based scholarships or other aid. Many schools offer merit-based aid for students with a high school GPA of a certain level or with a certain level of SAT scores in order to attract more students to their school. Check with your program's academic department to see if they maintain a bulletin board or other method of posting available scholarships.

While you are looking for sources of scholarships, continue to enhance your chances of winning one by participating in extracurricular events and volunteer activities. You should also obtain references from people who know you well and are leaders in the community, so you can submit their names and/or letters with your scholarship applications. Make a list of any awards you've received in the past or other honors that you could list on your scholarship application. There are many scholarships awarded to students planning careers in fitness. To find more sources, search the Internet using terms such as "fitness" and "scholarship."

A program benefiting mainly middle-class students is the Hope Scholarship Credit. Eligible taxpayers may claim a federal income tax credit for tuition and fees up to a maximum of $1,500 per student (the amount is scheduled to be reindexed for inflation after 2002). The credit applies only to the first two years of postsecondary education, and students must be enrolled at least half-time in a program leading to a degree or a certificate. To find out more about the Hope Scholarship Credit, log onto www.sfas.com.

For the Lifetime Learning Credit, eligible taxpayers may claim a federal income tax credit for tuition and fees up to a maximum of $1,000 per student through the year 2002. After the year 2002, eligible taxpayers may claim a credit for tuition and fees up to a maximum of $2,000 per student (unlike the Hope Scholarship Credit, this amount will not be reindexed for inflation after 2002). The Lifetime Learning Credit is not limited to the first two years of postsecondary education; students in any year can be eligible, and there is no minimum enrollment requirement. For more information about the Lifetime Learning Credit, log onto www.sfas.com.

The National Merit Scholarship Corporation offers about 5,000 students scholarship money each year based solely on academic performance in high school. If you are a high school senior with excellent grades and high scores on tests such as the ACT or SAT, ask your guidance counselor for details about this scholarship.

You may also be eligible to receive a scholarship from your state or school. Check with the higher education department of the relevant state or states (listed in Appendix A), or the financial aid office of the school you will attend.

Work-Study Programs

When applying to a college or university, you can indicate that you are interested in a work-study program. Their student employment office will have the most information about how to earn money while getting your education. Work options include the following:

- ▶ on- or off-campus
- ▶ part-time or almost full-time
- ▶ school- or nationally-based
- ▶ in some cases, in your program of study (to gain experience) or not (just to pay the bills)
- ▶ for money to repay student loans or to go directly toward educational expenses

If you're interested in school-based employment, the student employment office can give you details about the types of jobs offered (which can range from giving tours of the campus to prospective students to working in the cafeteria to helping other students in a student services office) and how much they pay.

You should also investigate the Federal Work-Study (FWS) program, which can be applied for on the Free Application for Federal Student Aid (FAFSA). The FWS program provides jobs for undergraduate and graduate students with financial need, allowing them to earn money to help pay education expenses. It encourages community service work and provides hands-on experience related to your course of study, when available. The amount of the FWS award depends on:

▶ when you apply (apply early!)
▶ your level of need
▶ the FWS funds available at your particular school

FWS salaries are the current federal minimum wage or higher, depending on the type of work and skills required. As an undergraduate, you will be paid by the hour (a graduate student may receive a salary), and you will receive the money directly from your school; you cannot be paid by commission or fee. The awards are not transferable from year to year, and not all schools have work-study programs in every area of study.

An advantage of working under the FWS program is that your earnings are exempt from FICA taxes if you are enrolled full-time and are working less than half-time. You will be assigned a job on-campus, in a private nonprofit organization, or a public agency that offers a public service. The total wages you earn in each year cannot exceed your total FWS award for that year and you cannot work more than 20 hours per week. Your financial aid administrator (FAA) or the direct employer must consider your class schedule and your academic progress before assigning your job.

For more information about National Work-Study programs, visit the Corporation for National Service website (www.cns.gov) and/or contact:

▶ **National Civilian Community Corps (NCCC)**—This AmeriCorps program is an 11-month residential national service program intended for 18–24-year-olds. Participants receive $4,725.00 for college tuition or to help repay education loan debt. Contact: National Civilian Community Corps, 1100 Vermont Avenue NW, Washington, DC 20525, 800-94-ACORPS.

▶ **Volunteers in Service to America (VISTA)**—VISTA is a part of ACTION, the deferral domestic volunteer agency. This program offers numerous benefits to college graduates with outstanding student loans. Contact: VISTA, Washington, DC 20525, 800-424-8867.

If you are already working in the field in which you intend to go to school, your employer may help you pay for job-related courses. Check with your employer for details.

Student Loans

Although scholarships, grants, and work-study programs can help to offset the costs of higher education, they usually don't give you enough money to entirely pay your way. Most students who can't afford to pay for their entire education rely at least in part on student loans. The largest single source of these loans—and for all money for students—is the federal government. However, you can also find loan money from your state, school, and/or private sources.

Try these sites for information about U.S. government programs:

www.fedmoney.org
This site explains everything from the application process (you can actually download the applications you will need), eligibility requirements, and the different types of loans available.

www.finaid.org
Here, you can find a calculator for figuring out how much money your education will cost (and how much you will need to borrow), get instructions for filling out the necessary forms, and even information on the various types of military aid (which will be detailed in the next chapter).

www.ed.gov/offices/OSFAP/students
This is the Federal Student Financial Aid Homepage. The FAFSA (Free Application for Federal Student Aid) can be filled out and submitted online. You can find a sample FAFSA in Appendix D, to help familiarize yourself with its format.

www.students.gov

This bills itself as the "student gateway to the U.S. government" and is run as a cooperative effort under the leadership of the Department of Education. You can find information about financial aid, community service, military service, career development, and much more.

You can also get excellent detailed information about different federal sources of education funding by sending away for a copy of the U.S. Department of Education's publication, *The Student Guide*. Write to: Federal Student Aid Information Center, P.O. Box 84, Washington, DC 20044, or call 800-4FED-AID.

Listed below are some of the most popular federal loan programs:

Federal Perkins Loans

A Perkins Loan has the lowest interest (currently, it's 5%) of any loan available for both undergraduate and graduate students, and is offered to students with exceptional financial need. You repay your school, which lends the money to you with government funds.

Depending on when you apply, your level of need, and the funding level of the school, you can borrow up to $4,000 for each year of undergraduate study. The total amount you can borrow as an undergraduate is $20,000 if you have completed two years of undergraduate study; otherwise, you can borrow a maximum of $8,000.

The school pays you directly by check or credits your tuition account. You have nine months after you graduate (provided you were continuously enrolled at least half-time) to begin repayment, with up to ten years to pay off the entire loan.

PLUS Loans (Parent Loan for Undergraduate Students)

PLUS Loans enable parents with good credit histories to borrow money to pay the education expenses of a child who is a dependent undergraduate student enrolled at least half-time. Your parents must submit the completed forms to your school.

To be eligible, your parents will be required to pass a credit check. If they don't pass, they might still be able to receive a loan if they can show that extenuating circumstances exist or if someone who is able to pass the credit check agrees to co-sign the loan. Your parents must also meet citizenship requirements and not be in default on any federal student loans of their own.

The yearly limit on a PLUS Loan is equal to your cost of attendance minus any other financial aid you receive. For instance, if your cost of attendance is $10,000 and you receive $5,000 in other financial aid, your parents could borrow up to, but no more than, $5,000. The interest rate varies, but is not to exceed 9% over the life of the loan. Your parents must begin repayment while you are still in school. There is no grace period.

Federal Stafford Loans

Stafford Loans are low-interest loans that are given to students who attend school at least half-time. The lender is the U.S. Department of Education for schools that participate in the Direct Lending program and a bank or credit union for schools that do not participate in the Direct Lending program. Stafford Loans fall into one of two categories:

Subsidized loans are awarded on the basis of financial need. You will not be charged any interest before you begin repayment or during authorized periods of deferment. The federal government subsidizes the interest during these periods.

Unsubsidized loans are not awarded on the basis of financial need. You will be charged interest from the time the loan is disbursed until it is paid in full. If you allow the interest to accumulate, it will be capitalized—that is, the interest will be added to the principal amount of your loan, and additional interest will be based upon the higher amount. This will increase the amount you have to repay.

There are many borrowing limit categories to these loans, depending on whether you get an unsubsidized or subsidized loan, which year in school you're enrolled, how long your program of study is, and if you are independent or dependent. You can have both kinds of Stafford Loans at the same time, but the total amount of money loaned at any given time cannot exceed $23,000 for a dependent undergraduate student and $46,000 as an independent undergraduate student (of which not more than $23,000 can be in subsidized Stafford Loans). The interest rate varies, but will never exceed 8.25%. An origination fee for a Stafford Loan is approximately 3% or 4% of the loan, and the fee will be deducted from each loan disbursement you receive. There is a six-month grace period after graduation before you must start repaying the loan.

State Loans

Loan money is also available from state governments. In Appendix A, you will find a list of the agencies responsible for giving out such loans, with websites and e-mail addresses when available. Remember that you may be able to qualify for a state loan based on your residency, your parents' residency, or the location of the school you're attending.

Alternative Loans

Alternative loans are loans either you, you and a co-borrower, or your parent can take out based on credit; usually the maximum you can borrow is for the cost of education minus all other financial aid received. Interest rates vary but are generally linked to the prime rate. Some of the many lenders who offer these types of loans are listed in the resources section at the end of this chapter. You can also ask your local bank for help or search the Internet for "alternative loans for students."

Questions to Ask Before You Take Out a Loan

In order to get the facts regarding the loan you are about to take out, ask the following questions:

1. What is the interest rate and how often is the interest capitalized? Your college's financial aid administrator (FAA) will be able to tell you this.

2. What fees will be charged? Government loans generally have an origination fee that goes to the federal government to help offset its costs, and a guarantee fee, which goes to a guaranty agency for insuring the loan. Both are deducted from the amount given to you.

3. Will I have to make any payments while still in school? It depends on the type of loan, but often you won't; depending on the type of loan, the government may even pay the interest for you while you're in school.

4. What is the grace period—the period after my schooling ends—during which no payment is required? Is the grace period long enough, realistically, for you to find a job and get on your feet? (A six-month grace period is common.)

5. When will my first payment be due and approximately how much will it be? You can get a good preview of the repayment process from the answer to this question.

6. Who exactly will hold my loan? To whom will I be sending payments? Who should I contact with questions or inform of changes in my situation? Your loan may be sold by the original lender to a secondary market institution, in which case you will be notified as to the contact information for your new lender.

7. Will I have the right to prepay the loan, without penalty, at any time? Some loan programs allow prepayment with no penalty but others do not.

8. Will deferments and forbearances be possible if I am temporarily unable to make payments? You need to find out how to apply for a deferment or forbearance if you need it.

9. Will the loan be canceled ("forgiven") if I become totally and permanently disabled, or if I die? This is always a good option to have on any loan you take out.

APPLYING FOR FINANCIAL AID

Now that you are aware of the types and sources of aid available, you will want to begin applying as soon as possible. You have heard about the Free Application for Federal Student Aid (FAFSA) many times in this chapter already, and should now have an idea of its importance. This is the form used by federal and state governments, as well as schools and private funding sources, to determine your eligibility for grants, scholarships, and loans. The easiest way to get a copy is to log onto www.ed.gov/offices/OSFAP/students, where you can find help in completing the FAFSA, and then submit the form electronically when you are finished. You can also get a copy by calling 1-800-4FED-AID, or by stopping by your public library or your school's financial aid office. Be sure to get an original form, because photocopies of federal forms are not accepted.

The second step of the process is to create a financial aid calendar. Using any standard calendar, write in all of the application deadlines for each step of the financial aid process. This way, all of your vital information will be in one location, so you can see at a glance what needs to be done and when it's due. Start this calendar by writing in the date you requested your FAFSA. Then, mark down when you received it and when you sent in the completed form (or just the date you filled the form out online if you chose to complete the FAFSA electronically). Add important dates and deadlines for any other applications you need to complete for school-based or private aid as you progress though the financial aid process. Using and maintaining a calendar will help the whole financial aid process run more smoothly and give you peace of mind that the important dates are not forgotten.

When to Apply

Apply for financial aid as soon as possible after January 1 of the year in which you want to enroll in school. For example, if you want to begin school in the fall of 2004, then you should apply for financial aid as soon as possible after January 1, 2004. It is easier to complete the FAFSA after you have completed your tax return, so you may want to consider filing your taxes as early as possible as well. Do not sign, date, or send your application before January 1 of the year for which you are seeking aid. If you apply by mail, send your completed application in the envelope that came with the original application. The envelope is already addressed, and using it will make sure your application reaches the correct address.

Many students lose out on thousands of dollars in grants and loans because they file too late. Don't be one of them. Pay close attention to dates and deadlines.

After you mail in your completed FAFSA, your application will be processed in approximately four weeks. (If you file electronically, this time estimate is considerably shorter.) Then, you will receive a Student Aid Report (SAR) in the mail. The SAR will disclose your Expected Family Contribution (EFC), the number used to determine your eligibility for federal student aid. Each school you list on the application may also receive your application information if the school is set up to receive it electronically.

You must reapply for financial aid every year. However, after your first year, you will receive a Student Aid Report (SAR) in the mail before the application deadline. If no corrections need to be made, you can just sign it and send it in.

Getting Your Forms Filed

Follow these three simple steps if you are not completing and submitting the FAFSA online:

1. Get an original Federal Application for Federal Student Aid (FAFSA). Remember to pick up an original copy of this form, as photocopies are not accepted.

2. Fill out the entire FAFSA as completely as possible. Make an appointment with a financial aid counselor if you need help. Read the forms completely, and don't skip any relevant portions or forget to sign the form (or forget to have your parents sign, if required).

3. Return the FAFSA long before the deadline date. Financial aid counselors warn that many students don't file the forms before the deadline and lose out on available aid. Don't be one of those students!

Financial Need

Financial aid from many of the programs discussed in this chapter is awarded on the basis of need (the exceptions include unsubsidized Stafford, PLUS, consolidation loans, and some scholarships and grants). When you apply for federal student aid by completing the FAFSA, the information you report is used in a formula established by the United States Congress. The formula determines your Expected Family Contribution (EFC), an amount you and your family are expected to contribute toward your education. If your EFC is below a certain amount, you will be eligible for a Pell Grant, assuming you meet all other eligibility requirements.

There is no maximum EFC that defines eligibility for the other financial aid options. Instead, your EFC is used in an equation to determine your financial needs. Eligibility is a very complicated matter, but it can be simplified to the following equation: your contribution + your parents' contribution = expected family contribution (EFC). Student expense budget/cost of attendance (COA) − EFC = your financial need.

The need analysis service or federal processor looks at the following if you are a dependent student:

▶ Family assets, including savings, stocks and bonds, real estate investments, business/farm ownership, and trusts
▶ Parents' ages and need for retirement income
▶ Number of children and other dependents in the family household
▶ Number of family members in college
▶ Cost of attendance, also called student expense budget; includes tuition and fees, books and supplies, room and board (living with parents, on campus, or off campus), transportation, personal expenses, and special expenses such as childcare

A financial aid administrator calculates your cost of attendance and subtracts the amount you and your family are expected to contribute toward that cost. If there's anything left over, you are considered to have financial need.

Are You Considered Dependent or Independent?

Federal policy uses strict and specific criteria to make this designation, and that criteria applies to all applicants for federal student aid equally. A dependent student is expected to have parental contribution to school expenses, and an independent student is not.

You're an independent student if at least one of the following applies to you:

▶ you were born before January 1, 1980 (for the 2003–2004 school year)
▶ you are married (even if you're separated)
▶ you have legal dependents other than a spouse who get more than half of their support from you and will continue to get that support during the award year
▶ you are an orphan or ward of the court (or were a ward of the court until age 18)
▶ you are a graduate or professional student

▶ you are a veteran of the U.S. Armed Forces—formerly engaged in active service in the U.S. Army, Navy, Air Force, Marines, or Coast Guard or as a cadet or midshipman at one of the service academies—released under a condition other than dishonorable. (ROTC students, members of the National Guard, and most reservists are not considered veterans, nor are cadets and midshipmen still enrolled in one of the military service academies.)

If you live with your parents, and if they claimed you as a dependent on their last tax return, then your need will be based on your parents' income. You do not qualify for independent status just because your parents have decided to not claim you as an exemption on their tax return (this used to be the case but is no longer) or do not want to provide financial support for your college education.

Students are classified as *dependent* or *independent* because federal student aid programs are based on the idea that students (and their parents or spouse, if applicable) have the primary responsibility for paying for their post-secondary education. If your family situation is unusually complex and you believe it affects your dependency status, speak to a financial aid counselor at the school you plan to attend as soon as possible. In extremely limited circumstances a financial aid office can make a professional judgment to change a student's dependency status, but this requires a great deal of documentation from the student and is not done on a regular basis. The financial aid office's decision on dependency status is *final* and cannot be appealed to the U.S. Department of Education.

Gathering Financial Records

Your financial need for most grants and loans depends on your financial situation. Now that you have determined if you are considered a dependent or independent student, you will know whose financial records you need to gather for this step of the process. If you are a dependent student, then you must gather not only your own financial records, but also those of your parents because you must report their income and assets as well as your own when you complete the FAFSA. If you are an independent student, then you need to gather only your own financial records (and those of your spouse if you're married). Gather your tax records from the year prior to the one in which you are applying. For example, if you apply for the fall of 2004, you will use your tax records from 2003.

Filling Out the FAFSA

To help you fill out the FAFSA, gather the following documents:

- U.S. Income Tax Returns (IRS Form 1040, 1040A, or 1040EZ) for the year that just ended and W-2 and 1099 forms
- records of untaxed income, such as Social Security benefits, AFDC or ADC, child support, welfare, pensions, military subsistence allowances, and veterans' benefits
- current bank statements and mortgage information
- medical and dental expenses for the past year that weren't covered by health insurance
- business and/or farm records
- records of investments such as stocks, bonds, and mutual funds, as well as bank certificates of deposit (CDs) and recent statements from money market accounts
- Social Security number(s)

Even if you do not complete your federal income tax return until March or April, you should not wait to file your FAFSA until your tax returns are filed with the IRS. Instead, use estimated income information and submit the FAFSA, as noted earlier, just as soon as possible after January 1. Be as accurate as possible, knowing that you can correct estimates later.

Maximizing Your Eligibility for Loans and Scholarships

Loans and scholarships are often awarded based on an individual's eligibility. Depending on the type of loan or scholarship you pursue, the eligibility requirements will be different. EStudentLoan.com (www.estudentloan.com) offers the following tips and strategies for improving your eligibility when applying for loans and/or scholarships:

1. Save money in the parent's name, not the student's name.
2. Pay off consumer debt, such as credit card and auto loan balances.
3. Parents considering going back to school should do so at the same time as their children. Often, the more family members in school simultaneously, the more aid will be available to each.
4. Spend student assets and income first, before other assets and income.
5. If you believe that your family's financial circumstances are unusual, make an appointment with the financial aid administrator at your school to review your case. Sometimes the school will be able to adjust your financial aid package to compensate.
6. Minimize capital gains.
7. Do not withdraw money from your retirement fund to pay for school. If you must use this money, borrow from your retirement fund.
8. Minimize educational debt.
9. Ask grandparents to wait until the grandchild graduates before giving them money to help with their education.
10. Trust funds are generally ineffective at sheltering money from the need analysis process, and can backfire on you.
11. If you have a second home, and you need a home equity loan, take the equity loan on the second home and pay off the mortgage on the primary home.

GENERAL GUIDELINES FOR LOANS

Before you commit yourself to any loans, be sure to keep in mind that they need to be repaid. Estimate realistically how much you will earn when you leave school, remembering that you will have other monthly obligations such as housing, food, and transportation expenses.

Once You're in School

Once you have your loan (or loans) and you are attending classes, don't forget about the responsibility of your loan. Keep a file of information on your loan that includes copies of all your loan documents and related correspondence, along with a record of all your payments. Open and read all your mail about your education loan(s).

Remember also that you are obligated by law to notify both your financial aid administrator (FAA) and the holder or servicer of your loan if there is a change in your:

- ▶ name
- ▶ address
- ▶ enrollment status (dropping to less than half-time means that you will have to begin payment six months later)
- ▶ anticipated graduation date

After You Leave School

After graduation, you must begin repaying your student loan immediately, or begin after a grace period. For example, if you have a Stafford Loan you will be provided with a six-month grace period before your first payment is due; other types of loans have grace periods as well. If you haven't been out in the working world before, your loan repayment begins your credit history. If you make payments on time, you will build up a good credit rating, and credit will be easier for you to obtain for other things. Get off to a good start, so you don't run the risk of going into default. If you default (or refuse to pay back your loan) any number of the following things could happen to you as a result. You may:

- ▶ have trouble getting any kind of credit in the future
- ▶ no longer qualify for federal or state educational financial aid
- ▶ have holds placed on your college records
- ▶ have your wages garnished
- ▶ have future federal income tax refunds taken
- ▶ have your assets seized

To avoid the negative consequences of going into default in your loan, be sure to do the following:

▶ Immediately open and read all mail you receive about your education loans.

▶ Make scheduled payments on time; since interest is calculated daily, delays can be costly.

▶ Contact your servicer immediately if you can't make payments on time; he or she may be able to get you into a graduated or income-sensitive/income contingent repayment plan or work with you to arrange a deferment or forbearance.

There are a few circumstances under which you won't have to repay your loan. If you become permanently and totally disabled, you probably will not have to (providing the disability did not exist prior to your obtaining the aid) repay your loan. Likewise, if you die, if your school closes permanently in the middle of the term, or if you are erroneously certified for aid by the financial aid office you will probably also not have to repay your loan. However, if you're simply disappointed in your program of study or don't get the job you wanted after graduation, you are not relieved of your obligation.

Loan Repayment

When it comes time to repay your loan, you will make payments to your original lender, to a secondary market institution to which your lender has sold your loan, or to a loan servicing specialist acting as its agent to collect payments. At the beginning of the process, try to choose the lender who offers you the best benefits (for example, a lender who lets you pay electronically, offers lower interest rates to those who consistently pay on time, or who has a toll-free number to call 24 hours a day, 7 days a week). Ask the financial aid administrator at your college to direct you to such lenders.

Be sure to check out your repayment options before borrowing. Lenders are required to offer repayment plans that will make it easier to pay back your loans. Your repayment options may include:

▶ *Standard repayment*: Full principal and interest payments due each month throughout your loan term. You will pay the least amount of interest using the standard repayment plan, but your monthly payments may seem high when you're just out of school.

▶ *Graduated repayment*: Interest-only or partial interest monthly payments due early in repayment. Payment amounts increase thereafter. Some lenders offer interest-only or partial interest repayment options, which provide the lowest initial monthly payments available.

▶ *Income-based repayment*: Monthly payments are based on a percentage of your monthly income.

▶ *Consolidation loan*: Allows the borrower to consolidate several types of federal student loans with various repayment schedules into one loan. This loan is designed to help student or parent borrowers simplify their loan repayments. The interest rate on a consolidation loan may be lower than what you're currently paying on one or more of your loans. The phone number for loan consolidation at the William D. Ford Direct Loan Program is 800-557-7392. Financial aid administrators recommend that you do not consolidate a Perkins Loan with any other loans since the interest on a Perkins Loan is already the lowest available. Loan consolidation is not available from all lenders.

▶ *Prepayment*: Paying more than is required on your loan each month or in a lump sum is allowed for all federally sponsored loans at any time during the life of the loan without penalty. Prepayment will reduce the total cost of your loan.

It's quite possible—in fact likely—that while you're still in school your Federal Family Education Loan Program (FFELP) loan will be sold to a secondary market institution such as Sallie Mae. You will be notified of the sale by letter, and you need not worry if this happens—your loan terms and conditions will remain exactly the same or they may even improve. Indeed, the sale may give you repayment options and benefits that you would not have had otherwise. Your payments after you finish school, and your requests for information should be directed to the new loan holder.

If you receive any interest-bearing student loans, you will have to attend exit counseling after graduation, where the loan lenders or financial aid office personnel will tell you the total amount of debt and work out a payment schedule with you to determine the amount and dates of repayment. Many loans do not become due until at least six to nine months after you graduate, giving you a grace period. For example, you do not have to begin paying on the Perkins Loan until nine months after you graduate. This grace period is to give you time to find a good job and start earning money. However, during this time, you may have to pay the interest on your loan.

If for some reason you remain unemployed when your payments become due, you may receive an unemployment deferment for a certain length of time. For many loans, you will have a maximum repayment period of ten years (excluding periods of deferment and forbearance).

THE MOST FREQUENTLY ASKED QUESTIONS ABOUT FINANCIAL AID

Here are answers to some of the most frequently asked questions about student financial aid:

1. *I probably don't qualify for aid—should I apply for it anyway?*
   Yes. Many students and families mistakenly think they don't qualify for aid and fail to apply. Remember that there are some sources of aid that are not based on need. The FAFSA form is free—there's no good reason for not applying.
2. *Do I have to be a U.S. citizen to qualify for financial aid?*
   Students (and parents, for PLUS Loans) must be U.S. citizens or eligible noncitizens to receive federal and state financial aid. Eligible noncitizens are U.S. nationals or U.S. permanent nonresidents (with "green cards"), as well as nonresidents in certain special categories. If you don't know whether you qualify, speak to a financial aid counselor as soon as possible.
3. *Do I have to register with the Selective Service before I can receive financial aid?*
   Male students who are U.S. citizens or eligible noncitizens must register with the Selective Service by the appropriate deadline in order to receive federal financial aid. Call the Selective Service at 847-688-6888 if you have questions about registration.

4. *Do I need to be admitted at a particular university before I can apply for financial aid?*

   No. You can apply for financial aid any time after January 1. However, to get the funds, you must be admitted and enrolled in school.

5. *Do I have to reapply for financial aid every year?*

   Yes, and if your financial circumstances change, you may get either more or less aid. After your first year you will receive a Renewal Application which contains preprinted information from the previous year's FAFSA. Renewal of your aid also depends on your making satisfactory progress toward a degree and achieving a minimum GPA.

6. *Are my parents responsible for my educational loans?*

   No. You and you alone are responsible, unless they endorse or co-sign your loan. Parents are, however, responsible for federal PLUS Loans. If your parents (or grandparents or uncle or distant cousins) want to help pay off your loan, you can have your billing statements sent to their address.

7. *If I take a leave of absence from school, do I have to start repaying my loans?*

   Not immediately, but you will after the grace period. Generally, though, if you use up your grace period during your leave, you will have to begin repayment immediately after graduation, unless you apply for an extension of the grace period before it's used up.

8. *If I get assistance from another source, should I report it to the student financial aid office?*

   Yes—and, unfortunately, your aid amount will possibly be lowered accordingly. But you will get into trouble later on if you don't report it.

9. *Are federal work-study earnings taxable?*

   Yes, you must pay federal and state income tax, although you may be exempt from FICA taxes if you are enrolled full time and work less than 20 hours a week.

10. *My parents are separated or divorced. Which parent is responsible for filling out the FAFSA?*

    If your parents are separated or divorced, the custodial parent is responsible for filling out the FAFSA. The custodial parent is the parent with whom you lived the most during the past 12 months. Note that this is not necessarily the same as the parent who has legal custody. The question of which parent must fill out the FAFSA becomes complicated in many situations, so you should take your particular circumstance to the student financial aid office for help.

FINANCIAL AID CHECKLIST

_____ Explore your options as soon as possible once you have decided to begin a training program.

_____ Find out what your school requires and what financial aid they offer.

_____ Complete and mail the FAFSA as soon as possible after January 1.

_____ Complete and mail other applications by the deadlines.

_____ Return all requested documentation promptly to your financial aid office.

_____ Carefully read all letters and notices from the school, the federal student aid processor, the need analysis service, and private scholarship organizations. Note whether financial aid will be sent before or after you are notified about admission, and how exactly you will receive the money.

_____ Gather loan application information and forms from your school or college financial aid office. You must forward the completed loan application to your financial aid office. Don't forget to sign the loan application.

_____ Report any changes in your financial resources or expenses to your financial aid office so they can adjust your award accordingly.

_____ Re-apply each year.

FINANCIAL AID ACRONYMS KEY

COA	Cost of Attendance (also known as COE, Cost of Education)
CWS	College Work-Study
EFC	Expected Family Contribution
EFT	Electronic Funds Transfer
ESAR	Electronic Student Aid Report
ETS	Educational Testing Service
FAA	Financial Aid Administrator
FAF	Financial Aid Form
FAFSA	Free Application for Federal Student Aid
FAO	Financial Aid Office/Financial Aid Officer

FDSLP   Federal Direct Student Loan Program

FFELP   Federal Family Education Loan Program

FSEOG   Federal Supplemental Educational Opportunity Grant

FWS   Federal Work-Study

PC   Parent Contribution

PLUS   Parent Loan for Undergraduate Students

SAP   Satisfactory Academic Progress

SC   Student Contribution

USED   U.S. Department of Education

FINANCIAL AID TERMS—CLEARLY DEFINED

accrued interest—interest that accumulates on the unpaid principal balance of your loan

capitalization of interest—addition of accrued interest to the principal balance of your loan that increases both your total debt and monthly payments

default (you won't need this one, right?)—failure to repay your education loan

deferment—a period when a borrower, who meets certain criteria, may suspend loan payments

delinquency (you won't need this one, either!)—failure to make payments when due

disbursement—loan funds issued by the lender

forbearance—temporary adjustment to repayment schedule for cases of financial hardship

grace period—specified period of time after you graduate or leave school during which you need not make payments

holder—the institution that currently owns your loan

in-school grace, and **deferment interest subsidy**—interest the federal government pays for borrowers on some loans while the borrower is in school, during authorized deferments, and during grace periods

interest-only payment—a payment that covers only interest owed on the loan and none of the principal balance

interest—cost you pay to borrow money

lender (originator)—puts up the money when you take out a loan; most lenders are financial institutions, but some state agencies and schools make loans too

origination fee—fee, deducted from the principal, which is paid to the federal government to offset its cost of the subsidy to borrowers under certain loan programs

principal—amount you borrow, which may increase as a result of capitalization of interest, and the amount on which you pay interest

promissory note—contract between you and the lender that includes all the terms and conditions under which you promise to repay your loan

secondary markets—institutions that buy student loans from originating lenders, thus providing lenders with funds to make new loans

servicer—organization that administers and collects your loan; may be either the holder of your loan or an agent acting on behalf of the holder

subsidized Stafford Loans—loans based on financial need; the government pays the interest on a subsidized Stafford Loan for borrowers while they are in school and during specified deferment periods

unsubsidized Stafford Loans—loans available to borrowers, regardless of family income; unsubsidized Stafford Loan borrowers are responsible for the interest during in-school, deferment periods, and repayment

FINANCIAL AID RESOURCES

In addition to the sources listed throughout this chapter, these are additional resources that may be used to obtain more information about financial aid.

Telephone Numbers

Federal Student Aid Information Center (U. S. Department of Education)	
Hotline	800-4FED-AID (800-433-3243)
TDD Number for Hearing-Impaired	800-730-8913
For suspicion of fraud or abuse of federal aid	800-MIS-USED (800-647-8733)
Selective Service	847-688-6888
Immigration and Naturalization (INS)	415-705-4205
Internal Revenue Service (IRS)	800-829-1040
Social Security Administration	800-772-1213
National Merit Scholarship Corporation	708-866-5100
Sallie Mae's college AnswerSM Service	800-222-7183
Career College Association	202-336-6828
ACT: American College Testing program (about forms submitted to the need analysis servicer)	916-361-0656
College Scholarship Service (CSS)	609-771-7725 TDD 609-883-7051
Need Access/Need Analysis Service	800-282-1550
FAFSA on the Web Processing/ Software Problems	800-801-0576

Websites

www.ed.gov/prog_info/SFAStudentGuide
The Student Guide is a free informative brochure about financial aid and is available online at the Department of Education's Web address listed here.

www.ed.gov\prog_info\SFA\FAFSA
This site offers students help in completing the FAFSA.

www.ed.gov/offices/OPE/t4_codes

This site offers a list of Title IV school codes that you may need to complete the FAFSA.

www.ed.gov/offices/OPE/express

This site enables you to fill out and submit the FAFSA online. You will need to print out, sign, and send in the release and signature pages.

www.career.org

This is the website of the Career College Association (CCA). It offers a limited number of scholarships for attendance at private proprietary schools. You can also contact CCA at 750 First Street, NE, Suite 900, Washington, DC 20002-4242.

www.salliemae.com

This is the website for Sallie Mae that contains information about loan programs.

www.teri.org

This is the website of The Educational Resource Institute (TERI), which offers alternative loans to students and parents.

www.nelliemae.com

This is the website for Nellie Mae; it contains information about alternative loans as well as federal loans for students and parents.

www.key.com

This is Key Bank's website, which has information on alternative loans for parents and students.

www.educaid.com

This is the website for Educaid, which offers both federal and alternative loans to students and parents.

Software Programs

Cash for Class

Tel: 800-205-9581

Fax: 714-673-9039

Redheads Software, Inc.

3334 East Coast Highway

#216

Corona del Mar, CA 92625

E-mail: cashclass@aol.com

C-LECT Financial Aid Module

Chronicle Guidance

Publications

P. O. Box 1190

Moravia, NY 13118-1190

Tel: 800-622-7284 or 315-497-

0330

Fax: 315-497-3359

Peterson's Award Search

Peterson's

P.O. Box 2123

Princeton, NJ 08543-2123

Tel: 800-338-3282 or 609-243-

9111

E-mail:

custsvc@petersons.com

Pinnacle Peak Solutions (Scholarships 101)

Pinnacle Peak Solutions

7735 East Windrose Drive

Scottsdale, AZ 85260

Tel: 800-762-7101 or 602-951-9377

Fax: 602-948-7603

TP Software—Student Financial Aid Search Software

TP Software

P.O. Box 532

Bonita, CA 91908-0532

Tel: 800-791-7791 or 619-496-8673

E-mail: mail@tpsoftware.com

Books and Pamphlets

The Student Guide
Published by the U.S. Department of Education, this is the handbook about federal aid programs. To get a printed copy, call 1-800-4FED-AID.

Looking for Student Aid
Published by the U.S. Department of Education, this is an overview of sources of information about financial aid. To get a printed copy, call 1-800-4FED-AID.

How Can I Receive Financial Aid for College?
Published from the Parent Brochures ACCESS ERIC website. Order a printed copy by calling 800-LET-ERIC or write to ACCESS ERIC, Research Blvd-MS 5F, Rockville, MD 20850-3172.

Cassidy, David J. *The Scholarship Book 2002: The Complete Guide to Private-Sector Scholarships, Fellowships, Grants, and Loans for the Undergraduate* (Englewood Cliffs, NJ: Prentice Hall, 2001).

Chany, Kalman A. and Geoff Martz. *Student Advantage Guide to Paying for College 1997 Edition.* (New York: Random House, The Princeton Review, 1997.)

College Costs & Financial Aid Handbook, 18th ed. (New York: The College Entrance Examination Board, 1998).

Cook, Melissa L. *College Student's Handbook to Financial Assistance and Planning* (Traverse City, MI: Moonbeam Publications, Inc., 1991).

Davis, Kristen. *Financing College: How to Use Savings, Financial Aid, Scholarships, and Loans to Afford the School of Your Choice* (Washington, DC: Random House, 1996).

Hern, Davis and Joyce Lain Kennedy. *College Financial Aid for Dummies* (Foster City, CA: IDG Books Worldwide, 1999).

Peterson's Scholarships, Grants and Prizes 2002 (Lawrenceville, NJ: Peterson's, 2001).

Ragins, Marianne. *Winning Scholarships for College: An Insider's Guide* (New York: Henry Holt & Company, 1994).

Scholarships, Grants & Prizes: Guide to College Financial Aid from Private Sources (Princeton, NJ: Peterson's, 1998).

Schwartz, John. *College Scholarships and Financial Aid* (New York: Simon & Schuster, Macmillan, 1995).

Schlacter, Gail and R. David Weber. *Scholarships 2000* (New York: Kaplan, 1999).

Other Related Financial Aid Books

Annual Register of Grant Support (Chicago, IL: Marquis, annual).

A's and B's of Academic Scholarships (Alexandria, VA: Octameron, annual).

Chronicle Student Aid Annual (Moravia, NY: Chronicle Guidance, annual).

College Blue Book. Scholarships, Fellowships, Grants and Loans (New York: Macmillan, annual).

College Financial Aid Annual (Englewood Cliffs, NJ: Prentice Hall, annual).

Directory of Financial Aids for Minorities (San Carlos, CA: Reference Service Press, biennial).

Directory of Financial Aids for Women (San Carlos, CA: Reference Service Press, biennial).

Financial Aids for Higher Education (Dubuque, IA: Wm. C. Brown, biennial).

Financial Aid for the Disabled and their Families (San Carlos, CA: Reference Service Press, biennial).

Leider, Robert and Ann. *Don't Miss Out: the Ambitious Student's Guide to Financial Aid* (Alexandria, VA: Octameron, annual).

Paying Less for College (Lawrenceville, NJ: Peterson's, annual).

THE INSIDE TRACK

Who: Yonny Acevedo
What: Personal Trainer
Where: Eastpm. Pennsylvania

Currently, I'm a self-employed personal trainer in Pennsylvania, specializing in bodybuilding, but I've always been involved in sports like soccer, basketball, baseball, and volleyball. The one sport I loved the most was cross-country running. In high school, I ran so much and performed so well that I got hooked, running one race after another, sometimes two in one day. I thought I was invincible. Like most young people, I was incredibly naïve and refused to acknowledge my own limits. So, it was only a matter of time before I got injured. My injuries forced me to undergo several months of physical therapy, during which I started weight training and saw a noticeable difference in my muscle development. Afterward, I was fully recovered, but no longer a competitive runner and had to find a different route to fitness. So, I joined a gym and started working out with a partner who got me involved in bodybuilding and personal training.

Soon after, I began working part-time at a gym, and my employer offered me the opportunity to enroll in the APEX personal training program, through which I received my ACE and NGA certifications. In the beginning, I started out with only a couple of clients at the gym where I worked, but after a while, I started picking up clients at other gyms. Now, I train clients in their own homes or in various gyms around the area, splitting a percentage of my fee with the facility owners. I have used ads to promote my business, but I attract most of my clients through word-of-mouth.

A good personal trainer is trustworthy with an energetic personality, strong motivational skills, and a lot of patience. It's also important to have good hygiene because you have to work so closely with clients. One thing I didn't realize about personal training before I got into it was how personal it really is. There are moments when you go beyond training and into therapy. Clients come to you with all kinds of emotions that need to be handled delicately. They trust and confide in you, and you become like a counselor to them. So, don't be surprised when they spill their problems out to you!

During my initial visit with a potential client, I conduct a comprehensive interview and give them a thorough evaluation in order to create the right training program for each individual. Then, I explain the benefits of every exercise, show them how to stretch properly, and in some cases, discuss a diet plan. Of course, all of this depends upon the client's specific goals. I've made lasting friendships with some of my clients. One of the most positive experiences I had was with a client that came to be with bone density loss. She was 50 years old and hunched over with a very low self-esteem. After eight months of training with me, she was completely transformed, not only physically but also emotionally. She still trains with me to this day and has more energy than ever. To top it all off, her bone density levels have improved.

I work between 50 and 60 hours a week, and my biggest challenge has been scheduling. When you first start training, you don't have many clients, but as business picks up, it becomes more and more difficult to fit them all in during the week and still leave enough time for yourself and your own training. In this profession, you have to be extremely mindful of your own health as well as your clients' because it's so easy to burn out.

In the end, the most important lesson I've learned is that injuries can sometimes teach us a great deal. In my case, they changed the course of my life, giving me the opportunity to become a personal trainer and natural body builder. I really love my job!

CHAPTER four

FINDING YOUR FIRST JOB

This chapter covers the job search process, explaining the many ways to locate a future employer once your fitness training is completed. You will learn how to conduct your search through networking, researching, using classified ads, reading industry publications, and utilizing online resources. Knowing how and where to find the best employment opportunities is the first step toward a successful job search.

ONCE YOU HAVE obtained a degree, certificate, or certification, you will be ready to find employment in your chosen field. The job market outlook is great, according to the U.S. Department of Labor. As mentioned in Chapter 1, the Bureau of Labor Statistics reports that they expect employment of fitness workers to increase 36% or more through 2010, meaning that the fitness industry is one of the fastest growing in the country. But even with an advantageous market, the search for a job can be time consuming and stressful.

If you are changing careers, or have otherwise conducted a search before, you are already familiar with the process. But whether a first-time job seeker or seasoned professional, you will be able to make the process more productive and enjoyable by following the advice in this chapter. Setting goals and formulating career and job objectives are the first steps. Then, take an organized approach to the whole procedure by establishing deadlines and staying on top of the details. To save you time and effort during the research phase of your search, you will learn how to identify and utilize the best resources available, including the Internet, your school's career placement office, and networking contacts.

Since so many in the fitness industry are in business for themselves, it is worth considering self-employment. Included in this chapter is a discussion of the benefits of entrepreneurship, as well as an examination of the important skills and strengths needed to succeed. Chapter 6 contains even more information on self-employment, with comprehensive listings of resources, contact information for associations and organizations that support entrepreneurs and their efforts, and some great ideas for growing your own business.

WHAT KIND OF JOB DO YOU REALLY WANT?

A "good job" means something different to everyone. Later in this chapter, a wide variety of employment choices and employers will be explored. Deciding on what is right for you is a highly personal, and very important, step. By formulating a job objective, you will focus your search, and help ensure that you end up where you want to be. Perhaps your goal is to someday be general manager of a corporation that owns thousands of health clubs. Or maybe you would like to begin teaching classes at the YMCA, and eventually buy and run your own studio. You might envision yourself as a personal trainer at a resort in a warm climate. Or, perhaps you are not sure what type of job you are looking for.

If that is the case, before you begin your job search, take the time to decide on long-term and short-term career goals. Proceed through the following steps even if you believe you already know these goals; clarifying your vision can only make your path toward satisfying, gainful employment more direct. Picture yourself in a fulfilling job next week, next year, and five years from now. Are you thinking in terms of one job, or several, moving up the corporate ladder? While thinking about your needs and wants, write them down. Use two columns, for short- and long-term planning. Keep in mind that your goals should:

▶ describe in detail what you want to accomplish

▶ be measurable, formulated in terms that can clearly be evaluated (for instance, "by next year, I will be employed at a corporate fitness center")

▶ be challenging, taking energy and discipline to accomplish

▶ be realistic and attainable

▶ have a definite point of completion (long-term goals should be broken up into short-term goals with definite, targeted completion dates)

▶ be flexible; sometimes great opportunities come along that take you in new directions, but still lead toward your long-term goals

If you have never envisioned your future career, you may be surprised by the direction in which it seems to point you. The process of thinking and writing down your goals can help to identify what has previously gone unacknowledged.

Take time to develop this vision of your career path, and write it down where you can refer to it as often as is necessary to remain focused. While it may seem like a low priority at this stage, a vision can help you avoid wasting time looking for, or even taking, jobs that are not right for you. No matter if you are searching for your first job, or are changing industries after a successful first career, knowing what you want is the best way to obtain it. Armed with this knowledge, you can begin the job search process with greater confidence. That alone can set you apart from the competition when it comes time to apply for a position.

TAKING A DEADLINE-ORIENTED APPROACH TO YOUR JOB SEARCH EFFORTS

As discussed earlier in this chapter, landing a job can be a difficult task. You have to find the opportunities, create a resume, write cover letters, schedule interviews, perform research on companies, participate in interviews, make follow-up calls, and keep track of all the potential employers you meet or correspond with. One way to help take the stress out of the procedure is to adopt an organized, deadline-oriented approach for finding a fitness job.

Begin by purchasing a traditional paper planner, such as a Day-Timer or Filofax, or a personal digital assistant (PDA), such as a Palm Pilot™ or Pocket

PC. Both systems work well; your choice will depend upon whether you prefer to write information in a calendar-type book, or use a more expensive, but more versatile, electronic device for the same purpose. Then, make a list of everything you will have to accomplish in order to land a job. Break up the big tasks into many smaller ones, which are easier to accomplish. Items you will probably put on your list include:

- writing or updating your resume
- getting your resume printed
- contacting those you know in the field about possible job openings
- purchasing outfits to wear to interviews
- bookmarking your favorite job-search and fitness industry websites, and visiting those sites regularly
- following up with interviewers after interviews

Once your list is complete, write down how long you think each task will take to accomplish. Next, prioritize your list. Determine which tasks need immediate attention, and which items can wait until later in the job search process. When you know what needs to be done and approximately how long it will take, create a schedule for yourself and set deadlines. Using your personal planner, calendar, or PDA, start at today's date and enter each job search-related task, one at a time. Leave yourself enough time to accomplish each one, and in your planner, mark down the date by which each should be completed.

Keep meticulous notes in your planner or on your PDA. Write down everything you do, with whom you make contact, the phone numbers and addresses of your contacts, topics of discussion on the phone or during interviews, the follow-up actions that need to be taken, and even what you wore to each interview. Throughout your job search process, keep your planner or PDA with you at all times. Refer to it and update it often to ensure that you remain on track.

During an interview, don't be afraid to take notes. If the interviewer wants to meet with you again, take out your planner or PDA and make the appointment on the spot. Not only will you keep yourself and your search organized, but you will also demonstrate this important quality to a potential employer.

RESEARCHING THE FIELD

Finding the right job means doing your homework. You need to know exactly what fitness positions you are qualified to fill, the jobs available, where they can be found, and how to land one. As stated in previous chapters, fitness instructors are employed in many settings, from small, privately owned establishments, to institutions such as schools and hospitals, to large clubs run by corporations. Five of the major employers of fitness instructors (chain clubs; smaller and privately owned clubs; corporate fitness/wellness centers; hospital- and other health care site-based fitness centers; resorts, spas, and cruise lines) are examined next, along with resources for finding the information you will want to have about a potential employer.

Large Chain Clubs

Chapter 1 discussed the pros and cons of working for a corporate-owned club (page 14). Chances are, there are a number of such clubs in your area. How can you find out about their owners and the differences between their facilities? The easiest way to get background information on a company is to contact it directly. Larger corporations maintain websites that contain facts and figures, as well as mission statements and lists of properties owned. You may also telephone a company's public relations office and ask for information. Request a copy of the company's annual report to the stockholders, which describes its corporate philosophy, history, products or services, goals, and financial status. Press releases, company newsletters or magazines, and recruitment brochures also can be helpful.

Background information on the organization also may be available at your public or school library. If you cannot get an annual report, check the library for reference directories that provide basic facts about the company, such as earnings, products and services, and number of employees. Some directories that are widely available in libraries include the following:

Dun & Bradstreet's Million Dollar Directory
Standard and Poor's Register of Corporations
Directors and Executives

Moody's Industrial Manual
Ward's Business Directory

The Internet is also an excellent resource for researching potential employers. To find lists of corporations that employ fitness instructors, try websites geared toward business news and information, such as www.business.com. Check out some of these other sites that may be useful in your search:

www.analysiszone.com
www.businessjeeves.com/MoneyComInd.html
www.corporateinformation.com
www.companydescriptions.com
www.planetbiz.com

Don't forget your school's placement office, which should also have information about nearby businesses that employ fitness instructors. They may even have valuable contacts with companies that routinely hire their graduates.

Independent Health Clubs, Gyms, and Studios

These employers may in some ways be harder to locate than their corporate counterparts. Many of them don't have websites, so the Internet cannot be relied upon as your best bet for finding them. However, they do all have phone service, so your first resource should be the local business phone directory. At this point, you are probably familiar with the names of the large chain clubs, so as you search under "health club," "spa," "gym," and "fitness," make a list of those who don't fall into that category.

To research the facilities on your list, you may then turn to the employer directly. Call each that interests you, and ask to speak to the manager. Introduce yourself, and ask if he or she would mind answering a few questions. They might prefer it if you visited and conducted an informational interview face-to-face. Check the later section on Networking for advice on how to handle telephone and in-person interviews. Either way, ask questions, which might include:

▶ "How many members do you have?"

▶ "What types of classes are offered? May I see a schedule?"

▶ "How many employees work here, and what does an average work schedule look like?"

▶ "What types of amenities are offered to members?"

▶ "Do instructors/trainers have other duties in addition to teaching/training?"

After you have spoken with the manager and visited the facility, there may still be information you would like to have about the employer. Check your local library for newspaper archives that might mention the business, and ask for the librarian's help in locating other types of information. Next, turn to the Internet. Search using the name of each club or fitness center to find their website, if they have one. You may also want to check for them on the websites of some of the large national associations, many of which have "corporate" members. Try the Aerobics and Fitness Association of America (www.afaa.com), the American Council on Exercise (www.acefitness.org), and the International Health, Racquet, and Sportsclub Association (www.ihrsa.org).

Corporate Fitness/Wellness Programs

There are a number of ways to get information about this fast-growing sector of the fitness industry. First, you will want to find out which companies in your area have gyms or fitness centers on site. Many of them directly hire personnel to run them, while others use businesses (consultants) that provide everything from the design of the center, to programming, and staffing. You will want to explore consultants as well as those who do more direct hiring of fitness instructors and personal trainers, in addition to exploring the possibility of contacting those companies that do not currently offer exercise programs to their employees.

To find out who may be hiring (that is, who has an onsite facility) networking or word-of-mouth may be your best bet. Read the section on networking at the end of this chapter for great advice on the entire process, from determining who is a contact, to making connections and organizing yourself.

Begin by asking instructors if they teach at local businesses, or know others who do.

Keep a detailed list of information regarding potential employers. You should have an entry for each company with an onsite facility, and leave plenty of room to note how hiring is done, with whom you spoke and when, etc. Add any information you may have gathered from instructors in your area. Then, scan the local classifieds, as well as those online, to check for corporate fitness job openings. You can use your local library's archives to search past issues of the local paper(s) as well. Add to your list those who are hiring or have hired in the past.

When you begin to make contact with the companies on your list, consult the section in Chapter 5 on "Interviewing Successfully." You will find great information that can help your first call to a potential employer to be well planned and professional. Determine during the course of the conversation whether their facility is staffed by direct hires or through a wellness company. If it is the latter, ask about that company, including contact information. Note this information on your list; you might not find an opening immediately, but will want a record of your research and contacts when you search again in the future.

In addition, check the phone book for fitness or exercise consultants and corporate wellness management companies. You can find out background information on many of them in the library, or by contacting the business directly. To learn more about corporate fitness consulting and management, look up the websites of some of the companies in the business, even if they are not in your geographical area. Check out www.corporatefitness.net, www.corporatefitnessworks.com, www.medifit.com, and www.fmconsulting. net. Finally, search the Internet with terms such as "corporate," "fitness," "wellness," and "management." You may find companies in your area, or others who can provide you with more information about this dynamic area of the fitness job market.

Hospital- and Other Healthcare Facility-based Fitness Centers

It can be somewhat difficult to find these centers, as there are no national or state listings available. By using the techniques detailed in the previous section on

Corporate Fitness/Wellness Programs, however, you should be able to locate a number of centers near you. As with the corporate facilities, they are run in one of two ways: staffed by direct hires, or staffed by a management company.

Begin your search by consulting your local library and telephone directory. Some centers may be listed individually, while others may be found by contacting hospitals, rehabilitation centers, assisted living centers, and long-term care facilities, and asking if they maintain fitness centers. You may also find listings of such potential employers on the Internet. Check sites such as www.hospitallink.com, www.hospitalsoup.com, and American Hospital Directory (www.ahd.com), which contain links to hundreds of hospitals' websites. Conduct your own search using terms such as "hospital wellness center" to find specific sites.

In addition, check out www.business.com. Their "Healthcare Facilities and Health Systems" page contains links to hundreds of sites, including those of industry associations, hospitals, and long-term care facilities. You can get financial, background, and contact information for thousands of these potential employers.

As with corporate fitness/wellness centers, some hospital-based facilities utilize the services of companies that provide turnkey management programs. If you are interested in working for such a company, you can research it as you would any other corporate employer. Visit the websites of some of the larger management companies and associations to get an idea of services offered, and even find site listings and job opportunities:

Healthcalc Network
16522 Westgrove Drive
Addison, TX 75001
Phone: 800-670-4316
Fax: 972-380-4400
www.healthcalc.net

Healthtrax
2345 Main Street
Glastonbury, CT 06033
Phone: 860-633-5572
Fax: 860-633-7472
www.healthtrax.net

Health Fitness Corporation

3500 West 80th Street, Suite 130

Minneapolis, MN 55431

Phone: 800-639-7913

Fax: 952-831-7264

www.healthfitnesscorp.com

L&T Health and Fitness

7309 Arlington Blvd. #202

Falls Church, VA 22042

Phone: 703-204-1355 ext. 29

Fax: 703-204-2332

www.ltwell.com

Medical Fitness Association

P.O. Box 73103

Richmond, VA 23235-8026

Phone: 804-327-0330

www.medicalfitness.org

The Resort Industry

The resort industry is made up of a number of sectors, including ski/mountain resorts, beach resorts, spas, clubs, and cruise lines; there are resorts that cater to golfers, scuba divers, tennis players, fishermen, and horseback riders. Most of these locations employ fitness instructors and personal trainers. When researching the industry for employment, keep in mind that resorts are usually corporate-owned. Once you have narrowed down the area(s) in which you have an interest, you can find out about potential employers as you would if seeking a position with any corporate-owned health club. Check back to page 113 for advice on gathering information about such employers.

In addition, many of the online resources listed later in this chapter, especially those that deal specifically with the fitness industry, contain job information and company profiles that may be of interest. Companies that place instructors exclusively in the resort setting include:

Fit Bodies—www.fitbodiesinc.com
Hospitality Online—www.hospitalityonline.com
NRG2GO—www.nrg2go.com
Professional Coaches Association—www.pcaholidays.com
Resort Jobs—www.resortjobs.com
The Riley Guide—www.rileyguidelcom
TravelJobz—www.traveljobz.com

Other ways to research the resort industry include the use of travel and leisure publications. Libraries usually have many of these resources, and may be especially helpful if you are interested in a local resort. There are also a number of travel websites that contain information on resorts, including:

www.resortsandlodges.com
www.resortsource.com
www.ski-guide.com
www.skiresortguide.com
www.spafinder.com
www.spaindex.com
www.vacation-hotline.com/resorts.htm

If you are interested in cruise line employment, your research will need to be somewhat different. Cruise ships are like floating hotels, and indeed, they employ fitness instructors and personal trainers much as a business would do on land. However, learning about job opportunities can be tricky. If you begin searching on the Internet, you will notice a number of products and services which purport to help you land cruise line jobs; they charge you a fee for printed material, an "application," a list of available cruise jobs, or a "placement" service that guarantees you will get a job. However, according to those who have work experience on ships, paying to find a job with a cruise line is unnecessary. In fact, some of the services are in business simply to take your money.

It is better to deal directly with the cruise lines, which maintain websites that give out plenty of information about their business, including employment opportunities. Note that some companies use agencies to fill certain types of positions, while others have labor agreements with unions in countries other than the United States (thus large numbers of job openings are only available to member of these unions). But Americans, Canadians, and British citizens fill the majority of fitness positions, which involve direct contact with the mostly English-speaking guests.

Use the list below to research some of the largest cruise lines. The business websites listed in the previous section on Corporations and Small Businesses are also worth checking out. You may want to read travel and resort publications, such as *Travel and Leisure* magazine, which rates cruise lines, and gives detailed (and less biased) descriptions of their services and reputations. You can also search the Internet with the terms "cruise and employment" to find more information (but beware of products or services that charge you money).

> Carnival Cruises: www.carnival.com
> Celebrity Cruises—www.celebrity-cruises.com
> Cunard—www.cunard.ine.com
> Disney—www.disney.go.com/DisneyCruise
> Holland America—www.hollandamerica.com
> Princess Cruises—www.princesscruises.com
> Radisson Seven Seas Cruises—www.rssc.com
> Royal Caribbean Cruise Line—www.rccl.com

FINDING AVAILABLE POSITIONS

There are a number of great ways to locate employment as a fitness instructor or personal trainer. Some have been around for years, such as classified ads and industry publications. Others are more recent additions to the job search arena, and offer great possibilities. They include Internet resources such as industry-specific sites (some of which list employment opportunities), and general career-related websites that offer advice on everything from writing your resume to researching potential employers to what to wear on an interview.

School Career Placement Centers

Almost every school has a career placement center, whose director has the job of helping you find employment when you graduate. A good placement office will have directories of businesses in the local area, information about job fairs, and copies of any industry publications that list fitness instructor job openings. A top placement director also maintains contacts with the business community, making his or her office one of the first places to hear about a job opening. Also use the placement office to find valuable general information about the market in your area.

Classified Ads

Conventional job-hunting wisdom says you should not depend too much on want ads for finding a job. However, this resource should not be overlooked, especially if you are still in school. By reading the classifieds, you can learn valuable information about the market for fitness professionals in your area. For instance, you will see at least a partial list of the places that hire instructors and trainers.

You can also get an idea of typical salaries and benefits in your area. Since one of the hardest questions to answer on an application or in an interview is "What is your desired salary?" it can be worthwhile to watch the ads and know the going rate ahead of time. You can also get information about part-time versus full-time jobs, learning what clubs expect if they hire you for full shifts as opposed to class or training session time only.

In addition to the educational aspect of want ads, reading and responding to them may actually lead to a position. Many clubs advertise fitness instructor positions in the classifieds, primarily because it is an inexpensive way to reach a large number of potential applicants. However, that means that, depending on your area, dozens of applicants will send a resume to an employer, and you will be competing with all of them. Don't wait to respond. If the ad appears in the Sunday newspaper, respond to it on Monday morning. If possible, call the club and ask if you can deliver your resume to the manager, creating an informal interview opportunity. Used properly, the classifieds will not only improve your knowledge of the job market, but it can lead to your first position as a fitness instructor.

Job Directories

While the Internet has probably surpassed the library in terms of usefulness in your job search, your local library and chamber of commerce are also good places to look. They are especially helpful if you want to work for a local employer who owns or manages a relatively small business. Both libraries and the chamber of commerce maintain directories of such employers. Two excellent sources organized specifically for job hunters are *The World Almanac National Job Finder's Guide* (St. Martin's Press) and the *Job Bank* series (Adams, Inc.). There are brief job descriptions and online resources in the *Job Finder's Guide*; the *Job Bank* books are published by geographic region and contain a section profiling specific companies, with contact information for major employers in your region sorted by industry.

Once you have identified companies of interest, use the resources at your local library to learn more about them. Your librarian can help you find public information about area businesses, including the names of company officers, the number of employees, a brief description of the company, news articles, and contact information.

Job Fairs

Attending job or career fairs is another way to find employment. Job fairs bring together a number of employers under one roof, usually at a hotel, convention center, or civic center. These employers send representatives to the fair to inform prospective employees about their company, accept resumes, and, occasionally, to conduct interviews for open positions. Many fairs are held specifically for health and fitness employers and prospective employees. They usually hold seminars for attendees covering such topics as resume writing, job hunting strategies, and interviewing skills.

The latest trend in job fairs is those offered online. The International Dance Exercise Association (IDEA) maintains one on their website, www.ideafit.com/JobFair/htm. A recent search of the Internet with the terms "job fair" and "exercise" resulted in thousands of hits. These sites are much like online classifieds in that they make available listings of employment opportunities, but usually also provide plenty of background information on the employers; some accept resumes and applications via e-mail.

Your school may be another venue for job fairs. Some physical education or exercise science departments invite representatives from dozens of companies each year before graduation. The emphasis at these fairs is usually on interviews; you can sign up for them with any or all of the attending companies, and gain valuable experience in the process. If your school does not hold job fairs, contact the information office of the convention center or civic center nearest you and ask if there is one their upcoming events calendar. The local newspaper or state unemployment office may also have relevant information. And, again, check the Internet with the search terms "job fair" and "fitness instructor."

While it's true that you will most likely be competing with many other job seekers at a job fair, your ability to impress an employer is far greater during an in-person meeting than it is if you simply respond to a classified ad by submitting your resume. By attending a job fair, your appearance, level of preparation, what you say and how you say it, and your body language can be used to help make an employer interested in hiring you. In the fitness industry, these are the very qualities that employers want to see and evaluate. When attending a job fair (other than one held at a school you are attending), your goal is to get invited to come in later for a formal in-person interview. Since you will have limited time with an employer at a job fair, typically between five and ten minutes, it is rare that an employer will hire someone on the spot.

Preparation on your part is vital. Determine beforehand which employers will be there and whether or not you have the qualifications to fill the job openings available. Begin your research by visiting the website created to promote the job fair you are interested in attending. The website typically lists detailed information about the companies attending and what types of jobs participating employers are looking to fill. Once you pinpoint those you are interested in, research them as if you are preparing for an actual in-person job interview.

Determine exactly how your qualifications and skills meet the needs of employers in which you are interested. Also, develop a list of questions to ask the employer during your in-person meeting at the job fair. Showing a sincere interest in working for an employer and asking questions that demonstrate your interest will help set you apart from the competition in a positive way.

Bring plenty of copies of your resume to the job fair, and begin by visiting with the employers for whom you are most interested in working. It is best to make contact with these clubs as early in the day as possible, when their representatives are fresh and most responsive. They may meet with dozens of potential employees daily, repeating the same information each time. You should be prepared to answer questions about why you want to work for them and how your skills and qualifications make you qualified to fill one of the positions the employer has available. As you meet with people, collect business cards and follow up your meetings later that day with a short letter, e-mail, or fax, thanking each person you met with for their time. Use this correspondence to reaffirm your interest in working for an employer.

Online Resources

As mentioned before in this chapter, one of the fastest growing and most comprehensive resources for job searching is the Internet. There are two types of sites that you should find to be of great use as you look for employment. The first, career-related websites, offer help with every step of the process from resume writing to researching a firm before accepting a job offer. You may also network with other people in your field, and obtain valuable career-related advice on some of these sites. The second type of site is fitness-related and contains lists of job openings geared specifically to your profession.

Career-Related Websites

Following are some of the online resources available to the job hunter. But don't limit yourself to this selection; using any Internet search engine or portal (such as www.dogpile.com, www.hotbot.com, or www.yahoo.com), you can enter a keyword such as: "resume," "job," "career," "job listings," or "help wanted" to find thousands of others.

Job Opportunities

- 6-figure Jobs—www.6figurejobs.com
- About.com—www.jobsearch.about.com/jobs/jobsearch
- America's Employers—www.americasemployers.com
- America's Job Bank—www.ajb.dni.us
- Boston Herald's Job Find—www.jobfind.com
- *Career Builder—www.careerbuilder.com
- Career.com—www.career.com
- CareerNet— www.careers.org
- CareerWeb—www.cweb.com
- College Central Network—www.employercentral.com
- Gary Will's Worksearch—www.garywill.com/worksearch
- JobBank USA—www.jobbankusa.com
- JobLynx— www.joblynx.com
- JobSource— www.jobsource.com
- Monster Board—www.monster.com
- *Occupational Outlook Handbook*—www.stats.bls.gov
- Salary.com—www.salary.com
- Vault.com—www.vault.com
- Wall Street Journal Careers—www.careers.wsj.com
- Yahoo Careers—http://careers.yahoo.com

*Career Builder lists ads from major newspapers, including the *Boston Globe*, *Chicago Tribune*, *Los Angeles Times*, *New York Times*, *San Jose Mercury News*, *Washington Post*, *Philadelphia Inquirer*, and *Southern Florida Sun-Sentinel*.

Fitness Instructor Employment Sites

These sites cover a wide range of fitness jobs, from instructors and trainers to more specialized positions in rehabilitation, corporate wellness, and sports medicine. Note that most of the industry associations and organizations listed in Appendix A include employment listings on their websites; they are therefore not listed below. In addition, many industry publications also include classifieds in their online and print versions. A listing of many of these publications may be found in the next section of this chapter. Finally, conduct a search on the Internet with terms such as "exercise instructor" and "employment" to find even more sites.

Health and Wellness jobs—www.healthandwellnessjobs.com
Health Career Web—www.healthcareerweb.com
Health Houndz—www.healthhoundz.com
Health Promotion Career—www.hpcareer.net/hpri_redirect.cfm
Idea Health and Fitness Association—www.ideafit.com/jobopp.htm
L&T Health and Fitness—www.ltwell.com/employment.htm
Office Workouts Inc.—www.officeworkouts.com
Women's Sports Services—www.womensportsjob.com

Industry Newsletters & Magazines

If you are already a member of one or more of the fitness industry associations, you are familiar with the publications they produce; if not, consult the list of associations in Appendix A. In addition to association newsletters and magazines, there are hundreds more that deal with the industry as a whole, as well as with specific segments of it. Many of them contain classified sections, in print or on their websites, in which job opportunities are listed.

By reading these publications, you will not only discover specific employment opportunies, but will also be able to keep abreast of the industry, tracking changes and identifying trends. Newsletters and magazines often announce breaking news and explain its significance. Being up on the latest exercise science research and health care trends will help convince potential employers that you will be a valuable asset to their business. It tells them you take the time to keep yourself well informed and ready to understand and face new challenges. As Cat Earisman, an instructor and trainer for over twenty years, notes:

> You need to keep reading and learning on your own, apart from formal education and certification. The more you know about the body and how it works, the better teacher you will be. I am constantly reading books on topics like exercise science. I feel I need to know as much as I can, because I don't want to mess around with someone's health.

The following list contains the names and websites for many of the top industry publications. Some offer most or all of their content online, while others provide some information on their websites, with offers to subscribe to a print edition. You may find other publications by searching the Internet with terms such as "magazine and fitness" or "newsletter and exercise," or try specific forms of exercise with the words *magazine*, *newsletter*, or *journal*.

Industry Publications

American Fitness (www.afaa.com)

American Journal of Health Promotion (www.healthpromotionjournal.com)

Athletic Business (www.athleticbusiness.com)

Certified News (www.ascm.org)

Club Business International (www.ihrsa.org)

Club Industry Magazine (www.industryclick.com)

Energy Magazine (www.energymagazine.com)

Exercise and Sports Sciences Reviews (www.ascm.org)

Fitness Management Magazine (www.fitnessmanagement.com)

Fitness Matters (www.ace.org)

Health and Fitness Journal (www.ascm.org)

HealthInvest Inc.—Innovative Work/Life Solutions (www.healthinvest.org)

IDEA Health and Fitness Source (www.ideafit.com)

IDEA Personal Trainer (www.ideafit.com)

IDEA Fitness Edge (www.ideafit.com)

International Electronic Journal of Health Education (www.iejhe.org)

Journal of Exercise Physiology (www.css.edu/asep)

Journal of the American Medical Association (http://jama.ama-assn.org/)

Muscle and Fitness (www.muscleandfitness.com)

National Council for Strength and Fitness Online Journal
    (www.ncsf.org/journal.htm)

New England Journal of Medicine (www.nejm.org)

Personal Fitness Professional (www.fit-pro.com)

Personal Trainer Magazine (www.nfpt.com/Library/magazine.htm)

Physician and Sports Medicine (www.physsportsmed.com)

Protraineronline.com (www.protraineronline.com)

Shape Magazine (www.shape.com)

Strength and Conditioning Journal (www.nsca-lift.org)

Thefitclub.com Magazine (www.thefitclub.com)

Training and Conditioning (www.athleticsearch.com)

Yoga International Magazine (www.yimag.com)

Yoga Magazine (www.yogamag.net)

Yoga Online (www.indigo.ie/~cmouze/yoga_online/yoga_online.htm)

CONSIDERING SELF-EMPLOYMENT

The Department of Labor estimates that out of about 160,000 fitness work-ers, 26,000 are self-employed, the majority of them as personal trainers. IDEA puts the figure even higher, noting that 37% of their personal trainer membership work for themselves. Fitness instructors are also moving more into the self-employment area, teaching as independent contractors, working as corporate fitness consultants, owning and running a franchise, or in a num-ber of other business endeavors.

Fran Scalessa, who teaches yoga in Summit, New Jersey, left a successful law practice to become a full-time instructor. In addition to teaching in clients' homes, he also holds classes at a private studio. After three years in the fitness industry, building up his business to six clients or classes per day, Fran is making an income similar to that earned while practicing law. His advice is to start small, gaining teaching experience at any location, and at any price. "You have to pay your dues," he explains. "Once you develop a following, you can teach on your own for higher rates. Word-of-mouth should be all the marketing you need, after you have taught enough classes at various clubs."

Mr. Scalessa's successful mix of studio and private home class locations can work for personal trainers as well as instructors. Renting space in an already existing gym, or creating a small workout area outfitted with the equipment you need in a space you own, can allow you the freedom to teach or work with clients outside of a club setting. You might also add time spent in a club or clubs as an independent contractor to boost your income and create exposure to more clients. More specific ideas about how to make a living as a full-time, self-employed fitness professional may be found in the section "Growing from Part-time to Full-Time," located in Chapter 6 (page 213).

Yet, as Irene Lewis McCormick, notes in an article in *Certified News*:

> Opening a fitness facility, an in-home personal training business, or a consulting service, requires a lot of research and pre-planning. Many of the business-oriented sessions at national conventions can assist in the conception, organization, and operation of a business start-up. The opportunities for networking can also contribute ideas that can help the new business thrive. But sharpening one's skills and determining that self-employment is the best option takes considerable thought, time, risk, and commitment.

Benefits of Self-Employment

There are many great fitness jobs listed earlier in this chapter, all of which involve working for another individual or company. Perhaps you have never considered working for yourself, or you are interested, but aren't sure what it entails. Why do so many in the fitness industry choose self-employment? There are a number of compelling reasons.

First is the potential for greater income. If you work full-time for a gym or health club, your salary will be set at a rate similar to that earned by every other employee. Perhaps you will receive bonuses or yearly increases, but unless you plan to move into management, the pay scale will remain fairly low. IDEA's Personal Fitness Trainer Fact Sheet quotes a survey of trainers as noting that a full-time employee trainer earned an average of $22,900 a year. Full-time self-employed personal trainers reported an average annual income of $33,800. The difference is due to the fact that those who are self-employed can charge higher rates for their services, even if they work at a club.

The International Sports Sciences Association (ISSA), whose unique certification program is geared toward to the entrepreneur, emphasizes the benefits of independent contracting when working at a club or gym. Their text, "Guide to Fiscal Fitness," explains how to negotiate a lucrative contract, even when most of the trainers or instructors working there are paid as part-time employees. By presenting yourself as a self-employed professional, whose education and experience can command a higher hourly rate, you can get work at clubs, many of which are eager to provide their members with the best instructors or trainers they can find.

Other benefits of self-employment are flexibility and creative freedom. You can teach or train when and where you want. As your own boss, you won't have to cater to someone else's whims or schedules. If you want to take time off to attend a seminar and learn something new that you can pass along to your clients, the choice is yours. As a self-employed instructor, you may develop your own class formats, using whatever equipment or music you prefer.

Do You Have What it Takes?

Being self-employed is more than just finding enough work at the right price to make a living. You will be running your own small business, responsible for marketing, purchasing health and liability insurance, accounting, customer relations, and more. Do you have what it takes to be a successful entrepreneur? To help determine whether you have the skills and personal attributes necessary to start your own business, read the following statements made by self-employed fitness professionals. The more statements you agree with, the better your chances of making a living with your own business.

> ▶ I am self-confident. I believe in myself. I can take responsibility for good and bad outcomes, and have a positive outlook that lets me learn from my mistakes and keep going forward.
> ▶ I understand the fitness industry. I keep up with clinical research and trends, knowing that my education must remain ongoing. I enjoy reading industry publications and attending workshops and seminars to learn more.
> ▶ I know the market that I work in. There is a demand for my skills and services in my area.
> ▶ I don't give up when things aren't going right. I have the strength and courage to keep trying, and to put in the hours it takes to succeed. If I've made a mistake, I can admit it, learn from it, and move on.

▶ I don't have problems with money. When things are tight, I know how to cut costs and where to find financing if I need it. I know how to keep accurate records and balance my books.

▶ I love working with others, and am described as a "people person." There are so many different personalities out there, and I enjoy interacting with all of them.

▶ I don't need someone to direct me; I can see what needs to be done, and do it.

▶ I like responsibility and being in charge. I can make decisions quickly when I need to.

▶ I'm organized. I like to make plans and follow through with them, paying attention to all the details.

▶ I'm trustworthy. I don't say things I don't mean, and I keep my word.

Resources for Entrepreneurs

Starting and running your own business doesn't mean you have to go it alone. There are a number of great resources in which you can find the knowledge and guidance you need to be a success. If you are planning to earn a degree or certificate before beginning your fitness career, consider enrolling in courses or choosing programs that offer instruction in areas that will benefit your new business. Many degree and non-degree programs offer instruction in record-keeping, marketing, and small-business management. Some certifying organizations (such as the ISSA, mentioned earlier in this chapter) also offer such instruction. You can sign up for individual classes at community or junior colleges in specific topics, or enroll in a fitness-related degree program that includes such instruction.

For instance, McHenry County College, in Crystal Lake, Illinois, offers a one-year certificate program entitled Fitness Instructor Technology (F.I.T.). Curriculum covers basic anatomy and physiology, applied kinesiology, fitness assessment and programming, and courses in business, stressing club business operations and member retention techniques. The Associate Degree in Fitness Leadership at Henry Ford Community College in Dearborn, Michigan, requires courses designed to benefit the future entrepreneur, including those in business and management.

There are a number of organizations at national and local levels that provide support and guidance to those starting their own businesses. Either by consulting their online resources, or attending meetings, you can find out about the differences between sole proprietorships and corporations, where to find reasonable rates on liability and health insurance, and how to write a business plan. The Service Corps of Retired Executives (SCORE) provides expert business advice via e-mail (www.score.org), or in person at their 400 chapters across the United States and in Puerto Rico. To find out the location of the nearest chapter, or to get more information, call SCORE at 800-634-0245.

The National Association for the Self-Employed (NASE) is another great resource. At a national level, this organization acts as an entrepreneur's advocate, promoting legislation such as the IRS's paperwork reduction act, and affordable health care. Directly to the small business owner, they provide free tax and financial advice, discounts on insurance, office supplies, other necessities, and access to special financing sources.

Entrepreneur Resources

Websites

ChamberBiz—www.chamberbiz.com

The Educated Entrepreneur—www.educatedentrepreneur.com

Entrepreneur Magazine—www.entrepreneur.com

Entrepreneurial Connection—www.entreprenerialconnection.com

The Entrepreneur's Help Page—www.tannedfeet.com

IRS's Small Business Pages—www.irs.gov/businesses/small/display/
    0,,i1%3D2&i2%3D23&genericId%3D20005,00.html

National Association for the Self-Employed—www.nase.org

Personal Training Business Consultants International—www.ptconsultants.com

Quicken.com Small Business—www.quicken.com/small_business

Small Business Administration—www.sba.gov

The Small Business Advancement National Center—www.sbaer.uca.edu/

The Small Business Knowledge Base—www.bizmove.com

United States Association for Small Business and Entrepreneurship—
    www.usasbe.org/

Young Entrepreneur's Organization—www.yeo.org

Books

Start Up: An Entrepreneur's Guide to Launching and Managing a New Business, by William J. Stolze (Career Press, 1999).

The Young Entrepreneur's Edge: Using Your Ambition, Independence, and Youth to Launch a Successful Business, by Jennifer Kushell, Bonnie Szymanski (Random House, 1999).

Starting Over: How to Change Careers or Start Your Own Business, by Stephen M. Pollan, Mark Levine (Warner Books, 1997).

Entrepreneur Magazine's 303 Marketing Tips: Guaranteed to Boost Your Business, edited by Rieva Lesonsky, Leann Anderson (Entrepreneur Media, 1999).

The Entrepreneur Magazine Small Business Advisor: The One-Stop Information Source for Starting, Managing and Growing a Small Business, by the Entrepreneur Media Inc. Staff (Entrepreneur Media, John Wiley & Sons, 1999).

NETWORKING

It is estimated that up to 90% of all jobs are filled by word of mouth. That means that someone you know, even perhaps an acquaintance, may be responsible for helping you find employment. But that doesn't mean you should sit around waiting for a phone call offering a job. Instead, be in active contact with those you know, form a network of them, and work your network as an integral part of your job search process.

Described in this way, the process probably sounds a lot less complicated and intimidating than the "networking" you may have heard of. Networking is simply the art of making contact with others to obtain information or get help meeting a specific goal. Successful people know that it is useful throughout a career, both when just starting out, and when looking to move ahead. But there are still some who picture it as insincere small talk or handshaking. Don't let that reputation get in the way: when done properly, networking is completely sincere, and can provide many benefits, such as:

► mentoring
► making contacts within a hiring company
► furthering training
► getting information about trends in the industry
► increasing business

The key to successful networking, no matter where you are in your career, is to break down the process into seven, easy-to-follow steps. An exploration of these steps follows, showing each one's direct application to a fitness instructor job search.

Step One: Identify Small Goals

Your ultimate goal, not only for networking, but for the entire job search process, is to find a great job. However, you should not approach day-to-day networking as a means to that larger goal. Instead, as your first step, identify smaller goals that can be met quickly. For instance, you have narrowed down your search to three clubs in your area. Now, you want to get "inside" information about them in order to decide whether or not to apply for a job with them. Or, you may simply be seeking advice from those already working in the field. Once your goals are identified, you can best determine how to meet them.

Step Two: Be Informed

If your goal is to seek advice about employers in your area, get as much information as you can first. Research the companies that hire fitness instructors as described earlier in this chapter. Understand the field in general, too. You want to sound like you have done your homework when you begin to make contacts.

This is also the step in which you should begin to make a list of potential contacts that may help you meet your goal(s). If you are in school, the person running the job placement office should be at the head of your list. Then, look to your research: you have probably read the names of others you can add to your list (heads of human resource departments, and others who do the hiring for their businesses). Others who may be of help to you are:

▶ friends and relatives
▶ current or former fellow students
▶ current or former teachers
▶ members of professional associations

> ▶ other professionals
> ▶ people who work for a club you would like to work for

Newsletters from your industry associations may list fitness instructors working in your area. The Internet is also a good place to find contacts. Industry association websites may provide you with leads, and there are an increasing number of sites that provide message boards on which job seekers can network. Check out some of the business sites listed on page 114, and find other sites by searching the Internet with terms such as "networking" and "job search."

Step Three: Make a Connection

Using the list of potential contacts you developed in step two, build your network. Connect with each person, and take the time to let him or her know about your job search. Tell them briefly about your background and education, and what makes you a superior candidate. Give them a good idea about the types of positions you are most interested in. In other words, be sure that everyone you know who may be able to help you land a job knows that you are looking for one!

During these contacts, work on developing a list of fitness instructors who work at the places where you are interested in finding employment. Call them, or visit them at work. Taking a class that they teach is a great way to introduce yourself. Although busy, most will take a few minutes to speak with a prospective newcomer. They were new to the business once themselves, so if you are careful not to take up too much of their time, they will probably be willing to give you some information. Begin by introducing yourself, showing that you are informed (step two) and interested in what they have to say. Then, ask if they are willing to help you.

Step Four: Ask for What You Want

If your contact indicates that he or she is willing to help you, be honest and direct about what you want. If your goal is to find out inside information about the club in which a contact works, tell him or her that you are thinking of applying to work there. Then, ask questions such as:

- ▶ "How do you like the club?"
- ▶ "What are the benefits of working here?"
- ▶ "What is the atmosphere like?"
- ▶ "Where else have you worked, and how does this facility compare?"
- ▶ "Do you have job responsibilities here other than teaching or training?"

Step Five: Expand Your Network

One of the most valuable pieces of information you can get from a contact is another contact. After you have obtained the information you need to meet your step one goal(s), simply ask if he or she would mind sharing with you the name of another person who might also be able to help you.

Also consider requesting *informational interviews* at clubs and other facilities that interest you. This type of interview is not granted in response to a job opening, but may be an excellent opportunity to:

- ▶ learn more about how the fitness center works
- ▶ gain interview experience
- ▶ make a contact that might help you get a job in the future
- ▶ understand the fitness industry better
- ▶ find out what kind of salary and benefits are offered

Step Six: Organize Yourself

Your list of contacts is drawn up, and you have begun the networking process in an organized fashion. Once you begin the process of speaking with some of your contacts, organization becomes even more important. You will need to keep track of them, and the information they impart. When you need to connect with a contact again, you will be able to easily access your information. There are software packages that can help you to keep track of your networking contacts, or, you can simply use a notebook and organize yourself. For each contact, note:

- ▶ Name
- ▶ Address
- ▶ E-mail address
- ▶ Phone number (work, pager, cellular phone, residence)
- ▶ Fax number
- ▶ Company name
- ▶ Job title
- ▶ First meeting—where, when, the topics you discussed
- ▶ Last contact—when, why, and how

Step Seven: Maintain Your Contacts

It is important to maintain your contacts once you have established them. Try to reach people again within a couple of weeks of meeting them. You can send a note of thanks, ask a question, or send a piece of information related to your conversation with them. This contact cements your meeting in their mind, so they will remember you more readily when you call them again in the future. If you haven't communicated with a contact for a few months, you might send him or her a note or e-mail about an article you read, relevant new technology, or other information, to remind them of your name and goal.

As you begin your job search, keep in mind that you are not just looking for a job; you are looking for a good job, one you will enjoy and feel challenged by. The process doesn't involve your begging for employment, but rather doing an efficient search for an employer who will be a match for your skills and talents. Once you have found an available position or positions that interest you, you will need to contact potential employers and express your interest. Chapter 5 explains how best to make that contact, from the initial phone call or letter, to the interview and job evaluation.

THE INSIDE TRACK

Who: Tracy Campoli
What: Certified Pilates Instructor
Where: New York, New York

I think it's very funny that I work primarily in a gym. Before becoming a Pilates Instructor, I never considered myself to be much of a "gym" person, having spent most of my time in a studio while attaining a BFA in dance prior to receiving my Pilates certification. But now I spend almost twenty hours a week in a gym!

Before choosing a training program, I spoke with several Pilates instructors that I liked and respected and asked them where they'd received their training. Soon after, I enrolled in a training program, performed an apprenticeship, and passed both written and practical exams to receive my Power Pilates Mat and IM=X Pilates Certifications, but it's extremely important to realize that a warm, trustworthy, and approachable personality is just as important as your certification. Ideally, a fitness instructor should also possess a practical knowledge of her specialty and be able to translate information in a variety of ways so that students of all levels will be able to under-stand it.

In order to find a job, I called every gym I could find and asked if they were in need of a Pilates trainer and I also made contacts with several Pilates and Yoga instructors in the area. It's always a plus to be able to "name drop" a little during an interview because it gives you more credibility and shows that you've taken the time to research your chosen field.

I've now worked at New York Sports Club for the past two-and-a-half years and also train students privately. As a Pilates instructor, I stretch my students and teach and demonstrate exercises, but in my private practice, I also book appointments and sometimes rent space to teach students. One of the most difficult aspects of being a Pilates Instructor is setting boundaries for yourself. Currently, I work about twenty-two to twenty-six hours a week, but a trainer could easily work twenty-four hours a day, seven days a week. Although it is very important to make yourself available to your students, it's equally important that you leave room for your personal life. At first, I found the hours to be extremely challenging because I wasn't used to getting up so early and also working late into the evening—often with long stretches not working in between. But after a while, I adjusted to the schedule and filled the down time pursuing my other interests.

As a Certified Pilates Instructor, I learn as much from my clients as they learn from me. My experiences working with students have really improved my people and communication skills. As a trainer, it is very important to listen to your clients so that you can tailor their workout to their specific needs. I've also realized how important trainers can be to their clients; clients' workouts are their "me time," and it's my responsibility to create both a challenging and fun environment. It's incredibly satisfying to watch a student improve and begin to feel and look stronger. I really enjoy my work because it has given me the opportunity to meet so many wonderful people and watch them grow both physically and emotionally.

CHAPTER five

JOB SEARCH SKILLS

Once you have pinpointed the job opportunities you are interested in pursuing, you will need to contact your potential employer to express your interest. The way you accomplish that contact can be just as important as your skills and training. This chapter will help ensure that the impression you leave is the very best possible, making you stand out as a superior candidate. Once you receive a job offer or offers, you will need to evaluate them and make a decision. At the end of the chapter, you will find tips on how to go about this final step on your path to employment.

YOUR FIRST CONTACT with a potential employer may be in person as you meet informally at a club or other worksite; through a phone call, mailed cover letter and resume, or e-mailed resume; or during an interview. Whatever the form, it is imperative that you use it to make an excellent impression. A resume full of spelling errors, an unprofessional sounding phone call, or an interview to which you arrive ten minutes late can all mean disaster to a job search. Once you are offered a job, you will need to handle the offer professionally, too.

It is not hard to master the job search skills you need to succeed, but it does take some time and effort. By carefully reading this chapter, you will learn how to land the job you want by writing great cover letters and resumes, interviewing with confidence, and assessing job offers thoroughly.

WRITING YOUR RESUME

Whether you are responding to an advertisement, following up on a networking opportunity, or making a cold contact, your resume is usually the first means by which a potential employer learns about you. Think of it as an advertisement you write to help sell yourself. A successful advertisement catches your attention by combining several elements: content, composition, clarity, and concentration. Falling short in any of these areas can cause a reader to pass over the ad; you want to make sure that a prospective employer will pay attention to yours.

As you write, edit, and proofread your resume, make an effort to keep all of the information short, to the point, and totally relevant. Anything you leave out can be discussed later, during a job interview. The purpose of your resume is to get an employer interested enough in you so you make it to the next level, getting invited for an interview.

Creating a powerful resume will take time and effort. Even if you have written dozens before, it is worth your while to seek out good resume-writing resources to help you draft one for your new career as a fitness instructor or personal trainer. While much has remained the same over the years, there are current standards and trends for resumes, including e-mailable and computer scannable resumes, that you should know about.

To start, check out your school's placement office, which may have copies of former students' resumes. Books such as *Great Resume* by Jason R. Rich (Learning-Express, 2000) contain excellent general guidelines. And there are plenty of online resources to help you create a winning resume, including the following:

- ▶ Resume Writing—www.abastaff.com/career/resume/resume.htm
- ▶ Accent Resume Writing—www.accent-resume-writing.com/critiques
- ▶ Damn Good Resume—www.damngood.com/jobseekers/tips.html
- ▶ The Elegant Resume—www.resumeadvice.tripod.com
- ▶ eResume Writing—www.eresumewriting.com
- ▶ JobStar—www.jobstar.org/tools/resume
- ▶ JobWeb—www.jobweb.com/catapult/guenov/restips.html
- ▶ Learn2Write a Resume—www.learn2.com/07/0768/0768.asp
- ▶ Monster.com Resume Center—http://resume.monster.com
- ▶ Rebecca Smith's eResumes & Resources—www.eresumes.com

- ▶ Resumania—www.resumania.com
- ▶ Resume Magic—www.liglobal.com/b_c/career/res.shtml
- ▶ Resume Tutor—www1.umn.edu/ohr/ecep/resume
- ▶ Resume Workshop—owl.english.purdue.edu/workshops/hypertext/ ResumeW/index.html
- ▶ 10 Minute Resume—www.10minuteresume.com

Content

Use the following questionnaire to gather the information needed for your resume. In the following sections, you will learn how to organize, format, and word it to make the best possible impression.

Contact Information

The only personal information that belongs on your resume is your name (on every page, if your resume exceeds one page in length), address, phone number, and fax number and e-mail address if you have them. Under no circumstances should you include personal information such as age, gender, religion, health or marital status, or number of children.

Full name: _____

Permanent street address: _____

City, State, Zip: _____

Daytime telephone number: _____

Evening telephone number: _____

Pager/cell phone number (optional): _____

Fax number (optional): _____

E-mail address: _____

Personal website address/online portfolio URL: _____

School address (if applicable): _____

Your phone number at school (if applicable): _____

Job/Career Objective(s)

Write a short description of the job you are seeking. Be sure to include as much information as possible about how you can use your skills to the employer's benefit. Later, you will condense this answer into one short sentence.

_____

_____

_____

_____

_____

What is/are the job title(s) you are looking to fill? _____

_____

Educational Background

Be sure to include your internship, if applicable, in this section. Gear your listing of any accomplishments, activities, and affiliations toward your future job. Include any internships, as well as the skills you learned which will be applicable to the position for which you are applying.

List the most recent college or university you have attended: _____

_____

City/State: _____

What year did you start?: _____

Graduation month/year: _____

Degree(s) and/or award(s) earned: _____

Your major(s): _____

Your minor(s): _____

List some of your most impressive accomplishments, extracurricular activities, club affiliations, etc.: _____

_____

List computer courses you have taken that help qualify you for the job you are seeking: _____

_____

_____

Grade point average (GPA): _____

Other college/university you have attended: _____

City/State: _____

What year did you start?: _____

Graduation month/year: _____

Degree(s) and/or award(s) earned: _____

Your major(s): _____

Your minor(s): _____

List some of your most impressive accomplishments, extracurricular activities, club affiliations, etc.: _____

_____

List computer courses you have taken that help qualify you for the job you are seeking: _____

_____

_____

Grade point average (GPA): _____

High school attended: _____

City/State: _____

Graduation date: _____

Grade point average (GPA): _____

List the names and phone numbers of one or two current or past professors/teachers (or guidance counselors) you can contact about obtaining a letter of recommendation or list as a reference: _____

_____

_____

_____

Personal Skills & Abilities

Your personal skill set (the combination of skills you possess) is something that differentiates you from everyone else. Skills that are marketable in the workplace are not always taught in school, however. Your ability to manage people, stay cool under pressure, remain organized, surf the Internet, use software applications, speak in public, communicate well in writing, communicate in multiple languages, or perform research, are all examples of marketable skills. When reading job descriptions or classified ads, pay careful attention to the wording used to describe what the employer is looking for. As you customize your resume for a specific employer, you will want to match up what the employer is looking for with your own qualifications as closely as possible. Try to utilize the wording provided by the employer within the classified ad or job description.

What do you believe is your most marketable skill? Why? _____

_____

_____

_____

List three or four specific examples of how you have used this skill in the past
    while at work. What was accomplished as a result?

    1. _____

    2. _____

    3. _____

    4. _____

What are keywords or buzzwords that can be used to describe your skill?

_____

_____

_____

What is another of your marketable skills? _____

_____

Provide at least three examples of how you have used this skill in the work-
    place:

    1. _____

    2. _____

    3. _____

What unusual or unique skill(s) do you possess that help you stand out from
    other applicants applying for the same types of positions as you?

_____

_____

_____

How have you already proven this skill is useful in the workplace?

_____

What computer skills do you possess? _____

_____

What computer software packages are you proficient in (such as Microsoft
    Office, Meeting Matrix, PowerPoint, Menu Maker, etc.)? _____

_____

Thinking carefully, what skills do you believe you currently lack?

_____

_____

What skills do you have that need to be polished or enhanced in order to
  make you a more appealing candidate? _____

_____

What options are available to you to either obtain or to brush up on the skills
  you believe need improvement (for example: evening/weekend classes at a
  college or university, adult education classes, seminars, books, home study
  courses, on-the-job-training, etc.)? _____

_____

_____

In what time frame could you realistically obtain this training?

_____

_____

Work/Employment History

Previous work experience is very important. Even if it had nothing to do with
your chosen field, every job you have ever had taught you something that will
make you a better fitness instructor or personal trainer. Experience in other
fields such as medicine, accounting, real estate, human resources, and insurance, is considered a hiring plus by potential employers. Don't overlook or
discount volunteer work for the same reason. You gained skills and experience, and your volunteering also indicates that you are committed to your
community. (Keep this in mind as you go through your training; if you are
short on experience, you might think about volunteering.)

Complete the following employment-related questions for all of your previous employers, including part-time or summer jobs held while in school, as
well as temp jobs, internships, and volunteering. You probably won't want to
reveal your past earning history to a potential employer, but you may want
this information available as reference when you begin negotiating your
future salary, benefits, and overall compensation package.

Most recent employer: _____

City, State: _____

Year you began work: _____

Year you stopped working (write "Present" if still employed): _____

Job title: _____

Job description: _____

_____

_____

Reason for leaving: _____

_____

_____

Of your accomplishments while holding this job, which three are you most proud of?

   1. _____

   2. _____

   3. _____

Contact person at the company who can provide a reference: _____

_____

Contact person's phone number: _____

Annual salary earned: _____

Employer: _____

City, State: _____

Year you began work: _____

Year you stopped working (write "Present" if still employed): _____

Job title: _____

Job description: _____

_____

_____

Reason for leaving: _____

_____

_____

Of your accomplishments while holding this job, which three are you most proud of?

1. _____
2. _____
3. _____

Contact person at the company who can provide a reference:_____
_____

Contact person's phone number:_____
Annual salary earned:_____

Military Service (if applicable)

Branch of service you served in:_____
Years served:_____
Highest rank achieved:_____
Decorations or awards earned:_____
Special skills or training obtained:_____

Professional Accreditations and Licenses

List any and all of the professional accreditations and/or licenses you have earned thus far in your career. Be sure to highlight items that directly relate to the job(s) you will be applying for. _____
_____
_____

Hobbies and Special Interests

You may have life experience that should be emphasized for potential employers. Did you help a spouse in a business? Were you a candidate for public office? Any number of experiences can add to your attractiveness as a job candidate. If you don't have a great deal of work experience, this part of your resume is very important. Think about the things you have done. Which have taught you lessons that are valuable for a fitness instructor or personal trainer to know? If you can't find a way to include those experiences on your resume, mention them in your cover letter.

List any hobbies or special interests you have that are not necessarily work-related, but that potentially could separate you from the competition. Can any of the skills utilized in your hobby be adapted for the workplace?

_____

_____

What non-professional clubs or organizations do you belong to or actively participate in? _____

_____

_____

Personal/Professional Ambitions

You may not want to share these on your resume, but answering the following questions will help you to focus your search, and prepare for possible interviewing topics.

What are your long-term goals?

Personal: _____

_____

_____

Professional: _____

_____

_____

Financial: _____

_____

_____

For your personal, professional, and then financial goals, what are five smaller, short-term goals you can begin working toward achieving right now that will help you ultimately achieve each of your long-term goals?

Short-Term Personal Goals:

1. _____
2. _____
3. _____
4. _____
5. _____

Short-Term Professional Goals:

1. _____
2. _____
3. _____
4. _____
5. _____

Short-Term Financial Goals:

1. _____
2. _____
3. _____
4. _____
5. _____

Will the job(s) for which you will be applying help you achieve your long-term goals and objectives? If 'yes,' how? If 'no,' why not? _____

_____

_____

_____

Describe your personal, professional, and financial situation right now:

_____

_____

_____

What would you most like to improve about your life overall? _____

_____

_____

What are a few things you can do, starting immediately, to bring about positive changes in your personal, professional or financial life? _____

_____

_____

_____

Where would you like to be (personally, professionally, and financially) five and ten years down the road? _____

_____

_____

_____

What needs to be done to achieve these long-term goals or objectives?

_____

_____

_____

_____

What are some of the qualities about your personality that you are most proud of? _____

_____

_____

_____

What are some of the qualities about your personality that you believe need improvement? _____

_____

_____

_____

What do others most like about you? _____

_____

_____

_____

What do you think others least like about you? _____

_____

_____

_____

If you decided to pursue additional education, what would you study and why? How would this help you professionally? _____

_____

_____

_____

If you had more free time, what would you spend it doing? _____

_____

_____

_____

List several accomplishments in your personal and professional life that you are most proud of. Why did you choose these things?

1. _____
2. _____
3. _____
4. _____
5. _____

What were your strongest and favorite subjects in school? Is there a way to incorporate these interests into the job(s) or career path you are pursuing?

_____

_____

_____

_____

What do you believe is your biggest weakness? Why would an employer not hire you? _____

_____

_____

_____

What would be the ideal atmosphere for you to work in? Do you prefer a large corporate atmosphere, working for yourself, or working in a small club or studio?

_____

_____

_____

List five qualities about a new job that would make it the ideal employment opportunity for you:

1. _____
2. _____
3. _____
4. _____
5. _____

What did you like most about the last place you worked? _____

_____

_____

What did you like least about the last place you worked? _____

_____

_____

What work-related tasks are you particularly good at?_____
_____
_____

What type of coworkers would you prefer to have?_____
_____
_____

When it comes to work-related benefits and perks, what is most important to
  you?_____
_____
_____

When you are recognized for doing a good job at work, how do you like to
  be rewarded?_____
_____
_____

If you were to write a "help wanted" ad describing your ideal dream job, what
  would the ad say?_____
_____
_____
_____

Composition

How your resume looks can be as important as what it says. Potential employers may receive a stack of resumes for one job opening, and they probably
spend less than one minute deciding which to review further and which to
throw away. The immediate toss-outs are usually the ones with glaring
errors—employers figure if you can't take the time to sell yourself properly,
what will your performance be like on the job? Your goal is to achieve an
overall look that is neat, clean, and within standard resume guidelines. Use
the following resume creation tips to help organize the material you gathered
in the questionnaire.

Resume Creation Tips

No matter what type of resume you are putting together, you want to ensure that your finished document has the most impact possible when a potential employer reads it. Bethany Palmer, a Senior Group Fitness Director with 70 instructors and trainers on her staff notes:

> Don't do anything fancy with your resume. Show that you take yourself and your profession seriously by keeping your resume traditional and well written. Most of the resumes I receive are done conservatively, on white, light gray, or cream paper with black ink, and that's what I like to see.

- Always use standard letter-size paper in ivory, cream, or another neutral color.
- Include your name, address, and phone number on every page.
- Make sure your name is larger than anything else on the page (example: your name in 14-point font, the rest in 12 point).
- Use a font that is easy to read, such as 12-point Times New Roman.
- Do not use more than three fonts in your resume.
- Edit, edit, edit. Read it forward and backward, and then have friends with good proofreading skills read it. Don't rely heavily on grammar and spell checkers, which can miss errors.
- Use bullet points for items in a list—they highlight your main points, making them hard to miss.
- Use keywords in the fitness industry.
- Avoid using excessive graphics such as boxes, distracting lines, and complex designs.
- Be consistent when using bold, capitalization, underlining, and italics. If one company name is underlined, make sure all are underlined. Check titles, dates, et cetera.
- Don't list your nationality, race, religion, or gender. Keep your resume as neutral as possible. Your resume is a summary of your skills and abilities.
- Don't put anything personal on your resume such as your birth date, marital status, height, or hobbies.
- One page is best, but do not crowd your resume. Shorten the margins if you need more space; if it's necessary to create a two-page resume, make sure you

balance the information on each page. Don't put just one section on the second page. Be careful about where the page break occurs.

■ Keep your resume updated. Don't write "9/97 to present" if you ended your job two months ago. Do not cross out or handwrite changes on your resume.

■ Understand and remember everything written on your resume. Be able to back up all statements with specific examples.

You can organize the information on your resume in a number of ways, depending on your work history, and how the hiring club wants the resume submitted. The three most common formats are:

▶ Chronological format
▶ Skills format (also known as a functional resume)
▶ Combination of chronological and skills formats

The most common resume format is *chronological*—you summarize your work experience year-by-year, beginning with your current or most recent employment experience and working backward. For each job, list the dates you were employed, the name and location of the company for which you worked, and the position(s) you held. Work experience is followed by education, which is also organized chronologically.

The *skills resume* (also known as the *functional resume*) emphasizes what you can do rather than what you have done. It is useful if you have little or no experience in your chosen field, have large gaps in your work history, or have relevant skills that would not be properly highlighted in a chronological listing of jobs. The skills resume concentrates on your skills and qualifications. Specific jobs you have held are listed, but they are not the primary focus of this type of resume.

You may decide a combination of the chronological and skills resumes would be best to highlight your education, experience, and talents. This is a popular choice for those entering the fitness industry, who may have relevant (rather than direct) work experience, such as working with the public. You can highlight the specific skills, recent certification workshops or degrees earned that directly relate to the jobs for which you are applying, while briefly mentioning where you have been and what you have done otherwise.

Special Note to Those Applying for Positions with Cruise Lines

Many large ship-owning companies use different processes for finding employees. Some companies ask for references to be submitted with a resume; others may demand a specific format for your resume. Whatever the instructions, it's vital that you follow them exactly, or your resume may never be considered.

Making Your Resume Computer-Friendly

One of the biggest trends in terms of corporate recruiting is for employers to accept resumes online via e-mail, through one of the career-related websites, or via their own website. If you are going to be applying for jobs online or submitting your resume via e-mail, you will need to create an electronic resume (in addition to a traditional printed resume).

Many companies scan all resumes from job applicants using a computer software program with optical character recognition (OCR), and then enter them into a database, where they can be searched using keywords. When e-mailing your electronic resume directly to an employer, as a general rule, the document should be saved in an ASCII, Rich Text or plain text file. Contact the employer directly to see which method is preferred.

When sending a resume via e-mail, the message should begin as a cover letter (and contain the same information as a cover letter). You can then either attach the resume file to the e-mail message or paste the resume text within the message. Be sure to include your e-mail address and well as your regular mailing address and phone number(s) within all e-mail correspondence. Never assume an employer will receive your message and simply hit "respond" using their e-mail software to contact you.

Guidelines for Creating an Electronic Resume to Be Saved and Submitted in ASCII Format

■ Set the document's left and right margins so that 6.5 inches of text will be displayed per line. This will ensure that the text won't automatically wrap to the next line (unless you want it to).

■ Use a basic, 12-point text font, such as Courier or Times Roman.

■ Avoid using bullets or other symbols. Instead, use an asterisk ("*") or a dash ("-"). Instead of using the percentage sign ("%") for example, spell out the word percent.

■ Use the spell check feature of the software used to create your electronic resume and then proofread the document carefully. Just as applicant tracking software is designed to pick out keywords from your resume that showcase you as a qualified applicant, these same software packages used by employers can also instantly count the number of typos and spelling errors in your document and report that to an employer as well.

■ Avoid using multiple columns, tables, or charts within your document.

■ Within the text, avoid abbreviations—spell everything out. For example, use the word "Director," not 'Dir." or "Vice President" as opposed to "VP." In terms of degrees, however, it's acceptable to use terms like "A.S.", or "B.A."

■ Use more than one page, if necessary. The computer can handle two or three, and the more skills you list in this extra space, the more "hits" you will get from the computer (a "hit" occurs when one of your skills matches what the computer is looking for).

Properly formatting your electronic resume is critical to having it scanned or read; however, it's what you say within your resume that will ultimately get you hired. According to the Rebecca Smith's eResumes & Resources website (www.eresumes.com), "Keywords are the basis of the electronic search and retrieval process. They provide the context from which to search for a resume in a database, whether the database is a proprietary one that serves a specific purpose, or whether it is a Web-based search engine that serves the general public. Keywords are a tool to quickly browse without having to access the complete text. Keywords are used to identify and retrieve resumes for the user. . . . Employers and recruiters generally search resume databases using keywords: nouns and phrases that highlight technical and professional areas of expertise, industry-related jargon, projects, achievements, special task forces and other distinctive features about a prospect's work history."

The emphasis is not on trying to second-guess every possible keyword a recruiter may use to find your resume. Your focus is on selecting and organizing your resume's content in order to highlight those keywords for a variety of online situations. The idea is to identify all possible keywords that are appropriate to your skills and accomplishments that support the kinds of jobs you are looking for. But to do that, you must apply traditional resume writing principles to the concept of extracting those keywords from your resume. Once you have written your resume, then you can identify your strategic keywords based on how you imagine people will search for your resume.

Examples of good keywords are:

Aerobics	Instructor
Certification	Organized and Dependable
Choreography	Personal Trainer
Client	Physical Therapy
Cross Training	Rehabilitation
Energetic	Resourcefulness
Exercise	Responsible
Exercise Science	Spinning
Flexible	Strength Training
Gym	Team Player

Look for other industry-related buzzwords, job-related technical jargon, licenses, and degrees as possible keywords to add to your electronic resume. If you are posting your resume on the Internet, look for the categories that websites use and make sure you use them too. Be sure the words "exercise," "fitness," "instructor," and/or "trainer" appear somewhere on your resume, and use accepted professional jargon.

The keywords you incorporate into your resume should support or be relevant to your job objective. Some of the best places within your resume to incorporate keywords are when listing:

▶ job titles
▶ responsibilities
▶ accomplishments
▶ skills

An excellent resource for helping you select the best keywords to use within your electronic resume is the *Occupational Outlook Handbook* (published by the U.S. Department of Labor). This publication is available, free of charge, online (www.stats.bls.gov/oco/oco1000.htm); however, a printed edition can also be found at most public libraries. Read the "Recreation and Fitness Workers" article, scanning for potential keywords.

Following is a list of skills almost any company or organization—from a large national club chain to a local private studio in Dayton, Ohio—will want in a fitness instructor or personal trainer, so any that you can include on your resume will give you an edge:

▶ flexibility and willingness to cover other employees' shifts
▶ team player
▶ understanding of body mechanics
▶ ability to handle classes attended by students with diverse abilities
▶ ability to handle disgruntled clients
▶ willingness to learn new formats and exercises, and keep classes and sessions fresh
▶ understanding of organizational relationships, roles, and functions
▶ adeptness at working independently, solving problems, and making decisions
▶ organizational skills to keep track of clients' progress
▶ ability to handle stress
▶ ability to maintain accurate records

Clarity

No matter how attractive your resume is, it won't do any good if a prospective employer finds it difficult to read. The most important rule is: Never send out a resume that contains mistakes. Proofread it several times and spell-check it. Then, ask one or two others to read it. If you are uncertain about a grammatical construction, seek out advice or change the wording to something you are sure is correct. Since writing a resume is often an ongoing process, remember to check for mistakes every time you make a change. There is absolutely no excuse for sending out a resume with misspelled words or grammatical errors.

In addition to checking spelling and grammar, your resume must be well written. Resume writing differs from other kinds of writing in that it does not use complete sentences. You should not write, "As manager of the physical therapy department, I managed 14 employees and oversaw over 700 hours of therapy weekly." Instead you should write, "Managed busy physical therapy department with 14 employees." However, all other rules of grammar apply. Tenses and numbers need to match, and double negatives and other awkward constructions are not acceptable.

It is also important to be concise, to help keep your resume at a manageable size, and to make important information stand out. In the two examples in the previous paragraph, the first requires 19 words; the second, just 8. They convey the same information, but the second does it more efficiently. By using a straightforward, brief style of wording, you highlight the fact that you have skills that are valued highly by employers. The ability to communicate and organize information well is vital to your future job success, and both can easily be reflected in your resume.

You demonstrate your communication abilities not only by making sure everything is spelled correctly and is grammatically accurate, but also by how well you write your resume. Word choice contributes greatly to clarity and persuasiveness. Experts have long recommended using verbs (action words) rather than nouns to promote yourself in a resume. Compare "managed busy physical therapy department with 14 employees" to "manager of physical therapy department." The first sounds much more impressive.

However, one caveat has recently been introduced to the verb preference rule. As discussed previously, computer resumes, whether scanned or e-mailed, are searched using keywords. These words tend to be nouns rather than verbs. Thus, when writing this type of resume, follow the keyword guidelines spelled out on page 159.

Concentration

Each time you send out a resume, whether in response to an ad, following up a networking lead, or even a cold contact, you should concentrate on tailoring your approach for the employer you are contacting. This means having more than one resume, or reconfiguring your resume before printing it so that it conforms better to the job opening for which you are applying.

For instance, Instructor A is interested in teaching yoga, but has work experience as a personal trainer. She is looking first for a position in a serious private yoga studio. But she might also be willing to take a position in a fitness club that is introducing yoga to its members just to get her foot in the door. Teaching classes in a corporate-owned chain might also be worth a try. Neither of these options is a first choice, but both can be good in the short term to develop a following, perhaps pick up some private students, and gain teaching experience. The yoga studio position is her dream job; the others are second-best choices. To apply for all of these jobs, Instructor A will need to alter her resume at least twice.

The resume for the yoga studio position will stress her two years of training and five years of yoga practice. She will also highlight her commitment to ongoing education through monthly attendance at workshops. For an instructor position in a fitness club, she will emphasize her previous work experience as a personal trainer, while making certain her desire to teach some yoga classes stands out as well.

Earlier in this chapter, you filled out a questionnaire that helped gather the information you need to write your resume. By keeping it close at hand, it should not be difficult to construct a resume that targets a particular job, concentrating your information so that a prospective employer will see that you are a likely candidate for their available position. In many cases, a few changes to a basic resume are enough to make it appropriate for a particular job opening.

An effective tool for tailoring your resume is to imagine what the job for which you are applying should be like. Based on the description of the position, what are the major daily tasks you will be expected to do? Compare these things with the inventory of your experience and education, and decide how to present your information so that the employer will know that you are capable of doing those tasks.

Finally, make sure you get your resume to the appropriate person in the proper way. If you got the person's name through a networking contact, deliver it in person unless the addressee specifies that you should mail it. If you are making a cold contact—that is, if you are contacting a firm that you found through your research that is not actively looking to fill a position—make sure you find out the name of the person doing the hiring, and deliver your resume to him or her. If you are responding to an ad, follow directions. If it specifies faxing your resume, do so. Demonstrate your ability to attend to detail.

Avoid Making These Common Resume Errors

- Stretching the truth. A growing number of employers are verifying all resume information. If you are caught lying, you will not be offered a job, or you could be fired later if it is discovered that you were not truthful.

- Including any references to money. Do not mention past salary or how much you are looking to earn anywhere within your resume and cover letter.

- Including the reasons why you stopped working for an employer, switched jobs, or are currently looking for a new job. Do not include a line in your resume saying, "Unemployed" or "Out of Work" along with the corresponding dates in order to fill a time gap.

- Having a typo or grammatical error in a resume. If you refuse to take the time necessary to proofread your resume, why should an employer assume you would take the time needed to do your job properly if you are hired?

- Using long paragraphs to describe past work experience. Consider using a bulleted list instead, which highlights important information. Remember that most employers will spend less than one minute initially reading a resume.

The following are sample resumes. The first is *chronological*, which highlights previous experience rather than education. The second is a *skills resume*; this applicant acquired many of the skills necessary for the position for which he is applying through internships held while in school, but has no employment history in the field. In the third resume sample, note the form, which is designed to be scanned.

Joyce Wilson
1562 State Street
Burlington, Vermont 05401
802-555-6646

OBJECTIVE

Professional in the fitness industry with extensive teaching experience seeks position as a personal trainer.

PROFESSIONAL BACKGROUND

Group Fitness Instructor
The Zone Club—Burlington, Vermont
June 2000–present
Classes include: group weight training, stretch and tone, and Spinning. Earned rapid promotion to Spinning coordinator based on performance. Made schedules for all instructors, communicated repair needs, acted as liaison between members and club management.

Personal Trainer
Stowe Health Club—Stowe, Vermont
January 2001–present
Currently work with four clients; three athletes involved in cross training, one rehabilitating knee injury.

Aerobics Instructor
Mountain Fitness—Waterbury, Vermont
September 1998–June 2000
Taught 10 step and floor aerobics classes per week.

EDUCATION

AFAA Certifications—aerobics (1998), weight training (2001)
American Red Cross CPR Certification
City Union High School, Burlington, Vermont, June 1998

Stephen Jones
300 W. Cloister Ave., Apt. 3
Redstone, PA 16842
814-555-9113

JOB OBJECTIVE
To find a position as a Pilates instructor.

EDUCATION
The Pennsylvania State University, University Park, PA
B.S., Exercise Science, 2001

The Pilates Center, University Park, PA
Pilates Mat Certification, 2001

INTERNSHIPS
Penn State Health Club, University Park, PA
Intern, September–December 2000
Performed various jobs within the club. Taught aerobics and stretching classes, assisted at front desk, handled membership paperwork.

Penn State Rehabilitation Center, University Park, PA
Intern, September–December 2001
Developed Pilates-based programs for rehabilitation patients, focusing on strength and flexibility work.

COMPUTER SKILLS
Experience with Microsoft Office and Web design.

CERTIFICATIONS
American College of Sports Medicine, 2001
International Sports Sciences Association, Specialist in Sports Conditioning, 2000
CPR

Danielle Jackson
15 Aspen Way
Sheridan, Illinois
818-555-2222

OBJECTIVE
Seeking a personal training position.

EDUCATION
Illinois State College (1997–2001)
Bachelor of Science degree in Physical Education

EMPLOYMENT
Health Club Assistant Manager, Group Fitness Instructor (Silver Gym Inc. May, 2001–Present):
Responsible for 5 classes per week, and:
- Human resource management (hiring, training, scheduling, and corrective action)
- Product ordering and receiving
- Coordination of maintenance services

Instructor (Exercise Plus 1999–2001):
Taught 8 classes per week: aerobics, kickboxing, step, and tone.
Assisted owner with training of new instructors.
Coordinated club instructors' attendance at continuing education workshops.

Instructor (YMCA 2000–2001):
Taught 6 classes per week: cycling, water aerobics, senior stretch.

PROFESSIONAL
American Council on Exercise Personal Trainer Certification, 2002
CPR Certification—Current

WRITING COVER LETTERS

Never send out a resume without a cover letter. While the former describes in detail why you are the person for the position, the latter aims the resume directly at the available job. If your cover letter is a failure, your resume may not be looked at at all. The four elements of the resume—composition, clarity, content, and concentration—are found in cover letters as well. However, their functions vary because the cover letter itself has a different purpose from the resume.

Composition

Your cover letter needs to grab the attention of the reader, while remaining within the guidelines discussed previously. As with your resume, avoid fancy fonts and stationery; choose something that matches or coordinates with your resume. Your cover letter should always be typed (printed) on good paper, using letterhead with your name, address, phone number, fax number, and e-mail address. Letterhead stationery can be done on your computer rather than ordered through a printing company.

A cover letter should be composed as a business letter. It should include the date, the name and address of the person the letter is to be sent to, and a salutation. At the end of the body of the letter, include a closing (such as "Sincerely"), your signature, and your name typed out below. You may use block paragraphs or choose to indent them. It is acceptable to type "enc." at the bottom, indicating there is material (your resume) enclosed with the letter.

Your cover letter should not exceed one page unless the employer specifically asks for more information than can reasonably fit on a single page. On occasion, an advertisement for a job will ask for a resume and a detailed statement of interest (or words to that effect). Sometimes ads will even ask you to address specific questions or issues in your letter, such as your goals, or what you can contribute to the organization. In such cases, you may need to write a letter that is more than one page.

Clarity

As with your resume, never send out a cover letter with a grammatical or spelling error. Even when you are pressed for time and rushing to get a letter out, make sure to spell-check it and proofread it carefully. Ask someone else to look it over as well. Your letter should be accurate, clear, and concise. It serves as a letter of introduction, an extension of your "advertisement," and needs to convince a prospective employer that you should be interviewed for the position.

Begin your cover letter with an introduction, followed by an explanation of why you are right for the available job, and end with a closing paragraph. As with your resume, it is vital that your cover letter be well written; however, it requires a different writing style. Sentence fragments and bulleted lists don't belong in a cover letter.

While a resume offers a somewhat formal presentation of your background, a cover letter should let your personality come through. View it as your first chance to speak with a prospective employer. The resume tells employers what you know and what you can do; the cover letter should tell them a little bit about who you are. However, even though it is somewhat less formal, don't use a conversational tone. Contractions ("I'll" instead of "I will," for example) and slang are not appropriate.

Content and Concentration

While it is important that your resume be tailored to specific job openings, it is even more important to target your cover letter. In fact, its major component should be its concentration on the particular job opening for which you are applying. Because it is so specific, you will need to write a new cover letter every time you send out your resume. It should never read like a form letter, nor should it just repeat the information in your resume. It tells the prospective employer why you are the one for the job.

In the first paragraph, indicate why you are writing the letter at this time. You may write something like:

▶ "I am applying for the position of Group Fitness Instructor advertised in the *Sunday Post*."
▶ "I am writing in response to your ad in the *Sunday Times*."
▶ "I am interested in obtaining a personal training position at your club."
▶ "We met last July at the Cleveland Fitness Expo. I will be graduating with my degree in exercise science in May, and recall that you mentioned you might have an opening for me at that time."

The first paragraph also usually indicates that your resume is enclosed for consideration, although this may be mentioned in the closing paragraph. If you learned about the position from a friend or acquaintance, be sure to name this mutual contact.

In the body of the letter, explain why your training and experience make you the right person for the job. Highlight and summarize the information in your resume, and take advantage of the opportunity to include more about yourself and your skills. For example, life experience that can't be easily incorporated into a resume can smoothly find its way into your cover letter. Instead of writing, "Before entering college, I worked at The Gym for two years, and before that at The Club for three years," try something like, "I have five years of teaching experience in which I interacted with a variety of students." The body of the letter is your opportunity to explain why the employer should care about your experience and training.

You can also include information about how soon you are available for employment or why (if it's the case) you are applying for a job out of town. You may also mention some of the things that you are looking for in a job—if they are either nonnegotiable or flattering to the employer. Make a direct reference to the specific position and organization. For example:

▶ "I will graduate on May 16 and will be available for employment immediately. A position with your facility appeals to me because it is known for its sports medicine department, and this is an area in which I have experience and am very interested in learning more about."

▶ "Although my internship was with Big Club International, I have come to realize that while that work was intensely interesting, I would prefer employment with a smaller facility. Rather than specialize in one small area, a position at a private club will afford me the opportunity to call on my comprehensive experience. I believe your club is the place for me and I am certain I would be an asset to you."

▶ "As you look at my resume, you will notice that although I am just now completing my education in fitness, I offer a background in teaching. Since your company has recently undergone a major expansion, I believe you would find me a valuable addition to your staff."

Finally, the last paragraph (some people prefer it to be two short paragraphs) should thank the reader, make a reference to future contact, and offer to provide further information. Examples of effective closing paragraphs include:

▶ "Thank you for your consideration. Please contact me at the address or phone number above if you need any further information."

▶ "I look forward to meeting with you to discuss this job opening."

▶ "Thank you and I look forward to speaking with you in the near future."

▶ "I would welcome the opportunity to discuss the match between my skills and your needs in more detail. You can contact me at the address or phone number above, except for the week of the 27th, when I will be out of town. Thank you for your time."

Jennifer Lee
1 First Avenue
Pasadena, California
555-123-4567
jlee@california.com

February 5, 2002

Dear Mr. Hart:

I am very interested in applying for the fitness instructor position listed in the *Sacramento Register* on May 4, 2001.

As you can see from my enclosed resume, I worked for a large club in Reno, Nevada for two years prior to moving to Sacramento. I enjoyed the work very much. I am an organized, detail-oriented person who gets along well with people. I was nominated for Employee of the Year twice in my previous position. I feel that these attributes, along with my work experience, qualify me for the position described in your advertisement.

I would greatly appreciate the opportunity for a personal interview. You can reach me at 123-4567.

Thank you for your consideration.

Sincerely,
Jennifer Lee

INTERVIEWING SUCCESSFULLY

The last step in the job search process, and the one that causes the most anxiety among job seekers, is the interview. Your potential employer has seen your application and resume, and believes you may be a good candidate; a face-to-face meeting gives him or her the chance to decide if you are the right person for the job, and you the chance to decide if the job is right for you.

An interview for a fitness instructor or personal training position typically involves three distinct parts. First, the interviewer will sit down with you to discuss your resume, asking for further clarification or answers to any questions they may have about it. They will probably also ask you about the classes you like to teach, the clientele you feel you best relate to, what you feel you can bring to the club, and other subjective topics.

Next, you will be asked to hold a mock training session or teach all or part of a class. When setting up your interview, you will be told if this interview segment is to be included—you won't be asked off guard to perform. Finally, you will be given a tour of the facility. This gives the interviewer a chance to see how you interact with others in the club, and a better view of your personality. It is important to them to find team players who really fit in with the environment, clientele, and coworkers. While it is normal to be nervous during the interview process, there are many things you can do to calm your fears. By carefully reading the following information and taking the suggestions made, you will greatly improve your chances for interviewing success.

Be Prepared

Research your potential employer before your interview and be ready to demonstrate your knowledge. Learn about the workings of large chain operations, resorts, institutions, or family-owned businesses. The section in Chapter 4 entitled "Researching the Field" explained many ways to get the information you are looking for. Ask around your town or city about the hiring company; members, clients, instructors, and trainers are all great sources of local input. If you have already done your homework, be sure to refamiliarize yourself before an interview. If not, now is the time to get the research done.

Preparation should also include practice—find someone to act as an interviewer, and have him or her take you through a mock interview. Ask for an honest evaluation of your performance, and work on those areas your "interviewer" feels you can improve. Practice speaking about your experience, education, and skills. Now is not the time for modesty; you are selling yourself, so be upbeat and forthcoming.

Act Professionally

Take the interviewing process very seriously. Even though you and your colleagues will spend much of your day in workout garb, you are entering the professional world, and you want to show that you fit into that environment. Make several extra copies of your resume, letters of recommendation, and your list of references to bring to your interview. You will also want to bring your daily planner, along with your research materials, a pad, and a working pen. Fit this paperwork into a briefcase or portfolio. On your pad, write down the club name, interviewer's name, address, telephone number, and directions to the location of the interview.

It is very important to be on time for your interview. Allow extra time for traffic and getting lost if the interview is in an unfamiliar location. Schedule your travel time so that you arrive 10 minutes before your interview starts. This will give you time to relax before you begin.

Your appearance is the very first thing a potential employer will notice, so make a positive first impression. Be sure that your clothes and shoes are clean. If you must make a choice, it is better to be overdressed than underdressed. Personal hygiene is also critical. If you were asked to demonstrate your teaching or training ability during the interview, dress accordingly, while maintaining a clean, neat, and professional appearance.

On the morning of your interview, read a local newspaper and watch a morning news program so you are aware of the day's news events and will be able to discuss them with the interviewer. Many interviewers like to start off an interview with small talk. You want to appear knowledgeable about what is happening in the world.

Speak Confidently

Greet your interviewer with a firm handshake and an enthusiastic smile. Speak with confidence throughout your interview and let your answers convey your assumption that you will be offered the job. For example, phrase your questions this way: "What would my responsibilities consist of?" "How many instructors work here, and what class formats are offered?" Answer questions in complete sentences; however, don't ramble on too long answering any one question. Many hiring managers will ask questions that don't have a right or wrong answer; they ask such questions to evaluate your problem-solving skills.

Your personality is crucial to your success as an instructor or personal trainer, so try to "be yourself" as much as possible in the sometimes awkward situation of the interview. Remember that your interviewer wants to hire someone who is enthusiastic, motivating, friendly, and able to connect easily with other people.

A potential employer is not allowed to ask you about your marital status, whether you have children or plan to, your age, your religion, or your race (these kinds of questions may be asked on anonymous affirmative action forms). If you are asked such a question, you might say, "I don't understand the question; what is it you want to know?" Better yet, figure out why they are asking the question, and address that issue. Then, the answer to "Do you have children?" becomes "If you are asking if I can be flexible and work overtime, that's not a problem."

Follow these general guidelines when answering questions in an interview:

- Use complete sentences and proper English.
- Don't be evasive, especially if you are asked about negative aspects of your employment history.
- Never imply that a question is "stupid."
- Don't lie or stretch the truth.
- Be prepared to answer the same questions multiple times. Make sure your answers are consistent, and never reply, "You already asked me that."

▶ Never apologize for negative information regarding your past.

▶ Avoid talking down to an interviewer, or making them feel less intelligent than you are.

Ask Questions

You will usually be given the opportunity to ask the interviewer questions, so be prepared. Have a list of questions ready in advance. There is much you need to know about the club to determine if it is a good fit for you. The interview is not a one-way street—while you are being evaluated, you are also evaluating them. If you don't ask any questions, the interviewer may think that you aren't interested in the position.

Almost any type of question is acceptable. You may want to know about the class schedule, whether you will be working under one person or a number of people, or if continuing education opportunities are offered on site. These are all legitimate questions. You may also have questions about the resources of the company, such as its purchasing and use of the latest equipment, and whether employees receive training in its use.

Anticipate the Questions You Will Be Asked

As part of your job interview preparation, think about the types of questions the interviewer will ask. Obviously, since you are applying for a job as a fitness instructor or personal trainer, you should anticipate detailed questions about the skills you possess and the experience you have using those skills.

Spend time developing well-thought-out, complete, and intelligent answers. Thinking about them, or even writing out answers on paper will be helpful, but what will benefit you the most is actual practice answering interview questions out loud. Stage a mock interview with someone you trust, who will evaluate your responses honestly.

Most of the questions you will be asked will be pretty obvious, but be prepared for an interviewer to ask you a few that are unexpected. By doing this, the interviewer will be able to see how you react and how well you think on your feet.

The following are common interview questions and suggestions on how you can best answer them:

▶ What can you tell me about yourself? (Stress your skills and accomplishments. Avoid talking about your family, hobbies, or topics not relevant to your ability to do the job.)

▶ Why have you chosen to pursue a career as a fitness instructor or personal trainer? (Give specific reasons and examples.)

▶ In your personal or professional life, what has been your greatest failure? What did you learn from that experience? (Be open and honest. Everyone has had some type of failure. Focus on what you learned from the experience and how it helped you to grow as a person.)

▶ Why did you leave your previous job? (Try to put a positive spin on your answer, especially if you were fired for negative reasons. Company downsizing, a company going out of business, or some other reason that was out of your control is a perfectly acceptable answer. Remember, your answer will probably be verified.)

▶ What should you consider to be your biggest accomplishments at your last job? (Talk about what made you a productive employee and valuable asset to your previous employer. Stress that teamwork was involved in achieving your success, and that you work well with others.)

▶ In college, I see you were a (insert subject) major. Why did you choose (insert subject) as your major? (Explain your interest in the subject matter, where that interest comes from, and how it relates to your current career-related goals.)

▶ What are your long-term goals? (Talk about how you have a career path, and where you believe this pre-planned career path will take you in the future. Describe how you believe the job you are applying for is a logical step forward.)

▶ Why do you think you are the most qualified person to fill this job? (Focus on the positive things that set you apart from the competition. What is unique about you, your skill set and past experiences? What work-related experience do you have that relates directly to this job?)

▶ What have you heard about our facility that was of interest to you? (Focus on the club's reputation. Refer to positive publicity, personal recommendations from employees, or published information that caught your attention. This shows you have done your research.)

▶ What else can you tell me about yourself that isn't listed in your resume? (This is yet another opportunity for you to sell yourself to the employer. Take advantage of it by mentioning any other positive information that you didn't have a chance to bring up previously.)

Avoid Common Interview Mistakes

Once you get invited to come in for an interview, do everything within your power to prepare, and avoid the common mistakes often made by applicants. Remember that for every job you apply for, there are probably dozens of other fitness instructors or personal trainers who would like to land that same position.

The following are some of the most common mistakes applicants make while preparing for or participating in job interviews, with tips on how to avoid making these mistakes.

▶ Don't skip steps in your interview preparation. Just because you have been invited for an interview, you can't afford to "wing it" once you get there. Prior to the interview, spend time doing research about the company, its products/services and the people you will be meeting with.

▶ Never arrive late for an interview. Arriving even five minutes late for a job interview is equivalent to telling an employer you don't want the job. The day before the interview, drive to the interview location and determine exactly how to get there and how long it takes. On the day of the interview, plan on arriving at least 10 minutes early and use the restroom before you begin the actual interview.

▶ Don't neglect your appearance. First impressions are crucial. Make sure your clothing is clean, your hair is well groomed, and your make-up (if applicable) looks professional. Always dress well for an interview, even if that means a new pair of yoga pants, sweatshirt, or sneakers. Also, be sure to brush your teeth prior to an interview, especially if you have eaten recently.

▶ Prior to an interview, avoid drinking any beverages containing caffeine. Chances are, you will already be nervous about the interview. Drinking coffee or soda won't calm you down.

▶ Don't go into the interview unprepared. Prior to the interview, use your research to compile a list of intelligent questions to ask the employer. These questions can pertain to the club, its facilities, its methods of training employees, the responsibilities of the job you are applying for, or anything else you may be curious about. When it is time for you to answer questions, always use complete sentences.

▶ Never bring up salary, benefits, or vacation time during the initial interview. Instead, focus on how you (with all of your skills, experience, and education) can become a valuable asset to the company you are interviewing with. Allow the employer to bring up the compensation package to be offered.

▶ Refrain from discussing your past earning history or what you are hoping to earn. An employer typically looks for the best possible employees for the lowest possible price. Let the employer make you an offer first. If asked, tell the interviewer you are looking for a salary/benefits package that is in line with the standard in the industry for someone with your qualifications and experience. Try to avoid stating an actual dollar figure.

▶ During the interview, avoid personal topics. There are questions that an employer cannot legally ask during an interview situation (or on an employment application). In addition to these topics, refrain from discussing sex, religion, politics, or any other highly personal topics.

▶ Never insult the interviewer. It is common for an interviewer to ask what you might perceive to be a stupid or irrelevant question. In some cases, the interviewer is simply testing to see how you will respond. Some questions are asked to test your morals or determine your level of honesty. Other types of questions are used simply to see how you will react in a tough situation. Try to avoid getting caught up in trick questions. Never tell an interview their question is stupid or irrelevant.

▶ Throughout the interview, keep your body language from getting out of control. For example, if you tap your foot or bite your nails when you are nervous, make sure you are aware of your habits so you can control them in an interview situation.

▶ If your job interview takes place over lunch or dinner, refrain from drinking alcohol of any kind.

Following Up

It is a common belief that by conducting a job interview, the interviewer is simply doing his or her job, which is to fill the position(s) available. As a result of this belief, many job seekers show no gratitude to the interviewer. This is a mistake. Sending a personal and well-thought out note immediately after an interview will not only keep your name fresh in the hiring manager's mind, but will also show that you have good follow-up skills, and that you are genuinely interested in the job opportunity.

Individual and personalized thank-you notes should be sent out within 24 hours of your interview, to everyone you met with when visiting a potential employer. Send separate notes containing different messages to each person (if applicable), addressing each using the recipient's full name and title. Make sure you spell names correctly.

Thank-you notes may be typewritten on personal stationery, following a standard business letter format. A more personal alternative is to write your thank-you note on a professional looking note card that may be purchased at any stationery, greeting card, or office supply store. The personal touch will add much to further a positive impression and help to separate you from your competition.

Keep your message brief and to the point. Thank the interviewer for taking the time out of his or her busy schedule to meet with you, and for considering you for the job opening available. Make sure you mention the exact position for which you applied.

In one or two sentences, highlight the important details discussed in your interview. You want the interviewer to remember you. Do not mention issues under negotiation, such as salary, benefits, concerns, and work schedule. Finally, reaffirm your interest in the position and invite further contact with a closing sentence such as "I look forward to hearing from you soon."

Final Thoughts on Interviewing

There are two more important things to keep in mind while going through interviews. Both will help you to keep not only your interview, but the whole job search process, in perspective. The first is that even if you apply and interview for a job, you do not have to take it. The other is that good interviewers try to sell you on coming to work for them.

Understanding that you are not required to take a job just because it is offered makes the interview seem less like a life-or-death situation and more like an opportunity to get to know at least one person at the hiring company. You will feel a greater sense of confidence and ease when you keep this in mind. The position you are interviewing for is not the only one available, so if it feels like a bad fit for you, or for them, move on.

It is also helpful to realize that interviewers are trying to sell you on coming to work for them. A good interviewer has one goal in mind: finding a good person to fill the job opening. They already think you are a possibility, which is why you were invited to interview. Once you are there, it is the interviewer's job to convince you that you would be very happy working at his or her club. Evaluate the information you are given about the work environment; does it fit with what you see and have heard about the facility? Be attuned to the tactics of the interviewer. You are both present at the interview for a specific purpose—yours is to find employment, while his or hers is to fill a position.

EVALUATING A JOB OFFER

You have been offered the job. Now, you have to decide—or perhaps, choose between a number of offers. How should you go about it? First, take some time. The hiring company will not expect you to accept or reject an offer on the spot; you may be given a few days or a week to make up your mind.

Second, you will need to develop a set of criteria for judging the job offer or offers, whether this is your first job, you are reentering the labor force after a long absence, or you are changing jobs or careers. While determining in advance whether you will like the work may be difficult, the more you find out about it before accepting or rejecting the job offer, the more likely you are to make the right choice. Based on what you learned about the job during your initial research and during your interview, ask the following questions:

► Does the work match your interests and make good use of your skills? The duties and responsibilities of the job should have been explained in enough detail during the interview to answer this question.

► Were you comfortable with the interviewer or with the supervisor you will have (if you met her or him)?

► Is this the kind of atmosphere you would enjoy every day? As you walked through on the way to your interview, or as you were being shown around, did the other employees seem friendly and happy? If possible, find out the club's turnover rate, which will indicate how satisfied other instructors and trainers are with their job and the club.

► What hours does the job call for? In the fitness industry, you can expect them to be irregular, but some employers are better than others at making sure their employees aren't given difficult schedules very often. How are holidays, nights, and weekends staffed? Consider the effect of work hours on your personal life.

► What are the opportunities offered by the job? A good job usually offers you the chance to learn new skills, to increase your earnings, and to rise to a position of greater authority, responsibility, and prestige. A lack of opportunity for betterment can dampen interest in the work and result in frustration and boredom. The person who offers you the job should give you some idea of promotion possibilities within the organization. What is the next step on the career ladder? Is it a step you would want to take? If you have to wait for a job to become vacant before you can be promoted, how long is the wait likely to be? Employers have different policies regarding promotion from within the organization. When opportunities for advancement do arise, will you compete with applicants from outside the club? Can you apply for other jobs in the organization, or is mobility limited?

► What are the salary and benefits? As noted previously, during the interview, it is best to wait for the interviewer to introduce these subjects. (And he or she may not!) Many companies will not talk about pay until they have decided to hire you. Once they have made the offer, though, they are bound to mention pay, and in order to determine if their offer is reasonable, you need a rough estimate of what the job would pay.

To get an idea of what your salary would be, talk to friends or acquaintances who were recently hired in a similar jobs. You can also check out Salary.com (www.salary.com). If you have just finished school, ask your teachers and the staff in the college placement office about starting pay for graduates with your qualifications. Scan the classified ads in newspapers and see what salaries are being offered for similar jobs. You might even want to call some of the advertisers and ask about wages; some may not give out this information over the phone, but it is worth a try. Detailed data on wages and benefits are also available from The Bureau of Labor Statistics, Division of Occupational Pay and Employee Benefit Levels, 2 Massachusetts Ave. NE., Room 4160, Washington, DC 20212-0001; 202-606-6225.

If you are considering the salary and benefits for a job in another geographic area, be sure to make allowances for differences in the cost of living, which may be significantly higher in a large metropolitan area than in a smaller city, town, or rural area. Do take into account that the starting salary is just that. Your salary should be reviewed on a regular basis; many organizations do it every 12 months. How much can you expect to earn after one, two, or three or more years? Benefits can also add a lot to your base pay, but they vary widely. Find out exactly what the benefit package includes and how much of the cost you must bear for, say, medical or life insurance.

Finally, there will be an end to the job search process. You will be offered a position that meets your wants and needs, and you will accept it. Chapter 6 details what happens after you begin work, helping you to maximize your potential for success in your new career.

THE INSIDE TRACK

Who: Jane Vanderpool

What: Yoga Instructor

Where: Atlanta, Georgia

Currently, I'm an I.K.Y.T.A. (International Kundalini Yoga Teachers Association) certified yoga instructor. I teach classes at a fitness center called Pure Endorphins in Atlanta but also instruct clients privately. I received my I.K.Y.T.A. certifications through a year-long teacher training program with a master Kundalini yoga instructor. I had to complete a written test prepared by I.K.Y.T.A and was awarded my certification and spiritual name by the leader of Kundalini yoga in the United States. When choosing a teacher for your training, I would suggest that you be as practical as possible. Meet the person you will be training with beforehand and feel it out, asking as many questions as you need to, but also listening to your inner voice. Ask yourself, "Can I comfortably and effectively learn from this person?" That's an important question.

I got my very first teaching job at my regular gym, because they needed substitute yoga teachers and my instructor knew that I was involved in a teacher training program. I found it extremely helpful to start small because it was surprisingly scary to teach my first class. Afterward, the fitness coordinator met with me to give me feedback on my class, and, at first, I was hurt by the criticism. But, that criticism helped me become a better teacher. In the end, we established a great working relationship and she even helped me get my second job at another gym. Since then, I've worked for several different clubs, but most of my success has been through word-of-mouth—I got my first private client because her friend attended one of my yoga classes.

As a yoga instructor, I have to prepare each class by deciding which set of exercises work best for a given group (while still being flexible enough to change the set if a beginner walks in) and arriving ten minutes early to set up the room. When teaching, I not only demonstrate the correct posture, correct my students' postures, tell them the benefits of every pose, and make myself available for questions after class, but I also strive to inspire my students both physically and mentally. If, for some reason, I'm unable to make it to a class, I'm also responsible for finding a substitute teacher.

Kundalini yoga encourages instructor creativity, so my background in musical theater and my B.F.A. in acting have been extremely helpful. I use my musical ability to learn and teach yoga sets, which are inherently rhythmic, and my acting skills to enhance my performance as a teacher, maintaining a peaceful and loving presence no matter what. But most of the time, maintaining a loving presence doesn't require any acting because I truly enjoy my work! In my opinion, good yoga teachers must be accessible, yet demanding in order to both comfort and challenge their students. The most satisfying aspect of my work is being able to witness my students' personal and physical growth. I love to see my students "get it" and become more connected to themselves and the people around them.

One thing that most people don't realize is how exhausting my schedule is! Teaching yoga requires a lot of work, and it can be hard to wind down. I teach fifteen classes a week, which amounts to approximately fifteen hours, but including the time it takes me to travel to each separate gym or private home, I'd have to say I work closer to thirty hours a week. Teaching yoga is so different than having a desk job because you can't do it in your sleep. It's definitely worth it, but you really need to schedule regular vacations and maintain your own yoga needs because it's easy to burnout. Another challenge to consider when teaching yoga is that many yoga centers don't pay an equitable salary. I recently left two of the prominent yoga schools I'd been teaching at because the amount of money they offered was not commensurate to the time and energy required for me to teach there.

Although I love Kundalini yoga, I'm currently enrolled in a teacher training program for Phoenix Rising Yoga Therapy, one-on-one yoga that's all about empowering students to be fully present in their bodies and to transform their lives as they unfold. It's an endless exploration, the path I'm on—much more so than just making a living.

CHAPTER six

SUCCEEDING ON THE JOB

In this chapter, you will learn how to succeed after you have landed a job as a fitness instructor or personal trainer. You will find out how to fit in in your new work environment, whether you are employed at a health club, corporate fitness center, resort, or other work setting. Also discussed is the forming of positive relationships with the people you work with and for. Finally, included are a number of other ways in which you can put your career on the fast track, from effectively dealing with stress to handling criticism professionally.

ONCE YOU ARE employed in your chosen profession, your goal becomes succeeding on the job. You already have an understanding of a fitness instructor or personal trainer's basic duties and how to perform them, but your education didn't cover how to manage work relationships, or how to acclimate yourself to a new work environment. Even the valuable lessons learned during an internship aren't enough to prepare you completely for your new career. There is much to discover regarding how to perform well on the job, beyond what you were taught in a certification workshop or the classroom.

FITTING INTO THE WORKPLACE CULTURE

As a fitness instructor or personal trainer, you may find employment at a variety of facilities, including corporate-owned chain health clubs, resorts, hospital fitness centers, and small privately owned studios. Obviously, the workplace cultures of these employers vary. Even among large clubs you will find differences; one may be more hierarchical and business-like, another is relaxed and casual, and yet another lies somewhere in between.

You will need to fit in in your work environment in two distinct ways. One way is with your employer and the team that works at your facility. You may need to know how to sell memberships, learn the company philosophy, and play by your manager's rules. The other is with your students and clients. As a fitness instructor and/or personal trainer, much of your time will be spent with them. You will be in a position of authority as you lead your class or training session; it is your personality, skills, and knowledge that set the tone. However, students like the familiar, and can give new instructors a bit of a hard time if they don't lead their classes like the other instructors. Training clients also have preferences, but may be more willing to accept change.

Although a class or training session feels like your domain, you will be expected to do things in a manner accepted by your place of employment. And when you are not working directly with clients or students, this expectation will be even greater. In other words, there will be a presumption by your coworkers and even many superiors that you know, very quickly, how the club or center operates. The question is, how do you, as a new employee, learn the acceptable ways in which things are done in the most timely and thorough fashion?

Begin by being attuned to the environment, intent on learning as much as you can as quickly as you can. This should be a primary goal of your first weeks and months on the job; once you gain an understanding of the workplace culture, it will help you succeed in your new career by knowing what's expected of you, and what you can expect in return.

Whether you work in a small studio or chain club, spend time observing and imitating. If you are working with other instructors or trainers, or are in frequent contact with management, pay careful attention to the work habits of these coworkers, and follow suit. For instance, if management answers the phone at the front desk if they happen to be in the area, do the same. If morning instructors have lunch together after classes, make it a point to be there, too. After some time has passed, you will know better which customs and traditions are worth following and which you can deviate from.

Most new instructors and trainers begin employment under an evaluation period, which typically lasts between three and six months. During this time, you will be monitored by your manager, or a senior instructor or trainer. Use the evaluation period to your best advantage by asking questions when you are not sure how something should be done, and by requesting feedback from your monitor. Try to find out how you are doing before the time is up; allow yourself a few weeks to make changes and improve if you discover you are not performing as expected.

At the end of the evaluation period, you will find out just how well you have fit in. Your manager may give you an oral or written evaluation, and possibly a raise if the evaluation is positive. If there are any problems with your job performance, you will likely be given another period of time during which to correct them.

Large Chain Clubs

Corporate culture is becoming more pervasive in the fitness industry. In fact, just a handful of large corporations own the majority of health clubs in the country. If you have chosen employment with a large chain club, you should be aware of some of the standard operating procedures of these corporate-owned and run facilities. This culture relies on a hierarchy to accomplish defined goals (first and foremost, to maximize profits). Those who work at headquarters make many of the decisions regarding day-to-day operations of their clubs. They may dictate the hours the facilities are open for business, wages of all employees, marketing strategies, equipment purchased, and other important factors. The managers of individual clubs answer to headquarters, and must play by their rules; they expect their employees to do the same.

For instructors and trainers, there are some advantages to this type of culture, including the availability of additional training, and the ability to stay on the cutting edge. Disadvantages include layers of management that can be stifling; job duties that may include cleaning, sales, and paperwork; and an impersonal environment. Wages may be lower than what you would expect for such large employers, but you will have to do some local research in this area to determine whether chain clubs are paying standard hourly rates.

Cat Earisman is an instructor who has worked in some of the largest chain clubs as well as independent hotel fitness centers during her twenty years in the industry. She notes that:

> The bigger the corporation that owns the club, the bigger the pocketbook. Large chains can afford to buy the latest equipment and train their employees to use it. They provide continuing education, and have huge schedules that offer something for everyone. There are some downsides to working for them, but I still recommend these clubs to new instructors, because you will have more opportunities, get to meet more people, and develop a network more easily.

Smaller Clubs and Studios

There are also opportunities for fitness instructors and personal trainers in smaller clubs and studios, as discussed in detail in Chapter 1. In settings like these, you will have fewer managers working above you, and may be given more freedom to do things your way. Even so, there are unwritten rules that govern this type of workplace culture. As with employment at a large club, pay careful attention in your first few weeks on the job. You will want to project an image of competence and authority, especially with students and clients, while observing the workplace and gaining a good knowledge of the culture.

The downside of working in a smaller club or facility is that your employer probably won't have the resources of a large company to support the business. Your salary may be lower than that of a peer working for a chain club, and you may never see perks such as a pension plan or medical insurance. If you are working for someone new to the business, you may have to deal with the instability that comes with not knowing if you will have a job in the near future; the fitness industry is very competitive, and typically only those who show a profit will stay in business.

Hospital-Based Fitness Centers

If you find employment with a hospital-based fitness center, or a related medical facility, you will find a very different workplace culture. While the operation of the center may be similar to other types of exercise clubs, the emphasis is on health. Some of your students and clients will be combating illness and disease, others will be working to achieve or maintain a beneficial lifestyle, while still others will be rehabilitating. The center will have medical professionals working closely with other staff members, who may expect you to learn specific skills necessary to operations, such as conducting stress tests, monitoring heart rate and blood pressure, and so on.

Fitting in with these professionals will require some additional effort. You will come to the job with a combination of training, education, and experience, but you should not stop there. Continue to learn by reading industry publications, online medical journals, and other materials that may be suggested by your coworkers. Refer back to the list on pages 127–128 for more reading suggestions. Keep up with advances in sports and rehabilitative medicine. You will not only perform better on the job, but also earn the respect of your clients, coworkers, and superiors.

No matter where you begin working, you may find that after your first week on the job that you don't fit into the workplace culture. While first impressions are important, you should plan to spend some time in your new position before deciding for certain that it isn't working. As mentioned earlier, it takes time to understand an environment and learn all of its unwritten rules. Give yourself a number of weeks or even months to fully integrate yourself into the culture of your new workplace.

BUILDING SOLID WORK RELATIONSHIPS

Your success as a fitness instructor or personal trainer will depend in large part on the relationships you develop and cultivate. Making a conscious effort to respect others and becoming a "people person" and "team player" while on the job will help your career immensely. In your current position, you will gain the respect of those you work with daily. And when you are ready to move on to another, possibly higher-level, position, these relationships will aid you in networking your way up.

Basic Rules

When it comes to building and maintaining professional relationships, some basic rules apply. The first is, "Sometimes peace is better than justice." You may be absolutely, 100% sure you are right about a specific situation. Unfortunately, you may have clients or superiors who doubt you or disagree with you. This is a common occurrence in the workplace.

Sometimes, you will need to assert your position and persuade the disbelievers to trust your judgment. Your previous track record and reputation will go a long way in helping to convince people to trust your opinions, ideas, and decisions. But you must carefully consider the gravity of the situation before you stick your neck out. In other words, in a work environment, choose your battles wisely. Go ahead and argue your position if you can prevent a catastrophe, or if your leadership role demands it.

If you are having a debate about an issue of taste, opinion, or preference with your superiors, it is advisable to leave the situation alone or accept their decisions. It may be appropriate to let your recommendation(s) be known, but do not argue your point relentlessly. Sometimes you will be right and people will not listen to you. Always be open to compromise and be willing to listen to and consider the options and ideas of others.

In terms of students and clients, this rule holds fast. The club's bottom line counts on the renewal of memberships. It is your job to make certain everyone in your class or training sessions leaves satisfied, every time. The very few exceptions are when someone is abusive, using completely inappropriate words or actions. However, it is still your job to maintain your composure and handle the situation as peacefully as possible.

There is also the possibility that a student or client will insist on performing a contraindicated exercise, or incorrectly perform an otherwise safe exercise. Because of liability issues, it is your duty to inform him or her that what they are doing could cause injury. Kindly but firmly explain a better exercise or technique. Allowing them to continue without inserting your professional opinion could not only hurt them, but also leave you vulnerable to a liability suit. Refer to the upcoming section on professional liability insurance for more information regarding your responsibility in such instances.

The second basic rule of work relationships is, "Don't burn bridges." If you are in a disagreement, or if you are leaving one employment situation for another, always leave the work relationship on a good note. Keep in mind that your professional reputation will follow you throughout your career. It will take years to build a positive reputation, but only one mistake could destroy it.

When changing jobs, don't take the opportunity to vent negative thoughts and feelings before you leave. While it might make you feel good in the short term, it will have a detrimental, lasting effect on your career and on people's perception of you. Someone you insult today could become your boss some-day or be in a position to help you down the line.

If you do behave unprofessionally toward someone, even if you don't ever have contact with that person again, he or she will have contact with many other people and possibly describe you as hard to work with or even rude. Your work reputation is very important; don't tarnish it by burning your bridges.

Your Manager

Because no two managers are alike, it's impossible to give advice that will cover every situation; however, there are a few rules that you can apply to this important relationship that will minimize conflict and make it more reward-ing. Here are some suggestions to help you start building a cooperative rela-tionship with your manager.

▶ *Understand the general expectations regarding your position.*
If you don't have a formal, written job description and you feel even minimally comfortable asking for one, do so. It takes some tact to do this; you should start by explaining why you want one. Say something like "I know it's not possible to describe everything, but I don't want to leave anything undone that I'm responsible for." Ask for this informa-tion at the very beginning of your relationship, before any possible ten-sion has built up, so it won't seem like a challenge to authority.

▶ *If you don't understand your manager's instructions, ask for clarification.*

You cannot work effectively if you don't know what's expected of you. If instructions for doing a task are unclear, you must ask for further details. Don't be afraid of appearing stupid. Most managers would prefer that you ask for clarification rather than try to muddle through and make mistakes.

▶ *Be flexible.*

If your manager occasionally asks you to do something that's not in your job description—as long as the demand isn't unethical (dishonest or sexist, for example)—it's best to go ahead and do it. If you are rigid about what you will and won't do, your boss is liable to become rigid too. If she or he consistently expects you to perform tasks outside your job description—for example, things you feel are demeaning—eventually you might want to say, very diplomatically, that you are not comfortable doing them.

▶ *Make your manager and your team look good.*

This could go under the heading of "gym politics." It makes sense to do whatever you can to enhance the image of your superior and your team, because your success is related to the success of the club. By adding positive energy to upper management, you help the whole team, which can translate into a better business. And if the club is doing well, they have more to offer you in terms of salary, benefits, and opportunities for better positions.

▶ *Don't go over your boss's head except for the direst reasons.*

It is not an inviolable rule to never complain about your manager to a higher authority. In cases of actual discrimination or harassment, you should go to someone else. But in general, it's best to take complaints to him or her first and try to settle the matter privately—give your manager a chance to correct bad behavior or explain policies that seem unreasonable or unclear. This takes courage, but the payoffs are large. You may find there's a reason behind the "unreasonable" behavior that you never thought of.

Your Coworkers

Like managers, no two coworkers are alike, either. It's impossible to please everyone, but a good rule of thumb on how to deal with coworkers is to treat them the way you would like to be treated. Here are some suggestions to help you start building cooperative relationships with your coworkers.

▶ *Help others, especially new employees.*
Consistently show that you are part of the team. In particular, give new employees extra support. We're all familiar with that sweaty-palmed feeling of the first day of work, even the first weeks of work. Remember what it's like to be new, and empathize. Be willing to share some of the information you learned in your first weeks and months on the job, and help ease another's transition into employment with your club.

▶ *Be positive about others' achievements.*
Never undermine anyone in your establishment by devaluing their achievements, even if their "achievements" seem minor. Don't be afraid that another person will look better than you. In a good workplace, one in which teamwork is valued, there's room for everyone to look good.

▶ *Do not complain to your manager about a coworker's behavior.*
This is unacceptable, unless the matter is extremely serious. Even if the behavior of a coworker is really egregious, try every other avenue to resolve the situation before complaining to a superior. If a coworker is committing infractions that violate important ethical rules (consistent sexist or racist treatment of other employees would be an example) or that violate confidentiality or otherwise damage the club or its members, of course a complaint is in order. But for lesser matters—especially for interpersonal conflicts—complaints to the boss, reminiscent of tattling in grade school, have a way of backfiring. It's best to talk to the person involved, or, if it's something minor, simply to ignore the behavior.

▶ *Don't engage in gossip.*
Gossip hurts the person being talked about, will inevitably come back to haunt you, and also can make you look like you don't have enough to do.

▶ *When conflicts arise, attack the problem, not the other person.*

If the instructor teaching the class before yours is consistently late finishing its cooldown, making your class start late, talk to him or her when you can remain calm and focused. Keep the discussion centered on how the problem affects your job and your students, not on how terrible the other person is. Just as you would with your manager, speak to the coworker one-on-one, and keep the good of the team uppermost in your mind.

Instead of saying, "It's your responsibility to end your class on time. How am I supposed to teach my class when I have to start ten minutes late? From now on, I expect you to be out on time," say something like, "Could we work something out about when your class ends? If I get into the studio ten minutes late, I don't have time to teach a full fifty-minute class, and my students get upset." If the other person ignores your request, repeat it at intervals. Chances are you will wear him or her down, or your manager will notice the bad behavior and do something about it.

▶ *Understand that your managers and coworkers have problems too.*

When someone has authority over you, it may be hard to remember that they are just human. They have kids at home who misbehave, cats that need to go to the vet, deadlines to meet, bosses of their own—sometimes, difficult ones—overseeing their work. If your manager occasionally acts unreasonably, don't take it personally, as it might have nothing to do with you. Of course, if his or her behavior is consistently abusive, you will have to do something about it. But occasional mood swings are something we are all entitled to.

The best way to handle demands that aren't horrendous but only annoying—failure to make priorities clear, for example—is to ask for a one-on-one conference to clarify things. If you keep focused during the conference on the needs of the team, it will probably go smoothly, and your work life will be more pleasant and rewarding.

Your Students and Clients

These are the people on whom your success and job satisfaction depend. As an instructor or trainer, you will work directly with students and clients; if they are happy, you and your manager will be, too. Let them know how important they are to you, and treat each person with dignity and respect. Remember the rules of good ethics, which apply to every situation:

▶ *Take responsibility for your actions.*
Don't blame the club, your coworkers, or anyone else for your mistakes. When you are the one in the wrong, own up to it. In a well-run organization, it should not be grounds for firing to admit you have made an error. Conversely, don't grovel or say you are wrong when you don't believe you are.

▶ *Never take credit for another's ideas.*
Not only is it wrong, but chances are that eventually you will be found out.

▶ *Do not violate confidentiality.*
As a fitness instructor or personal trainer, you will be in a position of authority and as such be trusted with personal confidences. Although you may be tempted, do not violate confidentiality, as you can seriously damage your reputation and the trust you have established with your students and clients.

MANAGING LIABILITY RISKS

Once you begin work as an instructor or personal trainer, you will be asked for advice and guidance on a routine basis. On the positive side, your opinions and knowledge will be respected and in demand. On the negative side, you will be in a category with other professionals such as attorneys, doctors, and engineers, who need to protect themselves from so-called "third-party" lawsuits. These are essentially claims alleging negligence in the performance of a professional service or services. "Negligence," in this situation, refers to the failure to provide the degree of knowledge, care, or skill of the average industry peer under similar circumstances.

It is important for a number of reasons to know not only what you can do on the job to minimize your risk of exposure to a lawsuit, but also how to protect yourself with professional liability insurance in the event you are charged with negligence. The number of professional liability claims is on the rise, especially for personal trainers. Such claims, because they are based on personal services, name individuals (and their assets). Even though you are certain you will perform at the very highest level of skill and professionalism, there is always the possibility that you could have a claim filed against you. Such a claim, if won by the plaintiff (the person bringing the suit against you), could mean the loss of all of your personal assets if you don't have insurance coverage.

There are other possible losses to consider if a suit is filed against you. First, whether you win or lose, just being named in a liability claim could damage your reputation. The information could be easily passed along within the fitness community, and chances are much of it will be incorrect. It is difficult to defend your good name under such circumstances. Your ability to make a living could be affected if the suit, and the gossip that surrounds it, results in fewer referrals and new clients.

Second, you could lose time and money even if you win. Being named in a claim means you may have to attend a trial and give depositions during the time you could have been working. And third, you may have difficulty obtaining insurance in the future. Insurance companies have the right to deny coverage based on your previous claim history. If they choose to insure you, it could be at a much higher rate than if you had no claim history.

Reducing Your Exposure to Claims

Most of the items on the following list are things that any good instructor or trainer would do in the regular course of business. However, reducing your exposure to liability lawsuits is not a small matter. Understanding exactly what you can do to avoid claims against you is essential, and for that reason, you should take a look at this section of the book periodically during your career. Remind yourself every six months or so of the steps listed next, to protect both you and your clients.

1. *Documentation*: For personal trainers, it is important to document your clients' histories, treatments, and progress. It is possible misunderstandings could develop over the scope of service, so, the more accurate your documentation is, the easier it will be for a court to see that you acted appropriately.

2. *Communication*: Clients want a clear explanation of their program (without a guarantee of any specific outcome) and your fees. Proper communication is also vital with coworkers and other professionals in the industry with whom you have contact.

3. *Education:* This applies to both your clients and students and yourself. Those you work with should have a clear understanding of what you are doing and why. The more they know, the better; they won't have the chance to develop a misconception about what you can and will do for them if they understand what to expect at the onset of their program.

   Explain the benefits of each exercise, along with correct form, timing, and other issues. Refrain from using technical terminology that may not be understood. If you are working with someone rehabilitating an injury or recovering from an illness, provide them with written materials that help them understand their own condition(s), your procedures, and treatments. Encourage students and clients to ask questions whenever they are unsure about what you are doing and why you are doing it.

   Your continuing education is crucial to your success and your professional standing. If you ever have to face a lawsuit, your knowledge of new advances and technology within your particular specialty can only enhance your credibility and possibly weaken the case against you.

4. *Common Sense:* Many situations require that you rely on common sense, even though routine practice could suggest another course. Your instincts are incredibly valuable when dealing with the public and maintaining your professional standing.

As important as it is to understand what you should do to minimize your exposure to liability lawsuits, you must also know what not to do. There are a number of common mistakes that can increase your risk; all are completely avoidable if you know about them and their importance ahead of time. Many of these mistakes have to do with those working in a healthcare facility, or with clients who are recovering or rehabilitating. But they are all worth a look by anyone in the fitness industry, as the line between the medical and fitness communities is beginning to blur. Increasingly, doctors are "prescribing" physical activity for their clients, and recommending exercise classes and personal training services.

Seven Common Mistakes of Personal Trainers and Fitness Instructors

Any of the following can encourage liability claims and/or make it harder to defend against such claims if they are filed against you.

1. Altering a client's records

2. Not documenting procedures and treatments

3. Failing to follow standard policies and procedures

4. Speaking down to a client, making him or her feel ignored or unimportant, and/or using fitness jargon that may not be understood

5. Blaming a client's problem on a coworker

6. Failing to obtain proper documentation, such as informed consent, from the client

7. Breaching confidentiality by talking about a client with family and friends

Purchasing Liability Insurance

In addition to being certain you are doing everything in your power to minimize your liability risk exposure, you will want to obtain appropriate insurance coverage. Liability insurance will pay for legal defense in the event of a lawsuit, and pay medical and/or property claims for which you are found legally liable, up to the limits of the policy. It is an essential cost of doing business as an independent contractor, and even if you are an employee and your employer provides it, it may still be worth it to pay for your own liability coverage.

When assessing various policies, compare them in the following categories. Numbers in parentheses refer to typical levels of coverage.

▶ *Annual protection*: there will most likely be an annual limit and a per incident limit ($1 million per occurrence, $4 million annual limit)

▶ *Property damage*: again divided into per occurrence and annual limits; there may be a deductible for this type of coverage ($500–$5,000; $500 deductible)

▶ *Defense costs*: pay 100% of the fees for services of an experienced malpractice attorney, whether the case is won or lost

▶ *Defendant's reimbursement*: "pays" you for your time in court (if you are in court, you are not at work, which may mean you aren't collecting wages) ($500/day, $10,000 incident)

▶ *First aid*: covers first aid received after a covered injury to a client

Group policies tend to be much less expensive than individual policies, so it makes sense to check with organizations and associations in the industry. Many of them offer their members very competitive rates for group insurance. You might choose to join one over another because it offers the best liability coverage.

Liability Coverage

Use the following as a guide; all figures were current at the time of publication. Numbers in the first group refer to per-occurrence and annual coverage limits. The second group for personal trainers refers to coverage purchased by an employee who is already listed under an employer's policy (see the box below regarding the possible need for this additional coverage).

Professional Liability—Instructor

500,000	Full or part time, employed or self-employed: $205
1,000,000	Full or part time, employed or self-employed: $260
2,000,000	Full or part time, employed or self-employed: $302

Professional Liability—Personal Trainer

	Full-time	Part-time	Employed
200,000/600,000K	275	137	85
500,000/1,000,000	322	161	99
1,000,000/1,000,000	365	182	150
1,000,000/6,000,000	390	195	120
2,000,000/4,000,000	476	238	155

Four Reasons Why You May Need Insurance Even if You Are Covered by Your Employer's Liability Policy

1. The limits of your employer's liability policy may not be enough to cover you.

2. Your employer's limits probably cover all employees; if the same lawsuit names more than one employee, or different lawsuits within the same policy year are filed, shared limits may be exceeded, leaving you without coverage.

3. Coverage from your employer will most likely only be in effect when you are on their property. If you have private clients, or work independently off your employer's premises, you need your own policy to protect you when working at these other locations.

4. You could be named by your employer in a lawsuit, or named in a lawsuit in which it is to your employer's advantage to blame you. If you carry your own coverage, you will be covered under any of these circumstances.

Informed Consent and Other Paperwork

As mentioned previously, in your capacity as an instructor or personal trainer, you will be asked for advice and guidance. This is something you will have in common with other professionals such as attorneys, doctors, and engineers. All of these professions use a variety of forms to explain the risks to their clients of following their advice and guidance. Once the risks are read and understood, the client must then put his or her signature to the form, stating that they give their consent to receive professional services, whether they be those of a doctor, engineer, or personal trainer. The piece of paper is typically referred to as an Informed Consent Agreement, and acts as a crucial part of the effort to reduce liability risk.

Those in the fitness industry use a number of other forms to both give and receive information to and from their clients. The forms help instructors and personal trainers to understand the limitations and histories of their clients, and to then put together an appropriate program. The following forms are samples used by many in the fitness industry. You may obtain such forms through organizations and associations, your employer, insurance agent, or peers in the field. Having such forms checked out by your attorney before using them is never a bad idea.

Waiver of Liability and Informed Consent

I agree to the following:

1. I am participating in a fitness program offered by _____ and recognize that it requires physical exertion that may be strenuous and may cause physical injury. I am fully aware of the risks involved.
2. I represent and warrant that I am physically fit and have no medical condition which would prevent my full participation in the fitness program. I understand it is my responsibility to consult with a physician prior to and regarding my participation in this or any other fitness program.
3. I agree to assume full responsibility for any risks, injuries, or damages, known or unknown, which might occur as a result of participating in the fitness program.
4. I waive any claim I may have against _____ for any injury or death caused by his negligence or other acts.
5. I, my heirs or legal representatives forever release, waive, discharge, and covenant not to sue _____ for any injury or death caused by his negligence or other acts.

I have read the above informed consent and waiver of liability and fully understand its contents. I hereby affirm that I am over 18, and I voluntarily agree to the terms and conditions stated above.

Signed _____ Date _____

Witness _____ Date _____

Exercise History

Are you currently involved in a regular exercise program? YES NO

Do you regularly walk or run one or more miles continuously?

YES NO DON'T KNOW

If yes, average number of miles you cover per workout or day: _____ miles

What is your average time per mile? _____ Minutes/Seconds DON'T KNOW

Do you practice weightlifting or home calisthenics? YES NO

Are you involved in an aerobic program? YES NO

If yes, your average aerobic points per week: _____

Have you taken in the past six months: 12 minute test ___ 1.5 mile ___

neither _____

If yes, your miles in 12 minutes _____ of time in 1.5 miles ___ Minutes/Seconds

Do you frequently compete in competitive sports? YES NO

If yes, which one or ones?

Golf ___ Volleyball ___ Bowling ___ Football ___ Tennis ___ Baseball ___

Handball ___ Track ___ Basketball ___ Soccer ___ Other ___

Average number of times per week ___

In which of the following high school or college athletics did you participate?

None ___ Track ___ Football ___ Swimming ___ Basketball ___ Tennis ___

Baseball ___ Wrestling ___ Soccer ___ Golf ___ Other ___

What activities would you prefer in a regular exercise program for yourself?

Walking and/or running ___ Bicycling (outdoors) ___ Swimming ___

Stationary running ___ Stationary biking ___ Tennis ___ Jumping rope ___

Handball, Basketball, or Squash ___ Other: ___

Comments: _____

_____

Medical/Health History

1.   During the past three months, approximately now many times have you experienced any pain, pressure, or discomfort in your chest?
     a. 0 (skip to question 3)
     b. 1–5
     c. 6–25
     d. 26+

2.   Describe the character of the discomfort (check all that apply)
     ___ sharp, fleeting, localized pain or "catch"
     ___ intensity changes if you take a deep breath or change positions
     ___ dull pressure, ache, tightness, pain, or burning
     ___ radiates or spreads to jaw, arm, neck, shoulder, or back
     ___ has awakened you from sleep
     ___ predictably brought on by exertion
     ___ predictably relieved by rest within 10 minutes
     ___ predictably relieved by nitroglycerine within 10 minutes

Circle YES or NO to the following questions:

3.   Has a doctor ever told you that you had an abnormal EKG indicating an enlarged heart (called left ventricular hypertrophy)? YES NO

4.   Have any of your blood relatives (father, mother, brothers, sisters) died of a heart attack before the age of 60 years? YES NO

5.   Have you ever had a heart attack? YES NO
     (if NO, skip to section General Medical and Health)

6.   How many heart attacks have you had? ___

7.   At what age was your first heart attack? ___

8.   Have you ever had bypass surgery? YES NO
     If yes, how long ago was your surgery? _____

9.   Have you ever had angioplasty? YES NO
     If yes, how long ago was your angioplasty? _____

10. Are you in a cardiac rehabilitation program? YES NO

General medical and health

1. How tall are you? (inches) _____
2. What is your current weight? (lbs.) _____
3. How old are you? _____
4. How you describe your body frame size?
    (circle one) small medium large
5. How would you describe your blood pressure?
    (circle one) don't know high normal low
6. What is your blood pressure now? (leave blank if unknown)
    systolic (higher number) _____
    diastolic (lower number) _____
7. Are you taking medication for high blood pressure? YES NO
8. What is your cholesterol level (based on blood test)? _____
9. What is your HDL cholesterol? (leave g. and h. blank if unknown)
    _____
10. Considering your age, how would you describe your overall physi-
    cal health?
    excellent
    fair
    good
    poor

Current health habits

1. Do you use tobacco products? YES NO
    If yes, how much and for how long? _____
    If you quit, describe how you accomplished that: _____
2. How much alcohol do you use per day? _____
3. How much coffee/caffeine do you use per day? _____
4. Does your job require:
    _____strenuous physical activity
    _____moderate physical activity
    _____little or no physical activity

5. In your leisure time, do you engage in:
    _____regular strenuous activity
    _____regular moderate activity
    _____occasional activity
    _____little or no activity

Answer with the appropriate number:

1. Never, hardly ever   2. Sometimes   3. Always, nearly always

_____Do you feel your eating habits are out of control?

_____How frequently do you put yourself on a diet?

_____Do you find yourself obsessed about food and your weight?

_____Do you find yourself engaging in eating episodes that you know
     are contrary to good health practices?

_____Do you ever feel that your consumption of alcohol is a problem?

_____Do you ever feel that your use of drugs is a problem?

_____How often do you bring work home from the office?

_____How often are you "on the run?"

_____How often do you arrive late for business appointments?

_____How often do you arrive late for social appointments?

_____How often do you take scheduled vacations?

_____Do you rush the conversation to "get to the point?"

Exercise profile

1. Do you have any physical problems or limitations that may affect your ability to exercise? YES NO

2. Have you ever had a serious back or knee problem? YES NO (if yes, check all appropriate)
    In the past 6 months: ____back pain ____back surgery
    ____knee pain ____knee surgery
    More than 6 months: ____back pain ____back surgery
    ____knee pain ____knee surgery

3. In an average week, how many times do you engage in physical activity? Include only activities that last for at least 20 consecutive minutes, make you breathe heavier, and make your heart beat faster.
    a. Never
    b. Less than one time per week
    c. 1 or 2 times per week
    d. 3-4 times per week
    e. 5 or more times per week

4. In a typical week, how many minutes do you perform aerobic exercise at an intensity sufficient to increase your heart beat, increase your breathing, and cause mild sweating? ____ minutes

5. Please use the scale below to indicate how often you do each of the following:
    1. Usually/frequently   2. Sometimes   3. Rarely/never
    (Rate from 1-3)

____ warm-up
____ cool-down
____ stretch
____ finish your workout with very high intensity (all out effort)
____ exercise with the proper activity-specific footwear
____ support structure of shoes deteriorate before undersoles wear out
____ exercise on hard surfaces
____ work out includes non-weight bearing activities (swim, cycle)
____ include strength training as part of your workout

6. During your leisure time, how many hours per week do you normally spend performing activities as described below (not applicable leave blank)

_____ very light intensity activities such as leisurely walking (as in shopping), bowling, golfing while using electric cart, gardening.

_____ light intensity activities such as brisk walking, doubles tennis, recreational volleyball, raking leaves, etc.

_____ moderate intensity activities such as very fast walking, very slow jogging, singles tennis, down hill skiing, etc.

_____ high intensity activities such as jogging/running, squash, singles racquetball, basketball, competitive cycling, etc.

_____ very high intensity activities such as full court basketball, competitive swimming and cycling, cross country skiing, running at 6.5 minutes per mile or faster, etc.

Nutrition Profile

The nutrition profile is a guide for professionals who work with clients that may need or wish for some nutritional information. When presenting comparisons, the chart below gives a good representation of two types of eating patterns. If the client's diet consists of mainly foods in the high-fat list, their diet is close to, or over 40% fat. If it more closely resembles the low-fat list, their diet is likely to be close to 30% fat or less. If they exclude all the foods in the high-fat list, their diet is likely to be 20% fat or less.

HIGH FAT DIET	LOW FAT DIET
Foods prominent in this diet include:	Foods prominent in this diet include:
• Whole milk, cheese, butter, cream	• Whole grain breads, cereals
• Meat with fat, poultry with skin	• Pasta, rice, potatoes, legumes
• Mayonnaise, margarine, oils	• Fruits
• Eggs	• Vegetables
• Olives, avocado, coconut, nuts	• Skim milk, low-fat cheese and yogurt
• Fried and deep fried foods	• Lean meat, poultry w/o skin
• Pastries, donuts, croissants	• Broiled, baked, or steamed foods
• Processed meats, cold cuts	• Fish
• Candy, cookies, cake, chips	• Popcorn (without butter)

1. Choose a % rate range below that you believe most closely represents your diet based on the above examples:
   a. 20% fat or less
   b. 20–26% fat
   c. 27–33% fat
   d. 34–39% fat
   e. 40% fat and higher

For each of the statements below, choose the answer that most accurately describes your response based on the scale below:

(1) 4 or more times per day   (2) 2–3 times/day   (3) once/day

(4) twice/week   (5) less than twice/week

_____ 1a. How often do you eat animal or vegetable protein foods such as meat, fish, poultry, eggs, milk, cheese, peanut butter, tofu, or legumes?

_____ 1b. How often do you eat broccoli, brussel sprouts, cabbage, cauliflower, or other vegetables in the cabbage family?

_____ 1c. How often do you eat apples, bananas, berries, melons, citrus, and other fruits?

_____ 1d. How often do you eat foods high in cholesterol such as processed meats, organ meats, cheese, eggs, whole milk, ice cream, sour cream, butter, shortening, etc.?

_____ 1e. How often do you eat foods high in vitamin A such as spinach, carrots, yams, cantaloupe, and other green leafy or yellow vegetables or fruits?

_____ 1f. How often do you eat foods high in vitamin C such as citrus fruits, tomatoes, strawberries, etc.?

2. How often do you eat out each week?

_____ 0 times _____ 1–3 times _____ 4–7 times _____ 8–12 times

3. Do you have business or social activities that include meals or refreshments? YES NO

4. Do you use nutritional supplements? YES NO

If yes, what type? _____

Frequency of use: _____

5. Have you recently made any changes in your eating habits?
YES NO

Screening Questionnaire

1. Has a doctor ever said you have heart trouble? YES NO
2. Have you ever had angina pectoris or sharp pain or heavy pressure in your chest as a result of exercise, walking, or other physical activity such as climbing a flight of stairs (Note: this does not include the normal out of breath feeling that results from normal activity)?
   YES NO
3. Do you experience any sharp pain or extreme tightness in your chest when you are hit with a cold blast of air? YES NO
4. Have you ever experienced rapid heart action or palpitations?
   YES NO
5. Have you ever had a real or suspected heart attack, coronary occlusion, myocardial infarction coronary insufficiency, or thrombosis? YES NO
6. Have you ever had rheumatic fever? YES NO
7. Do you have diabetes, high blood pressure, or sugar in your urine?
   YES NO
8. Do you or anyone in your family have high blood pressure, or hypertension? YES NO
9. Has more than one blood relative (parent, brother, sister, first cousin) had a heart attack or coronary artery disease before the age of 60? YES NO
10. Have you ever taken any medication to lower your blood pressure?
    YES NO
11. Have you ever taken medications or been on a special diet to lower your cholesterol level? YES NO
12. Have you ever taken digitalis, quinine, or any other drug for your heart? YES NO
13. Have you ever taken nitroglycerin or any other tablets for chest pain—tablets that you take by placing under your tongue? YES NO
14. Have you ever had a resting or stress electrocardiogram that was not normal? YES NO
15. Are you overweight? YES NO

MENTORS

Finding and learning from a mentor is probably one of the best ways to continue your education on the job, providing you with both a positive role model to learn from and a professional "coach," someone who sees your job performance and knows ways in which you can improve upon it. A mentor can give you the kind of insider information not covered during your training and help you develop a path for your career.

Finding a Mentor

You will probably need to actively search for a mentor, unless someone decides to take you under his or her wing and show you the ropes. A mentor can be anyone from another instructor, to a workshop leader, or a club manager. There is no formula for who makes a good mentor; title, level of seniority, or years in the field may be unimportant. Instead, the qualities of a good mentor are based on a combination of willingness to mentor, level of expertise in a certain area, teaching ability, and attitude.

Look for a mentor by getting involved in an alumni group or professional society. Attend conferences and ask for the e-mail addresses of those who you think may be good mentor candidates. Follow up by corresponding, and be frank about your interest in the person as a mentor.

In addition to professional associations and groups, you might also find a mentor at work. When looking within your place of employment, seek counsel from two kinds of mentors:

- ▶ a "higher up" (but not your boss, or you might be accused of simply currying favor) who can give you informal soundings on what your superiors think of your work
- ▶ a peer from another area of your place of employment, who can teach you about aspects of the club you do not yet know

When looking for a mentor, keep in mind the following questions:

▶ Who in your club/group/association has a great reputation as a true professional?

▶ Does the potential mentor tackle problems in a reasonable manner until they are resolved?

▶ What is it that people admire about the potential mentor? Do the admirable qualities coincide with your values and goals?

▶ Is he or she strong in areas that you are weak?

If you think you have found a mentor at work, spend time watching that person on the job. You can learn a lot about him or her through observation. When asked a question, does she take the time to help you find the solution, or does she point you toward someone else who can help you? The one who takes the time to help you resolve your question is the better choice for a mentor. Observe your potential mentor when he is working on a problem. Does he do so in a calm manner? Does the problem get resolved? If so, you may have found a good mentor.

Learning from a Mentor

Once you have entered into a mentoring relationship, intend to learn all you can. While there are no set rules about what a mentor can teach you, there are some specifics that are part of the "curriculum" in many mentoring relationships. The following is a list of things you may learn from a mentor:

▶ coworker interaction skills

▶ what to expect in your work environment

▶ how to communicate with the chain of command at your club

▶ in-depth knowledge about the equipment used at your club

▶ the best fitness industry magazines, websites, and other resource materials

▶ how to best advance in your career

▶ what conferences/classes/training programs you should attend

▶ advice on dealing with difficult students or clients

Once you find someone who seems to be the ideal mentor, don't feel compelled to stick with him or her forever. Career growth may open up possibilities to you in new areas of specialization. If that happens, you will probably want to find additional mentors who can show you the ropes in the new environment. However, maintain relationships with former mentors—the more allies you have in the industry, the easier it will be to succeed and advance in your career.

GROWING FROM PART-TIME TO FULL-TIME

Because the fitness industry is one of the fastest growing in the country, the number of entry-level jobs is large. It is relatively simple for instructors in most markets to find part-time employment with one or many clubs. The advantages of this arrangement to the clubs are numerous: they get a wide variety of teachers and trainers, pay them a (typically) low to moderate hourly wage, and skip the high cost of providing benefits and contributing to Social Security. For the instructors and personal trainers, though, there is a dilemma. They get to work at a job they love, but don't make enough money to support themselves. The challenge for many is to find or create a full-time job and make a living in the fitness industry.

It's not as easy as finding lots of part-time hours at various clubs to create a full-time schedule. The drawback to teaching exercise forty or more hours a week is the physical toll of the job. It's impossible to lead more than a certain number of classes each week and maintain your own health and physical well-being. Injuries such as shin splints and stress fractures can occur when too much aerobic exercise is had, and overworking muscles can cause damage not only to those muscles, but to joints and connective tissue as well.

One solution used by many instructors is to become certified and work as personal trainers. This enables them to be able to work more hours in a club, without the stress on their bodies. As a personal trainer, you may have to demonstrate many exercises, but you will not have to repeat them until the point of fatigue the way you would have to do when teaching a class. Bethany Palmer, a Senior Group Fitness Director with a staff of 50 instructors and 20 personal trainers, notes that she witnesses the rise of this trend as she interviews prospective employees:

I am seeing more and more instructors come in with dual certifications, in personal training and group exercise instruction. It's great to see this, because the process of becoming certified as a personal trainer is generally more rigorous than becoming an instructor. Trainers have a well-rounded concept and in-depth knowledge of the body and how it works. Plus, I worry less about injury to instructor/trainers, since it is less wear and tear on your body to conduct training sessions, even when working with small groups. You do more coaching and motivating instead of working out yourself. There are a lot of us at my club that do more than one thing, and I love to hire instructors who can do some personal training in addition to their classes.

In addition to blending instruction with personal training, there are other ways in which to generate a full time income. Irene Lewis McCormick, M.S., in an article published in *Certified News* (Volume 5, Number 6, Oct/Nov 1999), says "more and more group fitness instructors and personal trainers are taking their part-time positions and moving them into full-time careers by creating their own businesses and breaking into specialty markets." While the subject of self-employment was discussed in Chapter 4 in general terms, this chapter will look at four specific ideas for fitness businesses.

Gym Design

As a trainer or instructor, you will spend countless hours in gyms and fitness centers. You will develop a working knowledge of the best layouts of these spaces, the best equipment, even the best types of flooring and lighting if you are really paying attention. How can you use this knowledge to expand your business? One way is to provide your services as a gym designer.

A quick search of the Internet with the terms "gym design" turns up hundreds of web pages of personal trainers and other fitness professionals offering this service. Take a look at some of their sites for ideas on how to market yourself. To begin, you might consider partnering with an architect or interior designer who has clients interested in setting up home gyms. You can provide the professional fitness input necessary to design a space that meets clients' needs now, and can grow with them later.

There are also hundreds of businesses that deal exclusively with the design of home gyms, and many of them hire consultants. You could apply to work for one of them, gaining extra hours on the job, or the experience you need to venture out on your own. Gym design can be a great way to increase your income by adding it to your training or teaching schedule; or, you might decide that you like this type of work so much that it becomes the focus of your career.

Sales

Each day you work as an instructor or trainer, you come in contact with buyers or potential buyers of exercise equipment, fitness educational materials, nutritional supplements and other products. You may be purchasing such products already for yours or your clients' use. Therefore it is a small step from this limited involvement to a lucrative position as a salesperson.

The manufacturers and distributors of the products you use are always looking for people to sell them. If you have an interest in sales, this could prove a winning proposition for you. Some clubs prohibit their employees from marketing items while on the job, while others don't mind it. But you can always sell to private clients, and students in classes held in your own or rented space.

There are two ways to get started in sales. One is to contact the manufacturer of a product you are interested in selling. As professionals in the business themselves, they will be familiar with your advantageous contact with buyers, and may already use trainers and instructors to market and sell their wares. If not, you may have to explain why you feel you could add sales to your repertoire. The manufacturer can tell you whom in their organization to contact regarding employment; once you have a name, use the guidelines spelled out in Chapter 5 to make contact with him or her.

The second way to add to your income with sales of fitness-related products is to find a company that routinely uses fitness professionals as sales people. These businesses often provide sales training, promotional tools, and financial help with advertising, in addition to commission on every sale. Typically, the more you sell each month, the higher commission percentage you receive.

Partnering with other Professionals

If you are looking to expand your teaching or training hours into a full-time job, a great way to promote your services, build a client base, and generate more income, is to "partner" with professionals in other industries. Using many of the networking techniques described in Chapter 4, you can make contact and build business relationships with doctors, other health professionals, corporations and small businesses, product suppliers, and even architects and interior designers, who can refer clients to you.

"Cross-referrals and partnering services with medical professionals are increasing as is the number of trainers who work with clients who have special medical conditions or require post-rehabilitation services," says Kathie Davis, Executive Director of IDEA Health & Fitness Association and co-author of Personal Training Trendwatch 2001. (www.ideafit.com/PR2001Feb3.htm) Doctors, physical therapists, and nutritionists are just some of the partnering possibilities in the medical community.

What does partnering mean, specifically? Medical professionals are increasingly "prescribing" physical activity to their patients, and want to be sure that they follow appropriate, safe programs. If they know of a trainer or instructor whose skills they trust, they will be more than willing to recommend him or her. The referrals can go in the other direction as well: trainers and instructors may see clients who are in need of medical attention, and can refer them to the same doctor, physical therapist, or other medical professional who sends business their way.

Kathie Davis notes that:

One trainer in a hospital-based fitness center is working with the physical therapy department for referrals of discharged patients and offers lowered fees as an incentive to use his services. In a health club setting, some trainers get their post-rehabilitation clients from the club's physical therapist while another trainer provides all clients with a fitness and health assessment every three months and forwards the results to their primary care physician.

Who else can you partner with? How about those in the corporate world, who may be interested in having an instructor/trainer work in their in-house gym a few hours each week, developing programs for employees? Or even holding an aerobics or yoga class in a conference room after work? As more employers look for ways to combat the high cost of medical insurance, and decrease employee injuries and leave-taking, providing fitness and wellness programs becomes not just a nice perk, but a smart way to do business.

Look to professions known for a high level of stress. Can you develop a class in which you teach exercises known to reduce stress in the body? Perhaps you could develop a lecture series that explores stress from a number of angles: you could handle the physical aspects, a money manager could discuss stress as it relates to finances, a psychologist could talk about the mental and emotional toll of stress, etc. One-time seminars can impart useful information to employees in a corporate setting; you can fit many such seminars into your schedule, and as you develop a reputation for your expertise, you can charge high rates for your time.

You can also target the employers of workers prone to work-related musculoskeletal disorders (WMSDs), such as administrative assistants and others who spend hours at a keyboard. Learn all you can about WMSDs, including Computer Related Repetitive Strain Injuries (CRRSI), how best to avoid them, and how to alleviate symptoms. Become an "expert" in proper workstation setup, scheduling (how often to take a break from the computer or machinery), and appropriate exercises to relieve fatigue and strain on the body.

As evidence of the widespread nature of this problem, the Occupational Health and Safety Administration is considering the implementation of workplace ergonomic standards. If these standards become law, businesses around the country will need to hire trainers and other professionals to teach employees how best to physically perform their jobs.

But even without government regulation, many employers are interested in reducing the incidence of these injuries, because they result in lower productivity and millions of dollars of medical and workers' compensation insurance claims. The number of CTD related claims increases annually, and with our dependence on technology holding steady, they are likely to continue to grow. Employers who face this problem could be interested in hiring you to help them reduce the number of WMSDs in their workplaces. If this type of specialization interests you, check out www.ctsplace.com to read up on the latest research regarding diagnosis, treatments, cures, etc. of various WMSDs.

Buying a Franchise

Another idea for instructors who wish to be self-employed, or generate alternate sources of income, is franchise opportunities. Buying and running a franchise might be described as owning your own business with a built-in safety net. You won't be out on your own, trying to build name recognition, and struggling with the issues of entrepreneurship, because you will be part of a tested system of operations, provided with many layers of support. The success of the franchise company is directly related to the success of your venture. "90% of franchise businesses are still operating after 10 years, but 82% of independent business fail," according to the United States Department of Commerce.

As the owner of a fitness franchise, your income will be derived from membership fees, monthly dues, and, in some cases, pro-shop sales. Total expenses will include rent, advertising, utilities, payroll, insurance, and royalties, which are paid back to the franchise company. For an initial investment ranging from a few thousand to hundreds of thousands of dollars, you can get started, and be provided with services such as:

- ▶ assistance with financing
- ▶ training in management, sales, marketing
- ▶ access to proven marketing strategies
- ▶ volume buying power for equipment and supplies
- ▶ ongoing business counseling
- ▶ national advertising campaigns

Chapter 2 mentioned Jazzercise (page 41), which certifies instructors while making each one a franchisee. Jazzercise takes a percentage of each membership, and charges the franchise a yearly fee. But there are many more opportunities in the fitness industry which provide various levels of support, and charge different rates to their franchisees. A recent search for "fitness franchises" on www.google.com turned up almost 75,000 hits, some of which are listed below. There are also franchise sites that list opportunities by category, and provide information on issues relating to the purchase and running of a franchise. Some of the larger sites include:

www.bison.com
www.businessnation.com
www.nettizen.com
www.franchiseopportunities.com
www.franchise-update.com
www.franchisegator.com

Entrepreneur Magazine contains great information on specific franchise opportunities as well as advice for franchisees on a number of topics. Their start-up guides for self-employment are also popular. Find them at Entrepreneur Media Inc., 2445 McCabe Way, Irvine, CA 92614; 800-274-6229. Their website, www.entrepreneur.com, has even more valuable information on buying and running franchises.

Franchise Fitness Businesses
Contours Express—exercise and weight loss for women:
www.contoursexpress.com
Curves for Women—exercise and weight loss for women:
www.curvesforwomen.com
Gold's Gym—one of the largest fitness corporations:
www.goldsgym.com
Inches A Weigh—exercise and weight loss for women:
www.inchesaweigh.com
It Figures—exercise and weight loss for women: www.itfigures.biz
Lady of America, Inc.–Lotusea—corporate wellness programs:
www.lotusea.com
My Gym—children's fitness center: www.my-gym.com

PROMOTING YOURSELF

There are a number of other things you can do to keep your career moving in a positive direction. Don't wait for opportunities to land in your lap. Whether you are self-employed or work for a large chain club, you should create opportunities for career growth by being proactive. That can mean anything from promoting yourself while in your current position, solidifying your reputation as a highly competent professional, expanding your client base, and/or seeking out a promotion to a higher-level job.

Building on Your Reputation

No matter how well you work with others and how knowledgeable you are, in the end you will be judged by the product you put out. You want to develop a reputation as someone with a long list of satisfied customers, who gets results for students and clients. To accomplish this, take pride in everything you do, and make every person you encounter feel important and worth your very best effort.

Veteran instructor Cat Earisman gives this advice:

> Sell yourself while teaching each class. At the beginning and end of the hour, state your name, and when and what you will be teaching next. Tell the class how you are going to challenge them, with an upbeat attitude that's not intimidating. Learn students' names, and make sure they are having fun. You want them to leave eager to come back for more.

Perhaps most importantly, work toward increasing your abilities. You might decide to attend a seminar on a specialized topic such as rehabilitation or yoga ball. Or, you could join an industry association (see Appendix A for a listing of many organizations, with contact information), and get involved at a local level. Make it a point to visit informative websites such as Fitcommerce's www.clubmarket.com, which contain articles on industry trends and updates in the field.

Finally, regularly read one or more of the trade journals, listed in Chapter 4 (page 128—Industry Newletters and Magazines), on a regular basis. Actively pursue knowledge, experience, and greater involvement in the industry in which you work.

Dealing Positively with Criticism

When you do receive criticism about your job performance from a colleague or superior, you need to do three things. The first is to remain calm. You need to hear what is being said, and that is nearly impossible when you are upset. Listen and understand without trying to defend yourself or correcting the person who's critiquing your work.

Second, ask for clarification and concrete help to rectify the situation. If you have been told that a student in one of your classes was unhappy with you, find out exactly what the problem was. Was the music too loud, the content of the class too difficult, or is the student someone who loves to complain? Ask for specific information about the situation in a nonconfrontational way. If your manager or other instructors have dealt with this person, they may have good suggestions.

Third, follow any advice given, and ask the person who's critiquing you for help in the future. See if you can find a time when he or she can see how you have been doing things and make specific suggestions for changes. By keeping calm, and responding in a non-defensive, professional manner, you can turn a negative critique into an opportunity for positive growth and change.

Getting Promoted

Once you have been on the job for a while, you may decide that the position you hold isn't as challenging or rewarding as it once was. If you work for a large club, there may be promotion opportunities to seek out. Instructor and personal training jobs can lead to management positions with more responsibility and better pay.

If you decide you would like to seek a promotion, either immediately or in the future, prepare by taking four critical steps. If you plan well and think in terms of your career as a whole rather than just your first position in the industry, you will anticipate your rise through the ranks as soon as you land a job. The people who get promoted are those who:

1. know their club
2. maintain a positive attitude toward change
3. show genuine care for members and fellow employees
4. get to know upper management

The first step may take some time, but it's probably the easiest. You will need to become extremely well versed in your club's history, financial statements, operating procedures, training procedures and job duties. Some of this information may be presented during your training and first weeks on the job, while the rest may be learned later. Pay close attention, and really get to know and understand what your employer is all about. You will sound more authoritative when speaking about your club, and operate from a knowledgeable position as a team player.

Second, embrace the changes that will inevitably become a part of your "routine." The fitness industry is very sensitive to timing and trends, and therefore change is frequent. For instance, the changing of seasons plays a big part in the schedule-making process. In the summer, many members are home with school-aged children, and not available to attend the classes they normally frequent when school is in session. Summer also brings better weather, which lures members outside to get exercise by biking, running, swimming, and so on. Clubs often respond by cutting back on their class schedules.

There are also fitness trends to consider. The popularity of specific class formats is sometimes fleeting, and clubs need to keep up with the demand as long as it exists. While no one can accurately predict which trends will stay around, some general guidelines may apply. For instance, a class format or piece of equipment needs to meet the needs of many people. It must challenge the strong while remaining doable for beginners.

Other current trends include the popularity of mind-body workouts, such as yoga and tai chi. While they have been around for thousands of years, they have never been practiced as much as they are now. People are looking for calming, centering, relaxing forms of exercise, and these ancient forms fit the bill. Many fitness professionals believe this trend will last longer than many others because, among a handful of reasons, it is not the result of a gimmicky marketing campaign. The popularity of yoga has nothing to do with the sale and use of expensive props, and everything to do with the benefits its practice brings to students.

If club management responds to such trends by changing operational procedures, you need to be positive. Let your superiors know you will do all you can to support the new class format or equipment, contributing to its success. Change is the operative word in the industry; those who embrace it, and use it to increase sales, will probably be the ones who succeed.

Another attitude-oriented step toward promotion is showing genuine care and concern for others. Make every client feel important by focusing intently on them during training sessions. Don't get distracted by anything else going on in the workout room. After a program has been in place for a while, suggest to a client that you have been thinking about modifications, based on the progress you have evidenced.

Instructors, as mentioned previously, should learn students' names and use them in class. Don't point out someone's errors in a confrontational way, but rather encourage individuals when they are doing well. Let your students know that you love your job, and your time spent with them. Yoga instructor Fran Scalessa ends each class with this blessing: "Wishing compassion and contentment for all people."

Last, if you want to get promoted, you need to know club management. When you meet them, make a great impression. Discover ways to help them remember you, and play the politics of your company. It may take some time to understand how the game is played, but make it a priority to observe it at all times. Find out how those in management were promoted and why. Keep an ear open to inside information and gossip. Frequent your company's website and promotional material for other clues.

When it comes time to ask or apply for a promotion, be sure to understand your club's protocol. If applying in person, don't aggressively demand the job, but be prepared to explain why you are right for it. Your enthusiasm and confidence will show if you have researched the job, know you have the necessary skills, and are excited about taking on the extra responsibility. If you need to apply in writing, use the same care as if you were applying for your first position with the club. Update your resume to include your current job, pointing out the skills and responsibilities you possess that are needed for the new position.

Try to keep the application process low key. There's a possibility you won't get the promotion this time around, for any number of reasons. You don't want to hurt your chances in the future by exhibiting unprofessional behavior such as complaining about not getting the job. You are still employed, and still have duties to fulfill. Spend some time quietly figuring out why you weren't promoted; keep your ears open for any news about who did get the job and why. If it's appropriate, ask the person making the hiring decision for information about his or her choice. If there is something you can do to improve your chances in the future, begin to take steps to do so now.

FINAL THOUGHTS

As noted throughout this book, the hiring outlook for fitness instructors and personal trainers is outstanding, and doesn't appear likely to slow down in the future. Demand for those holding degrees in the industry is greatest; certification is necessary, and relatively easy to obtain. In order to stay competitive after you have been hired, don't let learning stop. Get involved in industry associations, regularly read career-specific publications, attend conferences and seminars, and keep your knowledge current.

Not only are there always a large number of job openings, but instructor and trainer positions are becoming more professionalized, offering a wider range of career directions than ever before. No matter where you are employed, however, you will be working directly with people. Always let them know that they are important, that your success and job satisfaction depends on them. Pursue each step toward your new career with diligence, compassion, and a commitment to excellence, and you will be well on your way to achieving success.

THE INSIDE TRACK

Who: Alexa Gray

What: Certified Fitness Instructor / Personal Trainer / Fitness Studio Owner

Where: Chatham, New Jersey

I am an Aerobics and Fitness Association of America (AFAA) and American College of Sports Medicine (ACSM) certified fitness instructor and personal trainer, and own my own studio in Chatham, New Jersey. I teach aerobics and weight training at the studio, and at a number of corporations in Morris County. I also provide fitness consulting services, including running programs at one client's on-site fitness center, and coordinating classes in stress reduction, exercise, and smoking cessation for another client.

I was a cheerleader in college, and have always been into fitness, and when I graduated (with a degree in education) I was thinking of ways to incorporate my love of fitness with my degree. I had contemplated becoming a gym teacher, but I knew in my heart that I wanted to work with adults. It didn't take me long to come to the conclusion that I wanted to get into the personal fitness field, but I was in the dark as where to begin. Keep in mind, this was in the early 1980s, and the industry wasn't quite as developed as it is today, so there wasn't as much opportunity.

To land my first job, I joined a club and started taking classes. After a couple of months, I approached the owner, and told her I was interested in teaching. Since she was always looking for new instructors, she was happy to train me and get me started. Word-of-mouth is a great way to find a job once you've got some experience. You get involved in the fitness community, and find out fast who is hiring, who is building a new facility, or expanding, and so on, an it will put you on the right track. I quickly learned that the best way of finding work is to network. And the best way to network in this field is to maintain business relationships with your competitors and colleagues. Even though someone at another club may be attracting your students today, they might be able to help you find a position tomorrow. It doesn't pay to alienate anyone. Make it a point to get to know instructors at other clubs, even if you have to take their classes to meet them initially. It's always a good idea to see what is going on out there, get new ideas, and make contacts.

As for certifications, I have held a number of them over the years, and have seen it all! There were certain certifications in the 1980s that involved taking a test very similar to the format of the SATs. It was really tough, and very few who took it passed. To get my ACSM certification, I also had to take a test, and show that I've had more than 300 hours of teaching experience, and hold another current certification as well as CPR certification. For my AFAA certification, I attended a weekend seminar and was given a written and practical exam at the end. The practical part was done in front of a large group, and was difficult for some of the new instructors. You had to teach part of a class to a room full of professionals, two of whom were grading you.

When you are ready to work, you will quickly find out that teaching can be really hard on your body. When you own a studio, you would think it would be easier in you, but it's just the opposite—you end up having to fill in for instructors who call in sick or have car trouble. You might have to teach when your body tells you it can't. Even if you're exhausted, have shin splints, or a bad blister, you've got to get out there and smile and do it anyway, it's your business, your livelihood. I usually end up working more than forty hours a week, with the all of the behind-the-scenes business of running the studio and consulting. Because of that, I try to teach only five classes a week.

From the boss's point of view, when I'm hiring, I look for a person who has some natural teaching ability. You can have a couple of degrees and certifications, and spend hours reading and studying, but it doesn't mean much if you can't get in front of a group of people and hold their interest. You need to be a motivator who seeks to bring out the best in people. Intelligence and a positive attitude are also high on the list.

If you think it's right for you, I would highly recommend entering the fitness field. It's hard work, but I am doing something I love, and have met so many wonderful people. Some of my students are now great friends, and some have even become colleagues. Good luck!

Appendix A

Professional Associations, National Accrediting Agencies, and State Higher Education Agencies

PROFESSIONAL ASSOCIATIONS

(Those offering certification are indicated with an asterisk *)

American College of Sports Medicine *
401 W. Michigan Street
Indianapolis, IN 46202-3233
www.acsm.org
Phone: 317-637-9200
Fax: 317-634-7817

America's Consumer Fitness Association
1809 Nottingham Drive, Suite 201
Winter Park, FL 32792
www.acfa.com
Phone: 407-657-1907
Fax: 407-678-6386

American Council on Exercise*
4851 Paramount Drive
San Diego, CA 92123
www.acefitness.org
Phone: 800-825-3636
Fax: 858-279-8064

American Fitness and Aerobics Association
  (AFAA) *
15250 Ventura Boulevard, Suite 200
Sherman Oaks, CA 91403
www.afaa.com
Phone: 877-968-7263
Fax: 818-788-6301
E-mail: afaa@afaa.com

American Fitness Professionals and
   Associates *
P.O. Box 214
Ship Bottom, NJ 08008
www.afpafitness.com
Phone: 609-978-7583
E-mail: afpa@afpafitness.com

American Society of Exercise Physiologists
1200 Kenwood Avenue
Duluth, MN 55811
www.css.edu/asep
Phone: 218-723-6297

American Yoga Association
P.O. Box 19986
Sarasota, FL 34276
www.americanyogaassociation.org
Phone: 941-927-4977
Fax: 941-921-9844
E-mail: info@americanyogaassociation.org

Aquatic Alliance International
59 Prospect Street #2
Lebanon, NH 03766
www.mindspring.com/~aai_getwet/
E-mail: vgoodric@night.vtc.vsc.edu

Aquatic Exercise Association
3439 Technology Drive, Unit 6
Nokomis, FL 34275-3627
www.aeawave.com
Phone: 888-AEA-WAVE
Fax: 941-486-8820

Ball Dynamics International Inc.*
14215 Mead Street
Longmont, CO 80504
www.fitball.com
Phone: 800-752-2255
Fax: 877-223-2962

Cooper Institute *
12330 Preston Road
Dallas, TX 75230
www.cooperinst.org
Phone: 972-341-3200
Fax: 972-341-3227

Fitness Resources*
P.O. Box 460610
Aurora, CO 80046
www.fitres.com
Phone: 303-400-4900
Fax: 303-680-6206
E-mail: BobDama@cs.com

International Dance Exercise Association
6190 Cornerstone Court East #204
San Diego, CA 92121
www.ideafit.com
Phone: 800-999-4332
Fax: 858-535-8234

International Fitness Association *
12472 Lake Underhill Road, #341
Orlando, FL 32828
www.ifafitness.com
Phone: 800-227-1976

International Fitness Professionals
   Association *
www.ifpa-fitness.com

International Health, Racquet and Sportsclub
   Association
263 Summer Street
Boston, MA 02210
www.ihrsa.org
Phone: 800-228-4772 or 617-951-0055
Fax: 617-951-0056
E-mail: info@ihrsa.org

International Personal Fitness Trainers'
   Association*
www.ipfta.com

International Sport Kickboxing Association
P.O. Box 90147
Gainesville, FL 32607
www.iska.com
Phone: 352-331-0260
Fax: 352-331-2119

International Sports and Fitness Trainers
   Association
P.O. Box 18971
Sarasota, FL 34276
www.isfta.com
Phone: 866-277-7773
Fax: 941-739-9691
E-mail: info@asfta.com

International Sports Sciences Association*
400 East Gutierrez Street
Santa Barbara, CA 93101
www.issaonline.com
Phone: 800-892-ISSA
Fax: 805-884-8119

Jazzercise, Inc.*
2460 Impala Drive
Carlsbad, CA 92008
www.jazzercise.com
Phone: 760-476-1750
Fax: 760-602-7180
E-mail: jazzinc@jazzercise.com

Madd Dog Athletics, Inc. (Spinning®)*
2111 Narcisus Court
Venice, CA 90291
www.spinning.com
Phone: 800-847-SPIN (7746)
Fax: 310-823-7408
E-mail: info@spinning.com

National Academy of Sports Medicine
26632 Agoura Road
Calabasas, CA 91302
Phone: 800-460-6276
Fax: 818-878-9288
www.nasm.org

National Association for Health and Fitness
401 West Michigan Street
Indianapolis, IN 46202-3233
www.physicalfitness.org
Phone: 317-955-0957
Fax: 317-634-7817
E-mail: info@physicalfitness.org

National Athletic Trainers' Association *
2952 Stemmons Freeway
Dallas, TX 75247-6916
www.nata.org
Phone: 214-637-6282
Fax: 214-637-2206

National Commission for Health Education Credentialing, Inc.*
944 Marcon Boulevard, Suite 310
Allentown, PA 18109
www.nchec.org
Phone: 888-624-3248
Fax: 800-813-0727

National Council of Strength and Fitness*
P.O. Box 43-0945
South Miami, FL 33243
www.ncsf.org
Phone: 800-772-NCSF

National Federation of Professional Trainers*
P.O. Box 4579
Lafayette, IN 47903-4579
www.nfpt.com
Phone: 800-729-6378
Fax: 765-471-7369
E-mail: info@nfpt.com

NESTA (National Endurance Sports Trainers Association) *
31441 Santa Margarita Parkway, Suite A-140
Rancho Santa Margarita, CA 92688-1835
www.nestacertified.com
Phone: 877-348-6692

National Institute for Fitness and Sport
250 University Boulevard
Indianapolis, IN 46202
www.nifs.org
Phone: 317-274-3432
Fax: 317-274-7408

National Strength and Conditioning Association *
1640 L Street, Suite G
Lincoln, NE 68508
www.nsca-lift.org
Phone: 888-746-2378
Fax: 402-476-7141
E-Mail: commission@nsca-cc.org

National Strength Professionals Association*
110 West Timonium Road
Timonium, MD 21113
www.nspainc.com
Phone: 800-494-6772
Fax: 301-947-0977

North American Academy of Health, Fitness and Rehabilitation Professionals (AAHFRP) *
3323 Watt Avenue #158
Sacramento, CA 95821
www.medicalexercisespecialist.com
Phone: 888-610-0923
Fax: 801-457-7844

President's Council on Physical Fitness and Sports (PCPFS)
Department W
200 Independence Avenue, SW,
Room 738-H
Washington, D.C. 20201-0004
www.fitness.gov
Phone: 202-690-9000
Fax: 202-690-5211

Professional Fitness, Inc. *
www.professional-fitness.com
Phone: 305-375-8121
E-mail: customerservice@professional-
fitness.com

Resist-A-Ball, Inc.*
4507 Furling Lane, Unit 202
Destin, FL 32541
www.resistaball.com
Phone: 877-269-9893
Fax: 850-837-1089
E-mail: info@resistaball.com

Wellness Councils of America
9802 Nicholas Street Suite 315
Omaha, NE 68114
www.welcoa.org
Phone: 402-827-3590
Fax: 402-827-3594
E-mail: wellworkplace@welcoa.org

Yoga Alliance
120 S. Third Avenue
West Reading, PA 19611
www.yogaalliance.org
Phone: 877-YOGAALL (964-2255)
Fax: 610-376-9896
E-mail: info@yogaalliance.org

United States Athletic Trainers Organization
www.usatrainers.com
Phone: 888-674-USAT
E-mail: usatrainers@nnng.com.

United States Yoga Association
2159 Filbert Street
San Francisco, CA 94123
www.usyoga.org
Phone: 415-931-YOGA

NATIONAL ACCREDITING AGENCIES

You may contact these agencies to request a list of the schools they accredit, or to ask about accreditation of a specific school.

Accrediting Commission for Career Schools
    and Colleges of Technology (ACCSCT)
2101 Wilson Boulevard, Suite 302
Arlington, VA 22201
703-247-4212; fax 703-247-4533
www.accsct.org

Accrediting Council for Independent
    Colleges and Schools (ACICS)
750 First Street NE, Suite 980
Washington, DC 20002-4241
202-336-6780; fax 202-842-2593
www.acics.org

Distance Education and Training Council
    (DETC)
1601 Eighteenth Street NW
Washington, DC 20009-2529
202-234-5100; fax 202-332-1386
www.detc.org

REGIONAL ACCREDITING AGENCIES

Middle States

Middle States Association of Colleges and
    Schools
Commission on Institutions of Higher
    Education
3624 Market Street
Philadelphia, PA 19104-2680
215-662-5606; fax 215-662-5950
www.msache.org

New England States

New England Association of Schools and
    Colleges
Commission on Institutions of Higher
    Education (NEASC-CIHE)
209 Burlington Road
Bedford, MA 07130-1433
781-271-0022, x313; fax 781-271-0950
www.neasc.org/cihe

New England Association of Schools and
    Colleges
Commission on Vocational, Technical, and
    Career Institution (NEASC-CTCI)
209 Burlington Road
Bedford, MA 01730-1433
781-271-0022, x316; fax 781-271-0950
www.neasc.org/ctci

North Central States

North Central Association of Colleges and
    Schools
Commission on Institutions of Higher
    Education (NCA)
30 North LaSalle, Suite 2400
Chicago, IL 60602-2504
312-263-0456; 800-621-7440; fax 312-263-
    7462
www.ncahihe.org

Northwest States

Northwest Association of Schools and
    Colleges
Commission on Colleges
11130 NE 33rd Place, Suite 120
Bellevue, WA 98004
425-827-2005; fax 425-827-3395
www.cocnase.org

Southern States

Southern Association of Colleges and
    Schools
Commission on Colleges (SACS)
1866 Southern Lane
Decatur, GA 30033-4097
404-679-4500; 800-248-7701; fax 404-679-
    4558
www.sacscoc.org

Western States

Western Association of Schools and
    Colleges
Accrediting Commission for Community and
    Junior Colleges (WASC-Jr.)
3402 Mendocino Avenue
Santa Rosa, CA 95403-2244
707-569-9177; fax 707-569-9179
www.accjc.org

Western Association of Schools and
    Colleges
Accrediting Commission for Senior Colleges
    and Universities (WASC-Sr.)
985 Atlantic Avenue, Suite 100
Alameda, CA 94501
510-632-5000; fax 510-632-8361
www.wascsenior.org/senior/wascsr.html

FINANCIAL AID FROM STATE HIGHER EDUCATION AGENCIES

You can request information about financial aid from each of the following state higher education agencies and governing boards.

Alabama

Alabama Commission on Higher Education
100 North Union Street
P.O. Box 302000
Montgomery, AL 36130-2000
334-281-1998; fax 334-242-0268
www.ache.state.al.us

State Department of Education
50 North Ripley Street
P.O. Box 302101
Montgomery, AL 36104
205-242-8082
www.alsde.edu

Alaska

Alaska Commission on Postsecondary
   Education
3030 Vintage Boulevard
Juneau, AK 99801-7100
907-465-2962; 800-441-2962;
   fax 907-465-5316
www.state.ak.us/acpe

State Department of Education
801 W. 10th Street, Suite 200
Juneau, AK 99801
907-465-2800; fax 907-465-3452
www.educ.state.ak.us

Arizona

Arizona Board of Regents
2020 N. Central Avenue, Suite 230
Phoenix, AZ 85004-4593
602-229-2500; fax 602-229-2555
www.abor.asu.edu

State Department of Education
1535 West Jefferson Street
Phoenix, AZ 85007
602-542-4361; 800-352-4558
www.ade.state.az.us

Arkansas

Arkansas Department of Higher Education
144 E. Capitol Avenue
Little Rock, AR 72201
501-371-2000
www.arkansashighered.com

Arkansas Department of Education
4 State Capitol Mall, Room 304A
Little Rock, AR 72201-1071
501-682-4474
arkedu.state.ar.us

California

California Student Aid Commission
P.O. Box 419027
Rancho Cordova, CA 95741-9027
916-445-0880; 888-224-7268;
   fax 916-526-8002
www.csac.ca.gov

California Department of Education
721 Capitol Mall
Sacramento, CA 95814
916-657-2451
goldmine.cde.ca.gov

Colorado

Colorado Commission on Higher Education
1380 Lawrence Street, Suite 1200
Denver, CO 80204
303-866-2723; fax 303-866-4266
www.state.co.us/cche_dir/hecche.html

State Department of Education
201 East Colfax Avenue
Denver, CO 80203-1799
303-866-6600; fax 303-830-0793
www.cde.state.co.us

Connecticut

Connecticut Department of Higher Education
61 Woodland Street
Hartford, CT 06105-2326
860-947-1800; fax 860-947-1310
www.ctdhe.org

Connecticut Department of Education
P.O. Box 2219
Hartford, CT 06145
860-566-5677
www.state.ct.us/sde

Delaware

Delaware Higher Education Commission
820 N. French Street
Wilmington, DE 19801
302-577-3240; 800-292-7935;
   fax 302-577-5765
www.doe.state.de.us/high-ed

District of Columbia

Department of Human Services
Office of Postsecondary Education,
   Research, and Assistance
2100 Martin Luther King Jr. Avenue SE,
   Suite 401
Washington, DC 20020
202-727-3685

District of Columbia Public Schools
Division of Student Services
4501 Lee Street NE
Washington, DC 20019
202-724-4934
www.k12.dc.us

Florida

Florida Department of Education
Turlington Building
325 West Gaines Street
Tallahassee, FL 32399-0400
904-487-0649
www.firn.edu/doe

Georgia

Georgia Student Finance Commission
State Loans and Grants Division
Suite 245, 2082 E. Exchange Place
Tucker, GA 30084
404-414-3000
www.gsfc.org

State Department of Education
2054 Twin Towers E., 205 Butler Street
Atlanta, GA 30334-5040
404-656-5812
www.glc.k12.state.ga.us

Hawaii

Hawaii Department of Education
2530 10th Avenue, Rm. A12
Honolulu, HI 96816
808-733-9103
www.doe.k12.hi.us

Idaho

Idaho Board of Education
P.O. Box 83720
Boise, ID 83720-0037
208-334-2270
www.sde.state.id.us/osbe/board.htm

State Department of Education
650 West State Street
Boise, ID 83720
208-332-6800
www.sde.state.id.us

Illinois

Illinois Student Assistance Commission
1755 Lake Cook Road
Deerfield, IL 60015-5209
708-948-8500
www.isac1.org

Indiana

State Student Assistance Commission of
    Indiana
150 W. Market Street, Suite 500
Indianapolis, IN 46204-2811
317-232-2350; 888-528-4719;
    fax 317-232-3260
www.in.gov/ssaci

Indiana Department of Education
Rm. 229, State House
Indianapolis, IN 46204-2798
317-232-2305
ideanet.doe.state.in.us

Iowa

Iowa College Student Aid Commission
200 10th Street, 4th Floor
Des Moines, IA 50309-2036
515-242-3344
www.state.ia.us/collegeaid

Iowa Department of Education
Grimes State Office Building
Des Moines, IA 50319-0146
515-281-5294; fax 515-242-5988
www.state.ia.us/educate

Kansas

Kansas Board of Regents
1000 SW Jackson Street, Suite 520
Topeka, KS 66612-1368
785-296-3421
www.kansasregents.org

State Department of Education
Kansas State Education Building
120 E. Tenth Avenue
Topeka, KS 66612-1103
785-296-3201; fax 785-296-7933
www.ksbe.state.ks.us

Kentucky

Kentucky Higher Education Assistance
    Authority
Suite 102, 1050 U.S. 127 South
Frankfort, KY 40601-4323
800-928-8926
www.kheaa.com

State Department of Education
500 Mero Street
Frankfort, KY 40601
502-564-4770; 800-533-5372
www.kde.state.ky.us

Louisiana

Louisiana Student Financial Assistance
    Commission
Office of Student Financial Assistance
P.O. Box 91202
Baton Rouge, LA 70821-9202
800-259-5626
www.osfa.state.la.us

State Department of Education
P.O. Box 94064
626 North 4th Street, 12th Fl.
Baton Rouge, LA 70804-9064
504-342-2098; 877-453-2721
www.doe.state.la.us

Maine

Finance Authority of Maine
5 Community Drive
P.O. Box 949
Augusta, ME 04333-0949
207-287-3263; 800-228-3734;
    fax 207-623-0095
www.famemaine.com/html/education

Maine Department of Education
23 State House Station
Augusta, ME 04333-0023
207-287-5800; fax 207-287-5900
www.state.me.us/education

Maryland

Maryland Higher Education Commission
Jeffrey Building, 16 Francis Street
Annapolis, MD 21401-1781
410-974-2971
www.mhec.state.md.us

Maryland State Department of Education
200 West Baltimore Street
Baltimore, MD 21201-2595
410-767-0100
www.msde.state.md.us

Massachusetts

Massachusetts Board of Higher Education
One Ashburton Place, Room 1401
Boston, MA 02108
617-727-9420
www.mass.edu

State Department of Education
350 Main Street
Malden, MA 02148-5023
781-338-3300
www.doe.mass.edu

Massachusetts Higher Education Information
    Center
700 Boylston Street
Boston, MA 02116
617-536-0200; 877-332-4348
www.heic.org

Michigan

Michigan Higher Education Assistance
 Authority
Office of Scholarships and Grants
P.O. Box 30462
Lansing, MI 48909-7962
517-373-3394; 877-323-2287
www.mi-studentaid.org

Michigan Department of Education
608 West Allegan Street, Hannah Building
Lansing, MI 48909
517-373-3324
www.mde.state.mi.us

Mississippi

Mississippi Postsecondary Education
Financial Assistance Board
3825 Ridgewood Road
Jackson, MS 39211-6453
601-982-6663

State Department of Education
Central High School
P.O. Box 771
359 North West Street
Jackson, MS 39205-0771
601-359-3513
www.mde.k12.ms.us

Minnesota

Minnesota Higher Education Services Office
1450 Energy Park Drive, Suite 350
Saint Paul, MN 55108-5227
651-642-0533; 800-657-3866;
 fax: 651-642-0675
www.mheso.state.mn.us

Department of Children, Families, and
 Learning
1500 Highway 36 West
Roseville, MN 55113
651-582-8200
www.educ.state.mn.us

Missouri

Missouri Coordinating Board for Higher
 Education
3515 Amazonas Drive
Jefferson City, MI 65109-5717
314-751-2361; 800-473-6757;
 fax 573-751-6635
www.cbhe.state.mo.us

Missouri State Department of Elementary
 and Secondary Education
P.O. Box 480
Jefferson City, MI 65102-0480
573-751-4212; fax 573-751-8613
www.dese.state.mo.us

Montana

Montana Higher Education Student
  Assistance Corporation
2500 Broadway
Helena, MT 59620-3104
406-444-6597; 800-852-2761 x 0606;
  fax 406-444-0684
www.mhesac.org

Montana Office of the Commissioner of
  Higher Education
2500 Broadway
P.O. Box 203101
Helena, MT 59620-3101
406-444-6570; fax 406-444-1469
www.montana.edu/wwwoche

State Office of Public Instruction
P.O. Box 202501
Helena, MT 59620-2501
406-444-3680; 888-231-9393
www.metnet.state.mt.us

Nebraska

Coordinating Commission for Postsecondary
  Education
P.O. Box 95005
Lincoln, NE 68509-5005
402-471-2847; fax 402-471-2886
www.ccpe.state.ne.us

Nebraska Department of Education
301 Centennial Mall S.
Lincoln, NE 68509-4987
402-471-2295
www.nde.state.ne.us

Nevada

Nevada Department of Education
700 East Fifth Street
Carson City, NV 89701-5096
775-687-9200; fax 775-687-9101
www.nde.state.nv.us

New Hampshire

New Hampshire Postsecondary Education
  Commission
2 Industrial Park Drive
Concord, NH 03301-8512
603-271-2555; fax 603-271-2696
www.state.nh.us/postsecondary

State Department of Education
State Office Park South
101 Pleasant Street
Concord, NH 03301
603-271-3494; fax 603-271-1953
www.state.nh.us/doe

New Jersey

State of New Jersey
20 West State Street
P.O. Box 542
Trenton, NJ 08625-0542
609-292-4310;
    fax 609-292-7225; 800-792-8670
www.state.nj.us/highereducation

State Department of Education
225 West State Street
Trenton, NJ 08625-0500
609-984-6409
www.state.nj.us/education

New Mexico

New Mexico Commission on Higher
    Education
1068 Cerrillos Rd.
Santa Fe, NM 87501-4925
505-827-7383; fax 505-827-7392
www.nmche.org

State Department of Education
Education Building
300 Don Gaspar
Santa Fe, NM 87501-2786
505-827-6648
www.sde.state.nm.us

New York

New York State Higher Education Services
    Corporation
One Commerce Plaza
Albany, NY 12255
518-473-1574; 888-697-4372
www.hesc.state.ny.us

State Education Department
89 Washington Avenue
Albany, NY 12234
518-474-3852
www.nysed.gov

North Carolina

North Carolina State Education Assistance
    Authority
P.O. Box 14103
Research Triangle Park, NC 27709
919-549-8614; fax 919-549-8481
www.ncseaa.edu

State Department of Public Instruction
301 N. Wilmington Street
Raleigh, NC 27601
919-807-3300
www.dpi.state.nc.us

North Dakota

North Dakota University System/State Board
   of Higher Education
10th Floor, State Capitol Building
600 East Boulevard Avenue Dept. 215
Bismarck, ND 58505-0230
701-328-2960; fax 701-328-2961
www.ndus.edu/sbhe

State Department of Public Instruction
State Capitol Building, 11th Floor
600 East Boulevard Avenue, Dept. 201
Bismarck, ND 58505-0164
701-328-2260; fax 701-328-2461
www.dpi.state.nd.us

Ohio

State Department of Education
25 South Front Street
Columbus, OH 43266-0308
614-466-2761; 877-644-6338
www.ode.state.oh.us

Oklahoma

Oklahoma State Regents for Higher
   Education
655 Research Parkway, Suite 200
Oklahoma City, OK 73104
405-225-9100; fax 405-225-9230
www.okhighered.org

Oklahoma Guaranteed Student Loan
   Program
P.O. Box 3000
Oklahoma City, OK 73101-3000
405-858-4300;
   fax 405-234-4390; 800-247-0420
www.ogslp.org

State Department of Education
Oliver Hodge Memorial Education Building
2500 North Lincoln Boulevard
Oklahoma City, OK 73105-4599
405-521-4122; fax 405-521-6205
www.sde.state.ok.us

Oregon

Oregon Student Assistance Commission
Suite 100, 1500 Valley River Drive
Eugene, OR 97401-2130
503-687-7400
www.osac.state.or.us

Oregon State System of Higher Education
P.O. Box 3175
Eugene, OR 97403
541-346-5700
www.ous.edu

Oregon Department of Education
255 Capitol Street NE
Salem, OR 97310-0203
503-378-3569; fax 503-378-2892
www.ode.state.or.us

Pennsylvania

Pennsylvania Higher Education Assistance
   Agency
1200 North Seventh Street
Harrisburg, PA 17102-1444
800-692-7392
www.pheaa.org

Rhode Island

Rhode Island Office of Higher Education
301 Promenade Street
Providence, RI 02908-5748
401-222-2088; fax 401-222-2545
www.ribghe.org

Rhode Island Higher Education Assistance
   Authority
560 Jefferson Boulevard
Warwick, RI 02886
800-922-9855; fax 401-736-1100
www.riheaa.org

State Department of Education
225 Westminster Street
Providence, RI 02903
401-222-4600
www.ridoe.net

South Carolina

South Carolina Higher Education Tuition
   Grants Commission
101 Business Park Boulevard, Suite 2100
Columbia, SC 29203-9498
803-896-1120; fax 803-896-1126
www.sctuitiongrants.com

State Department of Education
1429 Senate Street
Columbia, SC 29201
803-734-8500
www.sde.state.sc.us

South Dakota

Department of Education and Cultural Affairs
700 Governors Drive
Pierre, SD 57501-2291
605-773-3134
www.state.sd.us/deca

South Dakota Board of Regents
306 East Capitol Avenue, Suite 200
Pierre, SD 57501-2409
605-773-3455
www.ris.sdbor.edu

Tennessee

Tennessee Higher Education Commission
404 James Robertson Parkway, Suite 1900
Nashville, TN 37243-0820
615-741-3605; fax 615-741-6230
www.state.tn.us/thec

State Department of Education
6th Floor, Andrew Johnson Tower
710 James Robertson Parkway
Nashville, TN 37243-0375
615-741-2731
www.state.tn.us/education

Texas

Texas Education Agency
1701 North Congress Avenue
Austin, TX 78701-1494
512-463-9734
www.tea.state.tx.us

Texas Higher Education Coordinating Board
P.O. Box 12788
Austin, TX 78711
512-427-6101; 800-242-3062
www.thecb.state.tx.us

Utah

Utah System of Higher Education
#3 Triad Center, Suite 550
Salt Lake City, UT 84180-1205
801-321-7101
www.utahsbr.edu

Utah State Office of Education
250 East 500 South
Salt Lake City, UT 84111
801-538-7500; fax 801-538-7521
www.usoe.k12.ut.us

Vermont

Vermont Student Assistance Corporation
Champlain Mill
P.O. Box 2000
Winooski, VT 05404-2601
802-655-9602; 800-642-3177;
    fax 802-654-3765
www.vsac.org

Vermont Department of Education
120 State Street
Montpelier, VT 05620-2501
802-828-3147; fax 802-828-3140
www.state.vt.us/educ

Virginia

State Council of Higher Education for
   Virginia
James Monroe Building
101 N. 14th Street
Richmond, VA 23219
804-225-2628; fax 804-225-2638
www.schev.edu

State Department of Education
P.O. Box 2120
Richmond, VA 23218-2120
800-292-3820
www.pen.k12.va.us

Washington

Washington State Higher Education
   Coordinating Board
P.O. Box 43430
917 Lakeridge Way, SW
Olympia, WA 98504-3430
206-753-7800
www.hecb.wa.gov

State Department of Public Instruction
Old Capitol Building
P.O. Box 47200
Olympia, WA 98504-7200
360-725-6000
www.k12.wa.us

West Virginia

State Department of Education
1900 Kanawha Boulevard East
Charleston, WV 25305
304-558-2691
wvde.state.wv.us

State College and University Systems of
   West Virginia Central Office
1018 Kanawha Boulevard East, Suite 700
Charleston, WV 25301-2827
304-558-2101; fax 304-558-5719
www.hepc.wvnet.edu

Wisconsin

Higher Educational Aids Board
P.O. Box 7885
Madison, WI 53707-7885
608-267-2206; fax 608-267-2808
www.heab.state.wi.us

State Department of Public Instruction
125 South Webster Street
P.O. Box 7841
Madison, WI 53707-7814
608-266-3390; 800-541-4563
www.dpi.state.wi.us

Wyoming

Wyoming State Department of Education
Hathaway Building, 2300 Capitol Avenue,
  2nd Floor
Cheyenne, WY 82002-0050
307-777-7675; fax 307-777-6234
www.k12.wy.us/wdehome.html

Wyoming Community College Commission
2020 Carey Avenue, 8th Floor
Cheyenne, WY 82002
307-777-7763; fax 307-777-6567
www.commission.wcc.edu

Puerto Rico

Council on Higher Education
P.O. Box 19900
San Juan, PR 00910-1900
787-724-7100
·www.ces.gobierno.pr

Department of Education
P. O. Box 190759
San Juan, PR 00919-0759
809-759-2000; fax 809-250-0275

United States Department of Education

Students.Gov (Students' Gateway to the
  United States Government)
400 Maryland Avenue, SW
ROB-3, Room 4004
Washington, DC 20202-5132
www.students.gov

United States Department of Education
Office of Postsecondary Education
1990 K Street, NW
Washington, DC 20006
www.ed.gov/offices/OPE/

Appendix B

Additional Resources

For additional information on the topics discussed in this book, refer to the following reading lists, which are organized by subject, and the list of job-search-related websites.

BUSINESS WRITING

Bartell, Karen H. *American Business English* (Ann Arbor: University of Michigan, 1995).

Chesla, Elizabeth. *Improve Your Writing for Work, 2nd edition.* (New York: LearningExpress, 2000).

Danziger, Elizabeth. *Get to the Point! Painless Advice for Writing Memos, Letters and E-mails Your Colleagues and Clients Will Understand* (New York: Three Rivers Press, 2001).

Heller, Bernard. *The 100 Most Difficult Business Letters You'll Ever Have to Write, Fax, or E-Mail* (New York: HarperBusiness, 1994).

Kirschman, DeaAnne. *Getting Down to Business: Successful Writing at Work* (New York: LearningExpress, 2002).

Raphaelson, Joel, and Keith Roman. *Writing That Works, Third Edition* (New York: Harper Resource, 2000).

COLLEGES

Chronicle Vocational School Manual : A Directory of Accredited Vocational and Technical Schools 2001–2002. Moravia, NY: Chronicle Guidance, 2001.

The College Board, *The College Handbook* (annual). New York: College Entrance Examination Board.

Peterson's Guide to Distance Learning Programs (annual). Princeton, NJ: Peterson's.

Peterson's Guide to Two-Year Colleges (annual). Princeton, NJ: Peterson's.

COVER LETTERS

Beatty, Richard H. *The Perfect Cover Letter*, 2nd ed. (New York: Wiley, 1997).

Besson, Taunee. *The Wall Street Journal National Business Employment Weekly: Cover Letters*, 3rd ed. (New York: Wiley, 1999).

Enelow, Wendy and Louise Kursmark. *Cover Letter Magic* (Indianapolis: Jist Works, 2000).

Marler, Patty and Jan Bailey Mattia. *Cover Letters Made Easy* (Lincolnwood, IL: NTC Publishing, 1995).

Yates, Martin. *Cover Letters That Knock 'Em Dead* (Holbrook, MA: Adams Media, 2000).

FINANCIAL AID

Cassidy, Daniel. *Last Minute College Financing* (Franklin Lakes, NJ: Career Press, 2000).

College Board. *College Costs & Financial Aid Handbook 2002*, 19th ed. (New York: College Entrance Examination Board, 2001).

Finney, David F. *Financing Your College Degree: A Guide for Adult Students* (New York: College Entrance Examination Board, 1997).

Kaplan, Benjamin. *How to Go to College Almost For Free* (New York: HarperCollins, 2001).

INTERNSHIPS

Anselmi, John, et al. *The Yale Daily News Guide to Internships* (annual) (New York: Kaplan).

Ehrlich Green, Marianne. *Internship Success: Real-World, Step-By-Step Advice on Getting the Most Out of Internships* (New York: McGraw-Hill, 2000).

Hamadeh, Samer and Mark Oldham. *America's Top Internships* (annual) (New York: Random House).

INTERVIEWS

Bloch, Deborah. *How to Have A Winning Interview* (Lincolnwood, IL: VGM Career Horizons, 1998).

Eyre, Vivian, et al. *Great Interview: Successful Strategies for Getting Hired* (New York: LearningExpress, 2000).

Fry, Ron. *101 Great Answers to the Toughest Interview Questions* (Franklin Lakes, NJ: Career Press, 2000).

Medley, H. Anthony. *Sweaty Palms: The Neglected Art of Being Interviewed* (Berkeley, CA: Ten Speed Press, 1992).

JOB HUNTING

U.S. Department of Labor. *Occupational Outlook Handbook* (annual) (Lincolnwood, IL: NTC Publishing).

Bolles, Richard Nelson. *What Color Is Your Parachute? 2002: A Practical Manual for Job-Hunters and Career-Changers* (Berkeley: Ten Speed Press, 2001).

Cubbage, Sue, and Marcia Williams. *National Job Hotline Directory: The Job Finder's Hot List* (River Forest, IL: Planning/Communications, 1998).

OFFICE POLITICS

Bell, Arthur and Dayle M. Smith. *Winning With Difficult People* (New York: Barron's Business Success Series, 1997).

Dobson, Deborah Singer and Michael Singer Dobson. *Enlightened Office Politics* (New York: Amacom, 2001).

Hawley, Casey Fitts. *100+ Tactics for Office Politics* (New York: Barrons, 2001).

Tarbell, Shirley. *Office Basics Made Easy* (New York: LearningExpress, 1997).

Wall, Bob. *Working Relationships: The Simple Truth About Getting Along With Friends and Foes at Work* (Palo Alto: Davies-Black, 1999).

RESUMES

Rich, Jason R. *Great Resume: Get Noticed, Get Hired* (New York: Learning-Express, 2000).

Whitcomb, Susan. *Resume Magic: Trade Secrets of a Professional Resume Writer* (Indianapolis: Jist Works, 1998).

Yates, Martin. *Resumes That Knock 'Em Dead* (Holbrook, MA: Adams Media, 2000).

SCHOLARSHIP GUIDES

Cassidy, Daniel J. *The Scholarship Book: The Complete Guide to Private-Sector Scholarships, Fellowships, Grants, and Loans for the Undergraduate* (annual) (New York: Prentice Hall).

McKee, Cynthia Ruiz and Philip McKee. *Cash for College: The Ultimate Guide to College Scholarships* (New York: Quill, 1999).

Schlachter, Gail, et al. *Scholarships 2002* (New York: Kaplan, 2001).

STUDYING

Chesla, Elizabeth. *Read Better, Remember More*, 2nd ed. (New York: LearningExpress, 2000).

Wood, Gail. *How to Study*, 2nd ed. (New York: LearningExpress, 2000).

TEST HELP

Ehrenhaft, George, et al. *Barron's How to Prepare for the SAT: American College Testing Assessment*, 12th ed. (New York: Barron's Educational, 2001).

Meyers, Judith. *The Secrets of Taking Any Test*, 2nd ed. (New York: LearningExpress, 2000).

Robinson, Adam, et al. *Cracking the SAT & PSAT* (annual) (Princeton, NJ: Princeton Review).

Appendix C

Directory of Training Programs

TWO- AND FOUR-YEAR SCHOOLS OFFERING PROGRAMS AND/OR DEGREES IN EXERCISE SCIENCE, PHYSICAL EDUCATION, FITNESS INSTRUCTION, OR OTHER FITNESS-RELATED SUBJECTS

Two-Year Community Colleges Offering Certificate and Associate Degree Programs in Exercise Science

Albuquerque Technical Vocational Institute, NM

Allan Hancock College, CA

Allegany College of Maryland, MD

Allen County Community College, KS

Alvin Community College, TX

American River College, CA

Angelina College, TX

Anoka-Ramsey Community College, MN

Antelope Valley College, CA

Austin Community College, TX

Bainbridge College, GA

Barton County Community College, KS

Bellevue Community College, WA

Bergen Community College, NJ

Bowling Green State University—Firelands, OH

Butler County Community College, PA

Butler County Community College, KS

Camden County College, NJ

Carl Albert State College, OK

Carteret Community College, NC

Central Community College, NE

Central Florida Community College, FL

Central Piedmont Community College, NC

Cerritos College, CA

Chabot College, CA

Chattanooga State Technical Community College, TN

Chesapeake College, MD

Chipola Junior College, FL

Cisco Junior College, TX

Cloud County Community College, KS

Clover Park Technical College, WA

Coastal Carolina Community College, NC

Coastal Georgia Community College, GA

College of DuPage, IL

Columbus State Community College, OH

Community College of Allegheny, PA

Community College of Baltimore County—Catonsville, MD

Compton Community College, CA

County College of Morris, NJ

Cowley County Community College, KS

Cuesta College, CA

Cypress College, CA

Darton College, GA

Davidson County Community College, NC

Delaware Technical & Community College—Owens Campus, DE

Delaware Technical & Community College—Stanton/Wilmington,
    DE

Des Moines Area Community College, IA

Eastern Oklahoma State College, OK

Eastern Wyoming College, WY

Edison Community College, FL

El Camino College, CA

El Paso Community College District, TX

Enterprise State Junior College, AL

Everett Community College, WA
Fayetteville Technical Community College, NC
Finger Lakes Community College, NY
Front Range Community College, CO
Fullerton College, CA
Fulton-Montgomery Community College, NY
Galveston College, TX
Garland County Community College, AR
Garrett Community College, MD
Gateway Community College, CT
Glendale Community College, AZ
Glendale Community College, CA
Gogebic Community College, MI
Grays Harbor College, WA
Greenfield Community College, MA
Grossmont College, CA
Gulf Coast Community College, FL
Hagerstown Community College, MD
Herkimer County Community College, NY
Highland Community College, KS
Hocking Technical College, OH
Holyoke Community College, MA
Houston Community College System, TX
Howard Community College, MD
Hutchinson Community College and Area Vocational School, KS
Independence Community College, KS
Indian River Community College, FL
Iowa Central Community College, IA
Iowa Lakes Community College, IA
Iowa Western Community College, IA
Irvine Valley College, CA
James H. Faulkner State Community College, AL
Kansas City Kansas Community College, KS
Kauai Community College, HI
Kirkwood Community College, IA
Kishwaukee College, IL

Lake City Community College, FL

Lake Land College, IL

Lake Washington Technical College, WA

Lane Community College, OR

Laredo Community College, TX

Lincoln Land Community College, IL

Lorain County Community College, OH

Luzerne County Community College, PA

Madison Area Technical College, WI

Manchester Community College, CT

McHenry County College, IL

McLennan Community College, TX

Merced College, CA

Merritt College, CA

Miami-Dade Community College, FL

Mid Michigan Community College, MI

Mohawk Valley Community College, NY

Monroe County Community College, MI

Moraine Valley Community College, IL

Mott Community College, MI

Mt. San Antonio College, CA

Muskegon Community College, MI

Muskingum Area Technical College, OH

Naugatuck Valley Community College, CT

New Hampshire Community Technical College—Manchester, NH

New Mexico Junior College, NM

North Dakota State College of Science, ND

North Shore Community College, MA

Northampton Community College, PA

Northeastern Oklahoma Agricultural and Mechanical College, OK

Northwestern Connecticut Community College, CT

Norwalk Community College, CT

Oakland Community College, MI

Oakton Community College, IL

Ohlone College, CA

Okaloosa-Walton Community College, FL

Onondaga Community College, NY
Orange Coast College, CA
Orange County Community College, NY
Palm Beach Community College, FL
Palomar College, CA
Pasadena City College, CA
Pensacola Junior College, FL
Pima County Community College District, AZ
Portland Community College, OR
Quinsigamond Community College, MA
Rainy River Community College, MN
Raritan Valley Community College, NJ
Redlands Community College, OK
Rend Lake College, IL
Renton Technical College, WA
Ridgewater College, MN
Rochester Community and Technical College, MN
Rose State College, OK
Rowan-Cabarrus Community College, NC
San Bernardino Valley College, CA
San Jose City College, CA
San Juan College, NM
Santa Barbara City College, CA
Santa Rosa Junior College, CA
Shelton State Community College, AL
Skagit Valley College, WA
Southeastern Community College, NC
Southwest Wisconsin Technical College, WI
Southwestern College, CA
Spokane Community College, WA
Spokane Falls Community College, WA
SUNY College of Agriculture and Technology at Morrisville, NY
SUNY College of Technology—Alfred, NY
SUNY College of Technology—Delhi, NY
Sussex County Community College, NJ
Tallahassee Community College, FL

Technical College of the Lowcountry, SC
Tompkins-Cortland Community College, NY
Trident Technical College, SC
Triton College, IL
Tyler Junior College, TX
Ulster County Community College, NY
Vance-Granville Community College, NC
Ventura College, CA
Vincennes University, IN
Wayne County Community College, MI
West Valley College, CA
Western Iowa Tech Community College, IA
Western Nevada Community College, NV
William Rainey Harper College, IL

Colleges and Universities Offering Four-Year Degree Programs in Exercise Science, Exercise Physiology, Physical Education, Human Performance, and Kinesiology

[see www.css.edu/users/tboone2/asep/graduate.htm for links to schools]
Abilene Christian University
Andrews University
Appalachian State University
Arizona State University
Arkansas State University
Auburn University
Austin State University
Ball State University
Barry University
Baylor University
Bloomsburg University
Boise State University
Brigham Young University
Buena Vista University
Cal Poly State University
California State University, Fresno

California State University, Fullerton
California State University, Long Beach
California State University, Northridge
Centenary College of Louisiana
Chapman University
College of St. Scholastica
Colorado State University
Concordia University
Creighton University
Creighton College of Arts and Sciences
East Carolina University
East Stroudsburg University
East Tennessee State University
Eastern Washington University
Florida Atlantic University
Fort Lewis College
Frostburg State University
Furman University
George Washington University
Grand Canyon University
Gustavus Adolphus College
Humboldt State University
Illinois State University
Iowa State University
Indiana University
Jacksonville State University
Kansas State University
Kent State University
Kennesaw State University
Louisiana State University
Louisiana Tech University
Maharishi University of Management
Mankato State University
Marquette University
McNeese State University
Miami University

Michigan State University
Montana State University
Montclair State University
Murray State University
Norfolk State University
Northern Arizona University
Northeast Louisiana University
Northeastern University
Northern Illinois University
Oakland University
Old Dominion University
Oregon State University
Purdue University
Queens College, City University of New York
Radford University
Rice University
San Diego State University
San Francisco State University
Southern California College
Southern Connecticut State University
Southern Illinois University, Carbondale
Southeastern Louisiana University
State University of New York at Buffalo
St. Cloud State University
Syracuse University
Texas Woman's University
Thomas More College
Truman State University
Tulane University
University of California, Davis
University of Central Arkansas
University of Georgia
University of Colorado, Boulder
University of Connecticut
University of Dayton
University of Florida

University of Houston

University of Kansas

University of Kentucky

University of Illinois, Urbana-Champaign

University of Iowa

University of Louisville

University of Maryland, College Park

University of Massachusetts, Amherst

University of Memphis

University of Miami

University of Michigan, Ann Arbor

University of Minnesota

University of Minnesota, Duluth

University of Missouri, Columbia

University of Mississippi

University of Montana

University of Nebraska, Lincoln

University of Nebraska, Omaha

University of New Mexico, Albuquerque

University of North Carolina, Chapel Hill

University of North Carolina, Greensboro

University of North Dakota

University of North Texas, Denton

University of Northern Iowa

University of Oregon

University of Pittsburgh

University of San Francisco

University of Southern California, Los Angeles

University of Tennessee

University of Texas, Austin

University of Texas, Tyler

University of Utah

University of Wisconsin, Madison

University of Wisconsin, Milwaukee

Ursinus College

Utah State University

Virginia Tech
Wake Forest University
Washington State University
West Chester University
West Texas A&M University
West Virginia University
Western Maryland College
Western Michigan University
Willamette University
York University

YOGA TEACHER TRAINING SCHOOLS

Yoga Alliance (www.yogaalliance.org) has a directory of all schools in the United States that meet their educational standards. You may search the directory free, either by state, city, or school name, to find institutions that meet your criteria.

Various States

Atma Yoga
200-hour program
Massachusetts, North Carolina, and other
    locations.
413-528-6408

Integrative Yoga Therapy
200-hour teacher training. 500-hour yoga
    therapist training.

California, Florida, Ohio, and
    Massachusetts. Registered with Yoga
    Alliance.
800-750-9642

International Yoga
500-hour non-residential program
602-759-1972

Kundalini Yoga
(as taught by Yogi Bhajan)
200-hour teacher training program in 18
    countries
505-753-0423

Arkansas

Arkansas Barefoot Studio in Little Rock
200- and 500-hour programs
Registered by Yoga Alliance
501-661-8005

California

Bikram's Yoga College of India
90-day training
Beverly Hills, CA
310-854-5800

Planet Yoga
Two-week intensives followed by a
    mentoring program
Hermosa Beach, CA
310-376-5354

YogaFit
2.5-day program
Hermosa Beach, CA
310-798-8773

Sivananda
1-month residential programs
Locations in Woodburne, NY; Quebec,
    Canada; Jamaica; and Grass Valley, CA.
514-279-3545

Master Yoga Academy
9-month (500 hours) and 4-week (250 hours)
    programs
La Jolla, CA
800-LUV-YOGA or 858-454-6978

Stress Management Center of Marin
200- and 500-hour programs
Larkspur, CA
415-461-2288

Ananda
Month-long residential program
Nevada City, CA
800-346-5350

It's Yoga
14- and 28-day programs in Ashtanga
San Francisco, CA
415-543-1970

Integral Yoga Institute of San Francisco
4-both, part-time training (270 hours)
San Francisco, CA
415-821-1117

Santa Barbara Yoga Center
11-day intensives and full certification
    program
Santa Barbara, CA
805-965-6045

White Lotus
Two-week residential program
Santa Barbara, CA
805-964-1944

Kali Ray TriYoga
Ongoing teacher training intensives
Santa Cruz, CA and Great Barrington, MA
310-589-0600

Yoga Mandir
18 month Teacher and Director training
    program
Santa Monica, CA
310-395-0054

Yoga Research and Education Center
700-hour teacher training extending over 2
    years. 200-hour Viniyoga intensive.
Santa Rosa, CA
707-566-9000

American Yoga College

Registered with Yoga Alliance 200 and 500
   hour programs;

Locations in San Francisco Bay Area and
   national affiliates.

Walnut Creek, CA

888-949-9642

Mt. Madonna

Month-long residential Ashtanga program

Watsonville, CA

408-847-0406

Colorado

Gentle Touch Body Mind Spirit Connection

10 month, 250 hour training plus
   continuation education classes

Denver, CO

303-458-0922

Shoshoni Retreat Center

Month-long residential

Rollinsville, CO

303-642-0116

Florida

Yogi Hari's Ashram

2-week courses

Ft. Lauderdale, FL

954-563-4946

www.yogihari.com

Yoga and Inner Peace

Six-week, non-residential intensive

Lake Worth (near West Palm Beach), FL

651-641-8888

PremYoga

Exceeds Yoga Alliance requirements

Palm Beach, Fl

561-615-8603

Florida Institute for Integrated Yoga

Two-year weekend program, eclectic
   perspective

Tampa, FL

813-932-5456

Discovery Yoga

200-hour program, Yoga Alliance registered

St. Augustine, FL

904-827-9046

Georgia

Healthy Alternatives

Weekend program

Atlanta, GA

770-966-5184

Hawaii

American Viniyoga Institute

8-session program led by Gary Kraftsow

Makawao, HI

808-572-1414

Illinois

Kriya Yoga
Two non-resident programs: 210 hour Level I
program
100 hour Level II program
Chicago, IL
773-342-4600

Kansas

Kansas Barefoot Studio in Wichita
200 and 500 hour programs
Registered by Yoga Alliance
316-636-YOGA

Maine

Yoga Center of Maine and YOGAspirit
Studios
200-hour program. Yoga Alliance registered.
Auburn, ME
207-786-0100

Massachusetts

Kali Ray TriYoga
Ongoing teacher training intensives
Santa Cruz, CA and Great Barrington, MA
310-589-0600

Kripalu
1 month residential program or
3-segment option (3, 10-day segments)
Lenox, MA
800-741-7353

Kali Ray TriYoga Waltham
(Ongoing teacher training program)
Waltham, MA
781-863-1566

Michigan

Jonny Kest
Birmingham, MI
248-258-1777

New Jersey

The Energy Center
10–20 week yoga training; online; intensives
Berkeley Heights, NJ
908-464-6894

Freehold Yoga Center
6-month program
732-463-YOGA

Studio Yoga (Iyengar)
4 levels of non-resident teacher education
Madison, NJ
888-678-9642

Starseed
9-month part-time program
Montclair, NJ
973-783-1036

Yoga Synthesis
Various locations
973-962-4420

New Mexico

Kundalini Yoga
(as taught by Yogi Bhajan)
17 day teacher training intensive
1-888-346-2420

New York

Integral Yoga Institute
4 month, part-time program
New York, NY
212-929-0586

Rasa Yoga
300-hour teacher training program.
    Registered with Yoga Alliance.
New York, NY
866-875-0475

Sivananda
1 month residential programs
Locations in Woodburne, NY; Quebec,
    Canada; Jamaica; and Grass Valley, CA.
514-279-3545

Ohio

Bhumi's Yoga and Wellness Center
200 and 500 hour programs. Registered with
    Yoga Alliance.
Cleveland, OH
440-899-9569

T.R.Y. for Life Therapy
Cleveland, OH
Ursuline Sophia Center/East and St. Joseph
    Wellness Center/West
440-442-4160 x2 or 216-251-7062 x316

Ursuline Sophia Wellness Center
Yoga Teacher Certification Program
Pepper Pike, OH
440-442-4160 x2

Pennsylvania

Himalayan Institute
2-week residential program, plus ongoing
    correspondence course
Honesdale, PA
1-800-822-4547

Tennessee

The Southern Institute for Yoga Instructors
A 1,000-hour certification program at a Yoga
    Alliance registered school.
Nashville, TN
615-383-6197

Texas

Kundalini Yoga
8-month program
Austin, TX
512-326-3900

Living Yoga
200-hour certification
Austin, TX
512-266-7926

Virginia

One-Yoga
Rolling 1-year program taught by JJ Gormley
    and Suzie Hurley.
Arlington, VA
888-786-9642 (1-888-SUN-YOGA)

Integral Yoga International
1-month residential program
Buckingham, VA
800-858-YOGA (9642)

Washington

Discover Yoga
6-month intensive with Ellen Morell
Redmond, WA
425-861-1318

Center for Yoga of Seattle
2-year part-time program and 6-day
    intensives
800-964-2669 or 206-526-9642

Yoga Lodge on Whidbey Island
1-month residential program
Greenbank, WA
360-678-2120

PILATES TEACHER TRAINING SCHOOLS

California

On Center Conditioning
www.oncenterconditioning.com
Costa Mesa, CA
949-642-6970

The Energy Within
www.stottenergy.com
Encinatas, CA
760-942-0288

Colorado

The Pilates Center of Boulder
4800 Baseline Road, Suite D206
Boulder, CO 80303
303-494-3400

Florida

All American Pilates Certification
2730 South Ocean Boulevard
Palm Beach, FL 33480
561-795-1219

Polestar Education LLC
1500 Monza Avenue, Suite 350
Coral Gables, FL
800-387-3651

Inside Out Method
www.insideoutmethod.com
Miami, FL
305-573-4430

Massachusetts

Back and Body Studio
182 Summer Street
Kingston, MA 02364
781-585-1188

New Mexico

PhysicalMind Institute
1807 Second Street, Suite 40
Santa Fe, NM 87505
800-505-1990

Core Dynamics, Inc. (Michele Larsson)
www.coredynamicspilates.com
Santa Fe, NM
505-988-5076

Momentum
www.momentum-studio.com
Santa Fe, NM
505-992-8000

New York

Pilates Studio of New York
888-474-5283

The Physicalmind Institute
www.themethodpilates.com
84 Wooster Street
New York, NY 10012
800-505-1990

The Pilates Studio®
New York, NY
800-4-PILATES

Movements Afoot
www.movementsafoot.com
New York, NY
212-904-1399

The Inside Scoop
www.theinsidescoop.net
Plainview, NY
516-802-8248

In Balance Studio—On The Harbor
L.Salvani@aol.com
New York, NY
212-904-1399

Power Pilates
New York, NY
212-371-0700

North Carolina

Pilates Certification Center
3900 Merton Drive, Suite 100
Raleigh, NC 27609
919-787-0508

Texas

The Pilates Center of Austin
Austin, TX
512-467-8009

Glenn Studio, Inc.
Dallas, TX
1-877-528-3335

Certifying Studio List

All About Movement
www.allaboutmovement.com
Wellesley, MA
781-446-6224

Body By Design
cmcinri@aol.com
Providence, RI
401-351-0767

Bodywork/Mexa-Se Studio
Weston, CT
203-226-8550

Shore Pilates Center LLC
www.shorepilatescenter.com
Spring Lake Heights, NJ
732-282-0600

balanCenter
home.earthlink.net/~bcpilates
Bala Cynwyd, PA
610-747-0170

Body College
www.bodycollege.com
Washington, DC
202-237-0080

Body College
www.bodycollege.com
Rockville, MD
301-230-2526

Thinking Body
www.thinkingbody.com
Charlottesville, VA
434-975-0336

Center For Creative Healing
annmcconville@aol.com
Raleigh, NC
919-787-3818

Embodyment
www.embodymentstudio.com
Columbia, SC
803-256-2920

Balanced Movement
www.balancedbody.com
Bogart, GA
706-207-2805

Body Wise Studios
bodywisestudios@bellsouth.net
904-827-1669
St. Augustine, FL

Sanctuary 7
Miami, FL
305-794-2825

The B-Fit Center
www.bfitcenter.com
Tampa, FL
813-915-8223

Body firm
Louisville, KY
502-899-9890

Essence In Movement
taradance@cinci.rr.com
Cincinnati, OH
513-792-2300

Lonna Mosow's Center
for Mind Body Fitness
lonnamosow@aol.com
Eden Prairie, MN
612-941-9448

Body Evolve
bodyevolve@earthlink.net
Highland Park, IL
847-926-8490

Leslie's Total Fitness
LTFPilates@msn.com
Chicago, IL
312-751-1256

Wise Body Lafayette
wisebody@bellsouth.net
Lafayette, LA
337-593-9292

A Work In Progress
Tulsa, OK
918-743-1339

Oasis Mind-Body
Conditioning Center
www.oasisbody.com
Dallas, TX
214-692-6613

Dancescape Studio
www.dancescapestudio.com
Fort Worth, TX
817-924-4048

Eastside Studio
Houston, TX
713-526-8043

VIM Studio
www.vimpilates.com
Austin, TX
512-301-9599

Center Strength
Denver, CO
303-333-6674

Katrina Viehmann
www.personalizedpilates.com
Scottsdale, AZ
602-750-5799

Momentum
Santa Fe, NM
505-992-8000

Bodyline Fitness Studio
www.bodylinela.com
Beverly Hills, CA
310-274-2716

Synergy Systems
www.synergypilates.com
Encinitas, CA
760-632-5677

Center of Balance
www.centerofbalance.com
Mt. View, CA
650-967-6414

Mind-Body Connection
mindbody2@yahoo.com
Oakland, CA
510-420-0444

On Balance Inc.
onbalancestudio@hawaii.rr.com
Honolulu, HI
808-262-2528

Bodies In Balance
www.bodiesinbalanceofportland.com
Portland, OR
503-248-4483

Appendix D

Sample Free Application for Federal Student Aid (FAFSA)

On the following pages you will find a sample FAFSA. Use this sample to familiarize yourself with the form so that when you apply for federal, and state student grants, work-study, and loans, you will know what information you need to have ready. At print this was the most current form, and although the form remains mostly the same from year to year, you should check the FAFSA website (www.fafsa.ed.gov) for the most current information.

2002-2003

The FAFSA ℠

July 1, 2002 — June 30, 2003
Free Application for Federal Student Aid

OMB # 1845-0001

Use this form to apply for federal and state* student grants, work-study, and loans.

Apply free with FAFSA *on the Web* **www.fafsa.ed.gov**

1. If you are filing a **2001 federal income tax return,** we recommend that you complete it before filling out this form. However, you do not need to file your income tax return with the IRS before you submit this form.

If you or your family has **unusual circumstances not shown on this form** (such as loss of employment) that might affect your need for student financial aid, submit this form and then consult with the financial aid office at the college you plan to attend.

You may also use this form to apply for **aid from other sources, such as your state or college.** The deadlines for states (see table to right) or colleges may be as early as January 2002 and may differ. You may be required to complete additional forms. Check with your high school guidance counselor or a financial aid administrator at your college about state and college sources of student aid and deadlines.

2. Your answers on this form will be read electronically. Therefore:

- use black ink and fill in ovals completely:
- print clearly in CAPITAL letters and skip a box between words:
- report dollar amounts (such as $12,356.41) like this:

Correct ● Incorrect ⊗ ⊘

| 1 | 5 | | E | L | M | | S | T |

$ | | 1 | 2 | , | 3 | 5 | 6 | **no cents**

Blue is for students and purple is for parents.

If you have questions about this application, or for more information on eligibility requirements and the U.S. Department of Education's student aid programs, look on the Internet at **www.ed.gov/studentaid.** You can also call 1-800-4FED-AID (1-800-433-3243) seven days a week from 8:00 a.m. through midnight (Eastern time). TTY users may call 1-800-730-8913.

3. After you complete this application, make a copy of it for your records. Then **mail the original of only pages 3 through 6** in the attached envelope or send it to: Federal Student Aid Programs, P.O. Box 4001, Mt. Vernon, IL 62864-8601.

You should submit your application as early as possible, but no earlier than January 1, 2002. We must receive your application **no later than June 30, 2003.** Your college must have your correct, complete information by your last day of enrollment in the 2002-2003 school year.

You should hear from us within four weeks. If you do not, please check on-line at **www.fafsa.ed.gov** or call 1-800-433-3243.

4. Now go to page 3 and begin filling out this form.
Refer to the notes as instructed.

STATE AID DEADLINES

A R   April 1, 2002 *(date received)*
A Z   June 30, 2003 *(date received)*
*^C A   For initial awards – March 2, 2002
         For community college awards – September 2, 2002 *(date postmarked)*
* DC   June 28, 2002 *(date received by state)*
 DE   April 15, 2002 *(date received)*
 FL   May 15, 2002 *(date processed)*
^ I A   July 1, 2002 *(date received)*
 IL   For priority consideration, first-time applicants – September 30, 2002
       For priority consideration, continuing applicants – August 15, 2002 *(date received)*
^ IN   March 1, 2002 *(date postmarked)*
* KS   For priority consideration – April 1, 2002 *(date received)*
 KY   For priority consideration – March 15, 2002 *(date received)*
^ L A   For priority consideration – May 1, 2002
         Final deadline – July 1, 2002 *(date received)*
^ M A   For priority consideration – May 1, 2002 *(date received)*
 M D   March 1, 2002 *(date postmarked)*
 M E   May 1, 2002 *(date received)*
 M I   High school seniors – February 21, 2002
         College students – March 21, 2002 *(date received)*
 M N   June 30, 2003 *(date received)*
 M O   April 1, 2002 *(date received)*
 M T   For priority consideration – March 1, 2002 *(date postmarked)*
 NC   March 15, 2002 *(date received)*
 ND   April 15, 2002 *(date processed)*
 NH   May 1, 2002 *(date received)*
^ N J   June 1, 2002 if you received a Tuition Aid Grant in 2001-2002
         All other applicants
         – October 1, 2002, for fall and spring terms
         – March 1, 2003, for spring term only *(date received)*
*^NY   May 1, 2003 *(date postmarked)*
 OH   October 1, 2002 *(date received)*
 OK   For priority consideration – April 30, 2002
         Final deadline – June 30, 2002 *(date received)*
 OR   For priority consideration – March 1, 2002 *(date received)*
* P A   All 2001-2002 State Grant recipients and all non-2001-2002 State Grant recipients in degree programs – May 1, 2002
         All other applicants – August 1, 2002 *(date received)*
 PR   May 2, 2003 *(date application signed)*
 RI   March 1, 2002 *(date received)*
 S C   June 30, 2002 *(date received)*
 T N   May 1, 2002 *(date processed)*
*^W V   March 1, 2002 *(date received)*

Check with your financial aid administrator for these states: AK, AL, *AS, *CT, CO, *FM, GA, *GU, *HI, ID, *MH, *MP, MS, *NE, *NM, *NV, *PW, *SD, *TX, UT, *VA, *VI, *VT, WA, WI, and *WY.

^ *Applicants encouraged to obtain proof of mailing.*
* *Additional form may be required.*

STATE AID DEADLINES

Notes for questions 13–14 (page 3)

If you are an eligible noncitizen, write in your eight- or nine-digit Alien Registration Number. Generally, you are an eligible noncitizen if you are: (1) a U.S. permanent resident and you have an Alien Registration Receipt Card (I-551); (2) a conditional permanent resident (I-551C); or (3) an other eligible noncitizen with an Arrival-Departure Record (I-94) from the U.S. Immigration and Naturalization Service showing any one of the following designations: "Refugee," "Asylum Granted," "Indefinite Parole," "Humanitarian Parole," or "Cuban-Haitian Entrant." If you are in the U.S. on only an F1 or F2 student visa, or only a J1 or J2 exchange visitor visa, or a G series visa (pertaining to international organizations), you must fill in oval c. If you are neither a citizen nor eligible noncitizen, you are not eligible for federal student aid. However, you may be eligible for state or college aid.

Notes for questions 17–21 (page 3)

For undergraduates, full time generally means taking at least 12 credit hours in a term or 24 clock hours per week. 3/4 time generally means taking at least 9 credit hours in a term or 18 clock hours per week. Half time generally means taking at least 6 credit hours in a term or 12 clock hours per week. Provide this information about the college you plan to attend.

Notes for question 29 (page 3) — Enter the correct number in the box in question 29.

Enter **1** for 1st bachelor's degree
Enter **2** for 2nd bachelor's degree
Enter **3** for associate degree (occupational or technical program)
Enter **4** for associate degree (general education or transfer program)
Enter **5** for certificate or diploma for completing an occupational, technical, or educational program of less than two years
Enter **6** for certificate or diploma for completing an occupational, technical, or educational program of at least two years
Enter **7** for teaching credential program (nondegree program)
Enter **8** for graduate or professional degree
Enter **9** for other/undecided

Notes for question 30 (page 3) — Enter the correct number in the box in question 30.

Enter **0** for never attended college & 1st year undergraduate
Enter **1** for attended college before & 1st year undergraduate
Enter **2** for 2nd year undergraduate/sophomore
Enter **3** for 3rd year undergraduate/junior
Enter **4** for 4th year undergraduate/senior
Enter **5** for 5th year/other undergraduate
Enter **6** for 1st year graduate/professional
Enter **7** for continuing graduate/professional or beyond

Notes for questions 37 c. and d. (page 4) and 71 c. and d. (page 5)

If you filed or will file a foreign tax return, or a tax return with Puerto Rico, Guam, American Samoa, the U.S. Virgin Islands, the Marshall Islands, the Federated States of Micronesia, or Palau, use the information from that return to fill out this form. If you filed a foreign return, convert all figures to U.S. dollars, using the exchange rate that is in effect today.

Notes for questions 38 (page 4) and 72 (page 5)

In general, a person is eligible to file a 1040A or 1040EZ if he or she makes less than $50,000, does not itemize deductions, does not receive income from his or her own business or farm, and does not receive alimony. A person is not eligible if he or she itemizes deductions, receives self-employment income or alimony, or is required to file Schedule D for capital gains.

Notes for questions 41 (page 4) and 75 (page 5) — only for people who filed a 1040EZ or Telefile

On the 1040EZ, if a person answered "Yes" on line 5, use EZ worksheet line F to determine the number of exemptions ($2,900 equals one exemption). If a person answered "No" on line 5, enter 01 if he or she is single, or 02 if he or she is married.

On the Telefile, use line J(2) to determine the number of exemptions ($2,900 equals one exemption).

Notes for questions 47–48 (page 4) and 81–82 (page 5)

Net worth means current value minus debt. If net worth is one million or more, enter $999,999. If net worth is negative, enter 0.

Investments include real estate (do not include the home you live in), trust funds, money market funds, mutual funds, certificates of deposit, stocks, stock options, bonds, other securities, education IRAs, college savings plans, installment and land sale contracts (including mortgages held), commodities, etc. Investment value includes the market value of these investments as of today. Investment debt means only those debts that are related to the investments.

Investments do not include the home you live in, cash, savings, checking accounts, the value of life insurance and retirement plans (pension funds, annuities, noneducation IRAs, Keogh plans, etc.), or the value of prepaid tuition plans.

Business and/or investment farm value includes the market value of land, buildings, machinery, equipment, inventory, etc. Business and/or investment farm debt means only those debts for which the business or investment farm was used as collateral.

Notes for question 58 (page 4)

Answer **"No"** (you are not a veteran) if you (1) have never engaged in active duty in the U.S. Armed Forces, (2) are currently an ROTC student or a cadet or midshipman at a service academy, or (3) are a National Guard or Reserves enlistee activated only for training. Also answer "No" if you are currently serving in the U.S. Armed Forces and will continue to serve through June 30, 2003.

Answer **"Yes"** (you are a veteran) if you (1) have engaged in active duty in the U.S. Armed Forces (Army, Navy, Air Force, Marines, or Coast Guard) or as a member of the National Guard or Reserves who was called to active duty for purposes other than training, or were a cadet or midshipman at one of the service academies, **and** (2) were released under a condition other than dishonorable. Also answer "Yes" if you are not a veteran now but will be one by June 30, 2003.

The 2002-2003 FAFSA℠

Free Application for Federal Student Aid
For July 1, 2002 — June 30, 2003

OMB # 1845-0001

Step One: For questions 1-34, leave blank any questions that do not apply to you (the student).

1-3. Your full name (as it appears on your Social Security card)

1. LAST NAME

2. FIRST NAME

3. MIDDLE INITIAL

4-7. Your permanent mailing address

4. NUMBER AND STREET (INCLUDE APT. NUMBER)

5. CITY (AND COUNTRY IF NOT U.S.)

6. STATE

7. ZIP CODE

8. Your Social Security Number

9. Your date of birth   / / 1 9

10. Your permanent telephone number   ( ) –

11-12. Your driver's license number and state (if any)

11. LICENSE NUMBER

12. STATE

13. Are you a U.S. citizen? Pick one. **See page 2.**

a. Yes, I am a U.S. citizen. **Skip to question 15** .... ○ 1
b. No, but I am an eligible noncitizen. **Fill in question 14.** .... ○ 2
c. No, I am not a citizen or eligible noncitizen. .... ○ 3

14. ALIEN REGISTRATION NUMBER
A

15. What is your marital status as of today?

I am single, divorced, or widowed ..... ○ 1
I am married/remarried .... ○ 2
I am separated .... ○ 3

16. Month and year you were married, separated, divorced, or widowed

MONTH   YEAR   /

For each question (17 - 21), please mark whether you will be full time, 3/4 time, half time, less than half time, or not attending. **See page 2.**

17. Summer 2002	Full time/Not sure ○ 1	3/4 time ○ 2	Half time ○ 3	Less than half time ○ 4	Not attending ○ 5
18. Fall 2002	Full time/Not sure ○ 1	3/4 time ○ 2	Half time ○ 3	Less than half time ○ 4	Not attending ○ 5
19. Winter 2002-2003	Full time/Not sure ○ 1	3/4 time ○ 2	Half time ○ 3	Less than half time ○ 4	Not attending ○ 5
20. Spring 2003	Full time/Not sure ○ 1	3/4 time ○ 2	Half time ○ 3	Less than half time ○ 4	Not attending ○ 5
21. Summer 2003	Full time/Not sure ○ 1	3/4 time ○ 2	Half time ○ 3	Less than half time ○ 4	Not attending ○ 5

22. Highest school your father completed	Middle school/Jr. High ○ 1	High school ○ 2	College or beyond ○ 3	Other/unknown ○ 4
23. Highest school your mother completed	Middle school/Jr. High ○ 1	High school ○ 2	College or beyond ○ 3	Other/unknown ○ 4

24. What is your state of legal residence?   STATE

25. Did you become a legal resident of this state before January 1, 1997?   Yes ○ 1   No ○ 2

26. If the answer to question 25 is **"No,"** give month and year you became a legal resident.   MONTH   YEAR   /

27. Are you male? (Most male students must register with Selective Service to get federal aid.)   Yes ○ 1   No ○ 2
28. If you are male (age 18-25) and not registered, answer "Yes" and Selective Service will register you.   Yes ○ 1   No ○ 2

29. What degree or certificate will you be working on during 2002-2003? **See page 2** and enter the correct number in the box.

30. What will be your grade level when you begin the 2002-2003 school year? **See page 2** and enter the correct number in the box.

31. Will you have a high school diploma or GED before you enroll?   Yes ○ 1   No ○ 2
32. Will you have your first bachelor's degree before July 1, 2002?   Yes ○ 1   No ○ 2
33. In addition to grants, are you interested in student loans (which you must pay back)?   Yes ○ 1   No ○ 2
34. In addition to grants, are you interested in "work-study" (which you earn through work)?   Yes ○ 1   No ○ 2

35. Do not leave this question blank. Have you ever been convicted of possessing or selling illegal drugs? If you have, answer "Yes," complete and submit this application, and we will send you a worksheet in the mail for you to determine if your conviction affects your eligibility for aid.

No ○ 1
Yes ○ 3

DO NOT LEAVE QUESTION 35 BLANK

Step Two:
For questions 36-49, report your (the student's) income and assets. If you are married today, report your and your spouse's income and assets, even if you were not married in 2001. Ignore references to "spouse" if you are currently single, separated, divorced, or widowed.

36. For 2001, have you (the student) completed your IRS income tax return or another tax return listed in **question 37**?

a. I have already completed my return. ○ 1   b. I will file, but I have not yet ○ 2 completed my return.   c. I'm not going to file. **(Skip to question 42.)** ○ 3

37. What income tax return did you file or will you file for 2001?

a. IRS 1040 .... ○ 1
b. IRS 1040A, 1040EZ, 1040Telefile .... ○ 2
c. A foreign tax return. **See page 2.** .... ○ 3
d. A tax return for Puerto Rico, Guam, American Samoa, the U.S. Virgin Islands, the Marshall Islands, the Federated States of Micronesia, or Palau. **See page 2.** .... ○ 4

38. If you have filed or will file a 1040, were you eligible to file a 1040A or 1040EZ? **See page 2.**   Yes ○ 1   No ○ 2   Don't Know ○ 3

For questions 39-51, if the answer is zero or the question does not apply to you, enter 0.

39. What was your (and spouse's) adjusted gross income for 2001? Adjusted gross income is on IRS Form 1040–line 33; 1040A–line 19; 1040EZ–line 4; or Telefile–line I. $ ☐☐ , ☐☐☐

40. Enter the total amount of your (and spouse's) income tax for 2001. Income tax amount is on IRS Form 1040–lines 50 + 52; 1040A–lines 32 + 34; 1040EZ–line 11; or Telefile–line K(2). $ ☐☐ , ☐☐☐

41. Enter your (and spouse's) exemptions for 2001. Exemptions are on IRS Form 1040–line 6d or on Form 1040A–line 6d. For Form 1040EZ or Telefile, **see page 2.**   ☐☐

42-43. How much did you (and spouse) earn from working (wages, salaries, tips, etc.) in 2001? Answer this question whether or not you filed a tax return. This information may be on your W-2 forms, or on IRS Form 1040–lines 7 + 12 + 18; 1040A–line 7; or 1040EZ–line 1. Telefilers should use their W-2 forms.

You (42) $ ☐☐ , ☐☐☐
Your Spouse (43) $ ☐☐ , ☐☐☐

Student (and Spouse) Worksheets (44-46)

44-46. Go to page 8 and complete the columns on the left of Worksheets A, B, and C. Enter the student (and spouse) totals in questions 44, 45, and 46, respectively. Even though you may have few of the Worksheet items, check each line carefully.

Worksheet A (44) $ ☐☐ , ☐☐☐
Worksheet B (45) $ ☐☐ , ☐☐☐
Worksheet C (46) $ ☐☐ , ☐☐☐

47. As of today, what is the net worth of your (and spouse's) current **investments**? **See page 2.** $ ☐☐ , ☐☐☐

48. As of today, what is the net worth of your (and spouse's) current **businesses and/or investment farms**? **See page 2.** Do not include a farm that you live on and operate. $ ☐☐ , ☐☐☐

49. As of today, what is your (and spouse's) total current balance of **cash, savings, and checking accounts**? Do not include student financial aid. $ ☐☐ , ☐☐☐

50-51. If you receive veterans' education benefits, for **how many months** from July 1, 2002 through June 30, 2003 will you receive these benefits, and **what amount** will you receive per month? Do not include your spouse's veterans education benefits.

Months (50) ☐☐
Amount (51) $ ☐☐☐

Step Three:
Answer all seven questions in this step.

52. Were you born before January 1, 1979? ....   Yes ○ 1   No ○ 2

53. During the school year 2002-2003, will you be working on a master's or doctorate program (such as an MA, MBA, MD, JD, PhD, EdD, or graduate certificate, etc.)? ....   Yes ○ 1   No ○ 2

54. As of today, are you married? (Answer "Yes" if you are separated but not divorced.) ....   Yes ○ 1   No ○ 2

55. Do you have children who receive more than half of their support from you? ....   Yes ○ 1   No ○ 2

56. Do you have dependents (other than your children or spouse) who live with you and who receive more than half of their support from you, now and through June 30, 2003? ....   Yes ○ 1   No ○ 2

57. Are you an orphan, or are you or were you (until age 18) a ward/dependent of the court? ....   Yes ○ 1   No ○ 2

58. Are you a veteran of the U.S. Armed Forces? **See page 2.** ....   Yes ○ 1   No ○ 2

If you (the student) answer "No" to every question in Step Three, go to Step Four.

If you answer "Yes" to any question in Step Three, skip Step Four and go to Step Five on page 6.

(If you are a health profession student, your school may require you to complete Step Four even if you answered "Yes" in Step Three.)

Step Four: Complete this step if you (the student) answered "No" to all questions in Step Three.

59. Go to page 7 to determine who is considered a parent for this step. What is your parents' marital status as of today?

(Pick one.)   Married/Remarried ○ 1   Single ○ 2   Divorced/Separated ○ 3   Widowed ○ 4

60-63. What are the Social Security Numbers and last names of the parents reporting information on this form? If your parent does not have a Social Security Number, enter **000-00-0000**

60. FATHER'S/STEPFATHER'S SOCIAL SECURITY NUMBER ☐☐☐ – ☐☐ – ☐☐☐☐

61. FATHER'S/ STEPFATHER'S LAST NAME ☐☐☐☐☐☐☐☐☐☐☐☐☐☐☐☐

62. MOTHER'S/STEPMOTHER'S SOCIAL SECURITY NUMBER ☐☐☐ – ☐☐ – ☐☐☐☐

63. MOTHER'S/ STEPMOTHER'S LAST NAME ☐☐☐☐☐☐☐☐☐☐☐☐☐☐☐☐

64. Go to page 7 to determine how many people are in your parents' household. ☐☐

65. Go to page 7 to determine how many in question 64 **(exclude your parents)** will be college students between July 1, 2002 and June 30, 2003. ☐

66. What is your parents' state of legal residence?   STATE ☐☐

67. Did your parents become legal residents of the state in question 66 before January 1, 1997?   **Yes** ○ 1   **No** ○ 2

68. If the answer to question 67 is "No," give the month and year legal residency began for the parent who has lived in the state the longest.   MONTH ☐☐ / YEAR ☐☐☐☐

69. What is the age of your older parent? ☐☐

70. For 2001, have your parents completed their IRS income tax return or another tax return listed in **question 71**?

   a. My parents have already completed their return. ○ 1   **b.** My parents will file, but they have not yet completed their return. ○ 2   **c.** My parents are not going to file. **(Skip to question 76.)** ○ 3

71. What income tax return did your parents file or will they file for 2001?

   a. IRS 1040 .... ○ 1   **d.** A tax return for Puerto Rico, Guam, American Samoa, the U.S. Virgin Islands, the Marshall Islands, the Federated States of Micronesia, or Palau. **See page 2.** .... ○ 4

   b. IRS 1040A, 1040EZ, 1040Telefile ...... ○ 2

   c. A foreign tax return. **See page 2.** .... ○ 3

72. If your parents have filed or will file a 1040, were they eligible to file a 1040A or 1040EZ? **See page 2.**   **Yes** ○ 1   **No** ○ 2   **Don't Know** ○ 3

For questions 73 - 83, if the answer is zero or the question does not apply, enter 0.

73. What was your parents' adjusted gross income for 2001? Adjusted gross income is on IRS Form 1040–line 33; 1040A–line 19; 1040EZ–line 4; or Telefile–line I. $ ☐☐☐ , ☐☐☐

74. Enter the total amount of your parents' income tax for 2001. Income tax amount is on IRS Form 1040–lines 50 + 52; 1040A–lines 32 + 34; 1040EZ–line 11; or Telefile–line K(2). $ ☐☐☐ , ☐☐☐

75. Enter your parents' exemptions for 2001. Exemptions are on IRS Form 1040–line 6d or on Form 1040A–line 6d. For Form 1040EZ or Telefile, **see page 2.**   ☐☐

76-77. How much did your parents earn from working (wages, salaries, tips, etc.) in 2001? Answer this question whether or not your parents filed a tax return. This information may be on their W-2 forms, or on IRS Form 1040–lines 7 + 12 + 18; 1040A–line 7; or 1040EZ–line 1. Telefilers should use their W-2 forms.

   Father/ Stepfather (76) $ ☐☐☐ , ☐☐☐

   Mother/ Stepmother (77) $ ☐☐☐ , ☐☐☐

Parent Worksheets (78-80)

78-80. Go to page 8 and complete the columns on the right of Worksheets A, B, and C. Enter the parent totals in questions 78, 79, and 80, respectively. Even though your parents may have few of the worksheet items, check each line carefully.

   Worksheet A (78) $ ☐☐☐ , ☐☐☐

   Worksheet B (79) $ ☐☐☐ , ☐☐☐

   Worksheet C (80) $ ☐☐☐ , ☐☐☐

81. As of today, what is the net worth of your parents' current **investments**? **See page 2.** $ ☐☐☐ , ☐☐☐

82. As of today, what is the net worth of your parents' current **businesses and/or investment farms**? **See page 2.** Do not include a farm that your parents live on and operate. $ ☐☐☐ , ☐☐☐

83. As of today, what is your parents' total current balance of **cash, savings, and checking accounts**? $ ☐☐☐ , ☐☐☐

Now go to Step Six.

Step Five: Complete this step only if you (the student) answered "Yes" to any question in Step Three.

84. **Go to page 7** to determine how many people are in your (and your spouse's) household.

85. **Go to page 7** to determine how many in question 84 will be college students between July 1, 2002 and June 30, 2003.

Step Six: Please tell us which schools should receive your information.

Enter the 6-digit federal school code and your housing plans. Look for the federal school codes at **www.fafsa.ed.gov**, at your college financial aid office, at your public library, or by asking your high school guidance counselor. If you cannot get the federal school code, write in the complete name, address, city, and state of the college. For state aid, you may wish to list your preferred school first.

86. 1ST FEDERAL SCHOOL CODE **OR** NAME OF COLLEGE / ADDRESS AND CITY — STATE — HOUSING PLANS **87.** on campus 1 / off campus 2 / with parent 3

88. 2ND FEDERAL SCHOOL CODE **OR** NAME OF COLLEGE / ADDRESS AND CITY — STATE — **89.** on campus 1 / off campus 2 / with parent 3

90. 3RD FEDERAL SCHOOL CODE **OR** NAME OF COLLEGE / ADDRESS AND CITY — STATE — **91.** on campus 1 / off campus 2 / with parent 3

92. 4TH FEDERAL SCHOOL CODE **OR** NAME OF COLLEGE / ADDRESS AND CITY — STATE — **93.** on campus 1 / off campus 2 / with parent 3

94. 5TH FEDERAL SCHOOL CODE **OR** NAME OF COLLEGE / ADDRESS AND CITY — STATE — **95.** on campus 1 / off campus 2 / with parent 3

96. 6TH FEDERAL SCHOOL CODE **OR** NAME OF COLLEGE / ADDRESS AND CITY — STATE — **97.** on campus 1 / off campus 2 / with parent 3

Step Seven: Please read, sign, and date.

If you are the student, by signing this application you certify that you (1) will use federal and/or state student financial aid only to pay the cost of attending an institution of higher education, (2) are not in default on a federal student loan or have made satisfactory arrangements to repay it, (3) do not owe money back on a federal student grant or have made satisfactory arrangements to repay it, and (4) will notify your school if you default on a federal student loan.

If you are the parent or the student, by signing this application you agree, if asked, to provide information that will verify the accuracy of your completed form. This information may include your U.S. or state income tax forms. Also, you certify that you understand that **the Secretary of Education has the authority to verify information reported on this application with the Internal Revenue Service and other federal agencies**. If you purposely give false or misleading information, you may be fined $20,000, sent to prison, or both.

98. Date this form was completed.

MONTH / DAY / 2002 ○ or 2003 ○

99. Student signature (Sign in box)

1

Parent signature (one parent whose information is provided in Step Four) (Sign in box)

2

If this form was filled out by someone other than you, your spouse, or your parent(s), that person must complete this part.

Preparer's name, firm, and address

100. Preparer's Social Security Number (or 101)

— —

101. Employer ID number (or 100)

—

102. Preparer's signature and date

1

SCHOOL USE ONLY:

D/O ○ 1

FAA SIGNATURE

1

Federal School Code

MDE USE ONLY:

Special Handle —

Page 6

For Help — www.ed.gov/prog_info/SFA/FAFSA

Read these notes to determine who is considered a parent for purposes of this form. **Answer all questions in Step Four about them,** even if you do not live with them.

If your parents are both living and married to each other, answer the questions about them.

If your parent is widowed or single, answer the questions about that parent. If your widowed parent is remarried as of today, answer the questions about that parent **and** the person whom your parent married (your stepparent).

If your parents are divorced or separated, answer the questions about the parent you lived with more during the past 12 months. (If you did not live with one parent more than the other, give answers about the parent who provided more financial support during the last 12 months, or during the most recent year that you actually received support from a parent.) If this parent is remarried as of today, answer the questions on the rest of this form about that parent **and** the person whom your parent married (your stepparent).

Notes for question **64** (page 5)

Include in your parents' household (see notes, above, for who is considered a parent):
- your parents and yourself, even if you don't live with your parents, and
- your parents' other children if (a) your parents will provide more than half of their support from July 1, 2002 through June 30, 2003 or (b) the children could answer "No" to every question in Step Three on page 4 of this form, and
- other people if they now live with your parents, your parents provide more than half of their support, and your parents will continue to provide more than half of their support from July 1, 2002 through June 30, 2003.

Notes for questions **65** (page 5) and **85** (page 6)

Always count yourself as a college student. **Do not include your parents.** Include others only if they will attend at least half time in 2002-2003 a program that leads to a college degree or certificate.

Notes for question **84** (page 6)

Include in your (and your spouse's) household:
- yourself (and your spouse, if you have one), and
- your children, if you will provide more than half of their support from July 1, 2002 through June 30, 2003, and
- other people if they now live with you, and you provide more than half of their support, and you will continue to provide more than half of their support from July 1, 2002 through June 30, 2003.

Information on the Privacy Act and use of your Social Security Number

We use the information that you provide on this form to determine if you are eligible to receive federal student financial aid and the amount that you are eligible to receive. Sections 483 and 484 of the Higher Education Act of 1965, as amended, give us the authority to ask you and your parents these questions, and to collect the Social Security Numbers of you and your parents. We use your Social Security Number to verify your identity and retrieve your records, and we may request your Social Security Number again for those purposes.

State and institutional student financial aid programs may also use the information that you provide on this form to determine if you are eligible to receive state and institutional aid and the need that you have for such aid. Therefore, we will disclose the information that you provide on this form to each institution you list in questions 86–97, state agencies in your state of legal residence, and the state agencies of the states in which the colleges that you list in questions 86–97 are located.

If you are applying solely for federal aid, you must answer all of the following questions that apply to you: 1–9, 13–15, 24, 27–28, 31–32, 35, 36–40, 42–49, 52–66, 69–74, 76–85, and 98–99. If you do not answer these questions, you will not receive federal aid.

Without your consent, we may disclose information that you provide to entities under a published "routine use." Under such a routine use, we may disclose information to third parties that we have authorized to assist us in administering the above programs; to other federal agencies under computer matching programs, such as those with the Internal Revenue Service, Social Security Administration, Selective Service System, Immigration and Naturalization Service, and Veterans Administration; to your parents or spouse; and to members of Congress if you ask them to help you with student aid questions.

If the federal government, the U.S. Department of Education, or an employee of the U.S. Department of Education is involved in litigation, we may send information to the Department of Justice, or a court or adjudicative body, if the disclosure is related to financial aid and certain conditions are met. In addition, we may send your information to a foreign, federal, state, or local enforcement agency if the information that you submitted indicates a violation or potential violation of law, for which that agency has jurisdiction for investigation or prosecution. Finally, we may send information regarding a claim that is determined to be valid and overdue to a consumer reporting agency. This information includes identifiers from the record; the amount, status, and history of the claim; and the program under which the claim arose.

State Certification

By submitting this application, you are giving your state financial aid agency permission to verify any statement on this form and to obtain income tax information for all persons required to report income on this form.

The Paperwork Reduction Act of 1995

The Paperwork Reduction Act of 1995 says that no one is required to respond to a collection of information unless it displays a valid OMB control number, which for this form is 1845-0001. The time required to complete this form is estimated to be one hour, including time to review instructions, search data resources, gather the data needed, and complete and review the information collection. If you have comments about this estimate or suggestions for improving this form, please write to: U.S. Department of Education, Washington DC 20202-4651.

We may request additional information from you to process your application more efficiently. We will collect this additional information only as needed and on a voluntary basis.

Do not mail these worksheets in with your application.

Keep these worksheets; your school may ask to see them.

Worksheet A

Student/Spouse		Parent(s)
For question 44		**For question 78**
$	Earned income credit from IRS Form 1040–line 61a; 1040A–line 39a; 1040EZ–line 9a; or Telefile–line L(2).	$
$	Additional child tax credit from IRS Form 1040–line 63 or 1040A–line 40	$
$	Welfare benefits, including Temporary Assistance for Needy Families (TANF). Don't include Food Stamps or subsidized housing.	$
$	Social Security benefits received that were not taxed (such as SSI)	$
$ Enter in question 44.		Enter in question 78. **$**

Worksheet B

Student/Spouse		Parent(s)
For question 45		**For question 79**
$	Payments to tax-deferred pension and savings plans (paid directly or withheld from earnings), including, but not limited to, amounts reported on the W-2 Form in Boxes 12a through 12d, codes D, E, F, G, H, and S	$
$	IRA deductions and payments to self-employed SEP, SIMPLE, and Keogh and other qualified plans from IRS Form 1040–total of lines 23 + 29 or 1040A–line 16	$
$	Child support **received** for all children. Don't include foster care or adoption payments.	$
$	Tax exempt interest income from IRS Form 1040–line 8b or 1040A–line 8b	$
$	Foreign income exclusion from IRS Form 2555–line 43 or 2555EZ–line 18	$
$	Untaxed portions of IRA distributions from IRS Form 1040–lines (15a minus 15b) or 1040A–lines (11a minus 11b). Exclude rollovers. If negative, enter a zero here.	$
$	Untaxed portions of pensions from IRS From 1040–lines (16a minus 16b) or 1040A–lines (12a minus12b). Exclude rollovers. If negative, enter a zero here.	$
$	Credit for federal tax on special fuels from IRS Form 4136–line 10– nonfarmers only	$
$	Housing, food, and other living allowances paid to members of the military, clergy, and others (including cash payments and cash value of benefits)	$
$	Veterans' noneducation benefits such as Disability, Death Pension, or Dependency & Indemnity Compensation (DIC) and/or VA Educational Work-Study allowances	$
$	Any other untaxed income or benefits not reported elsewhere on Worksheets A and B, such as worker's compensation, untaxed portions of railroad retirement benefits, Black Lung Benefits, disability, etc. **Don't include** student aid, Workforce Investment Act educational benefits, or benefits from flexible spending arrangements, e.g., cafeteria plans.	$
$	Cash **received**, or any money paid on your behalf, not reported elsewhere on this form	XXXXXXXX
Enter in question 45.		Enter in question 79.

Worksheet C

Student/Spouse		Parent(s)
For question 46		**For question 80**
$	Education credits (Hope and Lifetime Learning tax credits) from IRS Form 1040-line 46 or 1040A-line 29	$
$	Child support **paid** because of divorce or separation. Don't include support for children in your (or your parents') household, as reported in question 84 (or question 64 for your parents).	$
$	Taxable earnings from Federal Work-Study or other need-based work programs	$
$	Student grant, scholarship, fellowship, and assistantship aid, including AmeriCorps awards, that was reported to the IRS in your (or your parents') adjusted gross income	$
$ Enter in question 46.		Enter in question 80. **$**